The Second Amendment and Gun Control

'*The Second Amendment and Gun Control: Freedom, Fear, and the American Constitution* provides a nicely balanced overview of a complex issue in American law and public policy. Yuill and Street have done a superb job of bringing together some of the leading scholars on the differing sides of this multi-layered controversy. The individual chapters are well done. You will agree with some, disagree with others, but in the end you will find that all of them make you think. It will be a must read for both students of the subject and general readers alike.'

Robert J. Cottrol, Harold Paul Green Research Professor of Law and Professor of History and Sociology, The George Washington University, USA and author of The Long, Lingering Shadow: Slavery, Race and Law in the American Hemisphere *(2013)*

The Second Amendment, by far the most controversial amendment to the US Constitution, will soon celebrate its 225th anniversary. Yet, despite the amount of ink spilled over this controversy, the debate continues on into the twenty-first century. Initially written with a view towards protecting the nascent nation from more powerful enemies and preventing the tyranny experienced during the final years of British rule, the Second Amendment has since become central to discussions about the balance between security and freedom. It features in election contests and informs cultural discussions about race and gender.

This book seeks to broaden the discussion. It situates discussion about gun controls within contemporary debates about citizenship, culture, philosophy, and foreign policy, as well as in the more familiar terrain of politics and history. It features experts on the Constitution, as well as chapters discussing the symbolic importance of Annie Oakley, the role of firearms in race, and filmic representations of armed Hispanic girl gangs. It asks about the morality of gun controls and of not imposing them.

The collection presents a balanced view between those who favour more gun controls and those who would prefer fewer of them. It is infused with the belief that through honest and open debate, the often bitter cultural divide on the Second Amendment can be overcome and real progress made. It contains a diverse range of perspectives including, uniquely, a European perspective on this most American of issues.

Kevin Yuill is Senior Lecturer in American History at the University of Sunderland. His research and teaching interests are broad and interdisciplinary. His concentration is on intellectual history of the United States. He has written on gun control in *A Cultural History of Firearms in an Age of Empire* (2013) and in journalistic articles. His monographs include *Richard Nixon and the Rise of Affirmative Action: The Pursuit of Racial Equality in an Era of Limits* (2006). He has also written on race and foreign policy in the United States at the turn of the century ("The spectre of Japan: the influence of foreign relations on race relations theory, 1905–24," *Patterns of Prejudice*, 2015) and is currently completing a manuscript on the 1924 Immigration Act.

Joe Street is Senior Lecturer in History at the Northumbria University, Newcastle. His work focuses on the San Francisco Bay Area in the post-war period and African American radicalism in the 1960s and 1970s. His publications include *Dirty Harry's America: Clint Eastwood, Harry Callahan, and the Conservative Backlash* (2016), *The Culture War in the Civil Rights Movement* (2007), and various articles on African American radicalism.

Controversies in American Constitutional Law
Series Editors:

Jon Yorke and Anne Richardson Oakes
Centre for American Legal Studies, School of Law, Birmingham City University, UK

Controversies in American Constitutional Law (CALS) presents and engages with the contemporary developments and policies which mould and challenge US constitutional law and practice. It deals with the full spectrum of constitutional issues, publishing work by scholars from a range of disciplines who tackle current legal issues by reference to their underlying legal and political histories and the philosophical perspectives that they represent. Its cross-disciplinary approach encourages analysis of past, present and future challenges to the idea of US constitutionalism and the power structures upon which it rests. The series provides a forum for scholars to challenge the boundaries of US constitutional law and engages with the continual process of constitutional refinement for the protection of individual rights and liberties, within an evolving framework of legitimate government.

CALS promotes research, scholarship, and educative programs in all areas of US law, and is the home of the *British Journal of American Legal Studies.* Faculty members have extensive experience in submitting *amicus curiae* briefs to the United States Supreme Court and lower federal courts, and advising on criminal justice issues in many states. CALS coordinates the largest British law undergraduate internship program to the United States. Through this program, and members' research, CALS has created relationships with over 100 partners in over 25 states. CALS faculty advise public bodies, provide professional training, and speak at conferences across the USA.

Recent title in this series

The United States Supreme Court's Assault on the Constitution, Democracy, and the Rule of Law
Adam Lamparello and Cynthia Swann
ISBN 978-1-1382-2243-4

Controversies in Equal Protection Cases in America: Race, Gender and Sexual Orientation
Anne Richardson Oakes
ISBN 978-1-4094-5427-4

Controversies in Tax Law: A Matter of Perspective
Edited by Anthony C. Infanti
ISBN 978-1-4724-1492-2

Controversies in Innocence Cases in America
Edited by Sarah Lucy Cooper
ISBN 978-1-4094-6354-2

The Second Amendment and Gun Control

Freedom, Fear, and the American Constitution

Edited by Kevin Yuill and Joe Street

Routledge
Taylor & Francis Group
LONDON AND NEW YORK

First published 2018 by Routledge

2 Park Square, Milton Park, Abingdon, Oxfordshire OX14 4RN
52 Vanderbilt Avenue, New York, NY 10017

Routledge is an imprint of the Taylor & Francis Group, an informa business

First issued in paperback 2019

British Library Cataloguing-in-Publication Data
A catalogue record for this book is available from the British Library

Library of Congress Cataloguing-in-Publication Data
Names: Yuill, Kevin L., 1962– author. | Street, Joe, author.
Title: The Second Amendment and gun control : freedom, fear, and the American Constitution / Kevin Yuill, Joe Street.
Description: Abingdon, Oxon [UK] ; New York : Routledge, 2017. | Series: Controversies in American constitutional law | Includes bibliographical references and index.
Identifiers: LCCN 2017019510 | ISBN 9781138706286 (hardback)
Subjects: LCSH: Firearms—Law and legislation—United States. | Gun control—United States. | United States. Constitution. 2nd Amendment.
Classification: LCC KF3941 .Y85 2017 | DDC 344.7305/33—dc23
LC record available at https://lccn.loc.gov/2017019510

ISBN: 978-1-138-70628-6 (hbk)
ISBN: 978-0-367-88747-6 (pbk)

Typeset in Galliard
by Apex CoVantage, LLC

Contents

Contributors

Saul Cornell is the Paul and Diane Guenther Chair in American History at Fordham University. He specializes in early American history and legal/Constitutional history. Professor Cornell has been a senior visiting research scholar at Yale Law School and The University of Connecticut Law School. He is the author of *The Other Founders: Anti-Federalism and the Dissenting Tradition in America, 1788–1828* (1999) and *A Well-Regulated Militia: The Founding Fathers and the Origins of Gun Control in America* (2006), and two edited volumes on the Second Amendment. His articles have appeared in *The Yale Law Journal, Constitutional Commentary, The UCLA Law Review, The Northwestern Law Review, The Journal of American History, The William and Mary Quarterly*, and *The Law and History Review*. He has also published opinion pieces in the *Atlantic, The New York Times, The Washington Post, The Chronicle of Higher Education, Slate, and Salon.*

Firmin DeBrabander is professor of philosophy at the Maryland Institute College of Art in Baltimore. He is author of *Spinoza and the Stoics* (Continuum Press, 2007) and *Do Guns Make Us Free?* (Yale University Press, 2015). He also writes social and political commentary, for a variety of national publications, including the *New York Times*, the *Baltimore Sun*, the *Washington Post*, the *Atlantic*, and *Salon*.

Emma Horrex recently successfully defended her PhD thesis at the University of Hull. Her research, funded in part by the Ann Watson Educational Trust and the Sidney Perry Foundation, explores the production, reception, and representation of girls in contemporary street gangs in American film. She teaches undergraduate modules in both American history and literature, and she has served as the Assistant Editor and Reviews Co-ordinator for *U.S. Studies Online*.

Karen Jones is Reader in History at the University of Kent and a nineteenth-century specialist with particular interests in environmental and cultural history. Her books include *Wolf Mountains: The History of Wolves Along the Great Divide* (2002) – a comparative study of the biology, mythology, and culture surrounding wolves in national parks in the Rockies – and *The American West: Competing Visions* (2009) – a post-revisionist take on the frontier experience. More recently, she has published on guns and empire; hunting with the camera; and animal exhibition and taxidermy. Her latest monograph, *Epiphany in the Wilderness: Hunting, Nature and Performance in the Nineteenth-Century American West* (2015), looks at the environmental and cultural imprint of hunting on the trans-Mississippi United States, with particular focus on human–animal encounter, storytelling, and gender tropes and transgressions.

David B. Kopel is Adjunct Professor of Constitutional Law at Denver University, Sturm College of Law; Research Director of the Independence Institute, in Denver; and an Associate Policy Analyst with the Cato Institute, in Washington, DC. He is also a member of the Colorado State Advisory Committee to the United States Commission on Civil Rights. Kopel writes for the *Washington Post* on its "Volokh Conspiracy" legal weblog. He is the author of seventeen books and over 100 scholarly articles. His books include the law school textbook *Firearms Law and the Second Amendment*, and most recently, *The Morality of Self-Defense and Military Action: The Judeo-Christian Tradition*. Kopel was a member of the Supreme Court oral argument team in *District of Columbia v. Heller*. His *Heller* and *McDonald* amicus briefs for a coalition of law enforcement organizations were cited by Justices Alito, Breyer, and Stevens. The federal Seventh Circuit Court of Appeals has lauded his scholarship as showing the proper model of the "originalist interpretive method as applied to the Second Amendment."

Emma Long is a lecturer in American Studies at the University of East Anglia. Her interests include the US Supreme Court, the Constitution, and the interplay of religion and politics. She has written on American evangelicalism, the language of post-war debate about religious liberty, and the Supreme Court. She is author of *The Church–State Debate: Religion, Education, and the Establishment Clause in Postwar America* (Bloomsbury, 2012).

Joyce Lee Malcolm is Patrick Henry Professor of Constitutional Law and the Second Amendment at Antonin Scalia Law School, George Mason University. She holds a PhD in history and specializes in Constitutional law, legal history, and law and war. Malcolm is the author of seven books, and numerous articles for legal and historical journals and the popular press. Her book *To Keep and Bear Arms: The Origins of an Anglo-American Right*, published by Harvard University Press, was cited in the Supreme Court's landmark Second Amendment opinions, *District of Columbia versus Heller* and *McDonald versus City of Chicago*. A second book, *Guns and Violence: The English Experience*, also published by Harvard University Press, tracks English laws on self-defense and firearms for their impact on crime in England. The book was recently translated into Portuguese by a Brazilian publisher. Malcolm's essays have been published in the *Wall Street Journal*, *The Financial Times*, *The London Telegraph*, *The Boston Globe*, *The Philadelphia Inquirer*, BBC News online, and other venues.

Rebecca Rössling holds a master's degree in American Studies from the University of Frankfurt, Germany. She is currently preparing her dissertation on black self-defense and the Second Amendment in post-civil rights America.

Peter Squires is a Professor of Criminology & Public Policy at the University of Brighton, United Kingdom, a role he has held since 2005. His work on firearm-enabled crime and gun politics dates back to 1994, since when he has written three books: *Gun Culture or Gun Control?* (2000); *Shooting to Kill?* (2010); and *Gun Crime in Global Contexts* (2014). His other areas of criminological interest include policing, gangs and gang culture, and the excessive propensity to criminalize in neoliberal political cultures. In 2012, his edited (with John Lea) collection *Criminalisation and Advanced Marginality*, critically exploring the work of Loic Wacquant, was published. In 2015, Peter Squires was elected president of the British Society for Criminology (for three years).

Simon Wendt is Assistant Professor of American Studies at the University of Frankfurt in Frankfurt, Germany. His research interests revolve around African American history,

American gender history, memory, nationalism, and the history of heroism. He is the author of *The Spirit and the Shotgun: Armed Resistance and the Struggle for Civil Rights* (2007) and coeditor of a number of books, including *Globalizing Lynching History: Vigilantism and Extralegal Punishment from an International Perspective* (2011), *Crossing Boundaries: Ethnicity, Race, and National Belonging in a Transnational World* (2013), and *Masculinities and the Nation in the Modern World: Between Hegemony and Marginalization* (2015). Simon Wendt is currently completing a book manuscript on the history of the Daughters of the American Revolution.

Kevin Yuill is Senior Lecturer in American history at the University of Sunderland. His research and teaching interests are broad and interdisciplinary, but he concentrates on American intellectual history of the late nineteenth and twentieth centuries. Using a historical approach, he investigates policy issues. He has written on gun control in *A Cultural History of Firearms in an Age of Empire* (Ashgate Publishing, 2013) and in journalistic articles. His monographs include *Assisted Suicide: The Liberal, Humanist Case Against Legalization* (Palgrave, 2013) and *Richard Nixon and the Rise of Affirmative Action: The Pursuit of Racial Equality in an Era of Limits* (Rowman and Littlefield, 2006). He has also written on the history of country music, race, and foreign policy in the United States at the turn of the century, and FDR and immigration. He is currently completing a manuscript on the 1924 Immigration Act.

Acknowledgements

The idea for this book came from a Firearms and Freedom Conference held on 11 June 2015 at the Eccles Centre for American Studies in the British Library, London, England. The conference was made possible by a grant from the United States Embassy in London. Thanks especially to Anneliese Reinemeyer, Fay Miller, Sarah-Jane Mayhew, and Bradley Moore from the Embassy. The Eccles Centre for American Studies also contributed enormously to the conference, providing a superb venue. The staff at the Eccles Centre, particularly Professor Phil Davies, Cara Rodway, and Jean Petrovic, helped enormously with ensuring the conference ran smoothly and efficiently. We would also like to acknowledge the support of the University of Sunderland, the University of Northumbria, Newcastle, The Institute of the Americas at University College, London. Thanks also to those who participated in the conference and made it the stellar event it was.

The publishers at Routledge have made publication of an edited collection, no easy feat, a smooth and easy process through their hard work and dedication. Thanks to Alison Kirk, Alexandra Buckley, Marie Roberts, and others behind the scenes for their skill and patience.

Finally, we should acknowledge our contributors, who, despite their very divergent views on the issues at hand, remained friendly, good humored, collegiate, and, above all, open-minded. Thanks to them, the spirit of that conference – one of debate and moving the discussion forward – runs throughout this book.

Introduction

> Hillary wants to abolish – essentially abolish the Second Amendment. By the way, if she gets to pick, if she gets to pick her judges, nothing you can do, folks. Although the Second Amendment people, maybe there is, I don't know.[1]

Republican presidential candidate Donald Trump ignited one of many campaign controversies with these words in Wilmington, North Carolina, as the presidential election headed towards its final months. As some pointed out, on the day Trump spoke, forty-one Americans were shot and killed.[2] Unsurprisingly, these words were pored over by political and media commentators for their deeper meaning. Clinton herself saw Trump's words as another demonstration of his lack of fitness for public office.[3] Bernice King, daughter of the Rev. Dr. Martin Luther King, Jr. was one among many who chastised Trump for his dangerous words. Gun control advocate Dan Gross denounced the words as 'repulsive.' The Democratic Senator Chris Murphy called the comments 'disgusting.' Even the Speaker of the House of Representatives, the Republican Paul Ryan, rebuked Trump's comments as a poor attempt at a joke.[4] Trump's response was typically robust. Refusing to apologize, he said, 'This is a political movement. This is a strong powerful movement, the Second Amendment, and there can be no other interpretation.'[5]

Whether they were deliberately calibrated to cause offense will never be known, but the ambiguity of Trump's terms was enough to excite the emotions of both sides of the gun debate. For the gun lobby, this was a thorough endorsement of their activities. Trump also slyly hinted at approval of vigilante action, previously considered the preserve of the more extreme wing of the gun rights firmament. For advocates of gun control, as suggested by King's and Gross's comments, these words were yet another vulgar demonstration of

1 Donald Trump quoted in Jeremy Diamond and Stephen Collinson, "Donald Trump: 'Second Amendment' Gun Advocates Could Deal With Hillary Clinton", *CNN.com*, August 10, 2016 at http://edition.cnn.com/2016/08/09/politics/donald-trump-hillary-clinton-second-amendment/index.html (accessed March 17, 2017).

2 Figures at www.gunviolencearchive.org/query/74821178-c890-448f-ba10-f39dccee70a8?page=6 (accessed March 17, 2017).

3 Clinton Says Trump Incited Violence With 'Second Amendment' Remarks, *BBC*, August 11, 2016 at www.bbc.co.uk/news/election-us-2016-37036856 (accessed March 17, 2017).

4 King, Gross, Murphy, Ryan cited or quoted in Nick Corasanti and Maggie Haberman, "Donald Trump Suggests 'Second Amendment People' Could Act Against Hillary Clinton", *New York Times*, August 9, 2016 at www.nytimes.com/2016/08/10/us/politics/donald-trump-hillary-clinton.html?_r=0 (accessed March 17, 2017).

5 Trump quoted ibid.

Trump's deplorable way with words and blithe inattention to the emotions that twenty-first-century politics – and particularly his campaign – excited. Both responses confirmed that emotions were running high, and perhaps even coming to dominate the debate over the Second Amendment. Trump's message tapped into so many of the fears that animate Americans regarding firearms in the twenty-first century – that guns will be 'grabbed,' that a government conspiracy to remove weapons from the hands of American citizens exists, but also that too many weapons are in 'unofficial' hands and that a violent core of Americans will resist any reforms they disagree with.

Trump is more equivocal regarding guns than this and some other of his recent pronouncements imply. As Marco Rubio noted, Trump wrote in his 2000 book, *The America We Deserve*, that he supported a ban on assault weapons and a slightly longer waiting period to buy a gun.[6] In an interview with Larry King, Trump expressed the wish that no one in the United States had guns.[7] Throughout the 2016 election campaign, he expressed fear of gun crime but constantly emphasized the importance of mental health. The real problem, he said, was not guns but the people who use them. 'The guns don't pull the trigger. It's the people that pull the trigger and we have to find out what is going on.'[8] With his emphasis on a law-and-order presidency, Trump has both emphasized the need for mental health checks and for more concealed carry laws, belying the same fear that animates those who would, if they could, remove all guns from American society.

Obama was perhaps less ambiguous in his approach. Consistently in favor of further gun controls, Obama was accused by Trump of taking 'baby steps' towards repeal of the Second Amendment through use of executive action. Trump mused: 'Whenever I see gun-free zones, that's a flag for the wackos to come in and start shooting people.'[9] Trump's comments came in response to a tearful Obama announcing gun control measures at which he said that 'too many' massacres had taken place in his country. Representative Gabrielle Giffords, herself a survivor of gun crime, was also present, thanks, according to Obama, only to the 'great' medical team who treated her and the support of her family. Obama went on to talk of the personal stories of those who had lost family members to gun crime, some of whom were arrayed behind him in the briefing room. Expressing exasperation that gun control had become such a partisan issue, Obama questioned, 'how did we get here?' 'We all have to be just as passionate' as the gun lobby, he urged gun control advocates.[10]

Obama was mocked by those who resist gun control for what some felt were faux emotions.[11] But Trump's response to Sandy Hook was, if anything, just as emotive as Obama's,

6 Marco Rubio, "Press Release: 'Get the Facts: Donald Trump's Anti-Second Amendment Record'" at www.presidency.ucsb.edu/ws/?pid=113161.

7 Andrew Kaczynski, "Trump Once Said of Guns: 'Nothing I Like Better than Nobody Has Them'" at www.buzzfeed.com/andrewkaczynski/trump-once-said-of-guns-nothing-i-like-better-than-nobody-ha?utm_term=.cr05DBeVQ#.syrjzpR48.

8 Trump, cited in Mark Hodge, "Donald Trump vs Hillary Clinton on Gun Control – What the US Election 2016 Candidates Have to Say", *The Sun*, November 4, 2016 at www.thesun.co.uk/news/2117620/donald-trump-hillary-clinton-gun-control-us-presidential-election-2016/.

9 Trump quoted in Mark Hensch, "Trump: Obama Taking 'Baby Steps' to Eliminate Second Amendment", *The Hill*, January 4, 2016 at http://thehill.com/blogs/ballot-box/presidential-races/264625-trump-obama-taking-baby-steps-to-no-second-amendment (accessed March 17, 2017).

10 Everett Rosenfeld, "Obama Announces Gun Control Plans: 'I Believe in the Second Amendment'", *CNBC*, January 5, 2016 at www.cnbc.com/2016/01/05/obama-announces-gun-control-plans-i-believe-in-the-second-amendment.html (accessed March 17, 2017). Some quotations derive from the embedded video in the article.

11 Brendan Gauthier, "Fox News Host Mocks Obama's Tears Over Sandy Hook: 'Check the Podium for a Raw Onion'", *Salon*, January 5, 2016 at www.salon.com/2016/01/05/fox_news_host_mocks_obamas_tears_over_sandy_hook_check_the_podium_for_a_raw_onion/ (accessed March 19, 2017).

albeit from a different perspective. As an American who has a concealed carry permit, not only has Trump promised to eliminate gun-free zones and said that a 'national right to carry' concealed weapons should be legal, but Trump advocates teachers with guns in schools.[12] Why? The Sandy Hook shooting is – thankfully – a very rare event. A simple breakdown of the statistics indicates the unnecessary nature of either gun control measures or arming teachers. American schools are amongst the safest places to be. Those aged 5–18 are extraordinarily unlikely to be the victims of homicide at school. There are about fifteen incidents of homicide per year in schools of those aged 5–18 in an average year,[13] in a population of some 50.4m school students,[14] which would make American schools, if they were a country, safer, in terms of homicide, than any other in the world.[15] It is ludicrous, as Trump and the National Rifle Association have done, to call for armed guards or teachers with loaded weapons in American schools. It simply is not necessary. But neither are gun control measures.

Characteristic of the discussion today is the ultra-partisan nature of positions in the United States on the Second Amendment. Obama noted that 90 per cent of Democrats in Congress supported the call for further background checks before any individual could purchase a gun, while 90 per cent of Republicans opposed the measure when it was introduced to Congress.[16] Just as shocking is the distance between grassroots Democrats and Republicans. Democrats have long been more likely than Republicans to favor controls on gun ownership over protecting gun rights. But what was a 27-percentage-point gap between supporters of Obama and John McCain on this question in 2008 surged to a historic 70-point gap between Clinton and Trump supporters in 2016.[17]

The issue of gun control is not only enmeshed in an increasingly bitter partisan divide between Red and Blue, but it has also transcended politics, and perhaps even rational thought, to become a core issue of American identity. The emotional response on both sides suggests that the Second Amendment, which guarantees to Americans the right to own guns, is central to American life and to Americans' views of themselves, their compatriots, their homes, their communities, and their nation. The argument over guns has become a battle for the souls of Americans. Initially written with a view towards protecting the nascent nation from more powerful enemies and guarding against tyranny from within, the Second Amendment is now fundamental to debates over American liberty and freedom, race and gender, politics and society.

What of the objects themselves – firearms? Pamela Haag has recently made a good, if seemingly obvious, point. Guns used to be no more than commodities, like paperclips, typewriters or men's shirts (Oliver Winchester's enterprise before he moved on to guns). The gun is fetishized.[18] Today it is the use of what is, more than 500 years after it first

12 Melissa Chan, "Donald Trump Says Some Teachers Should Have Guns in Classrooms", *Time*, May 22, 2016 at http://time.com/4344226/donald-trump-guns-teachers-classroom/ (accessed March 19, 2017).
13 https://nces.ed.gov/pubs2015/2015072.pdf (accessed March 19, 2017).
14 https://nces.ed.gov/fastfacts/display.asp?id=372 (accessed March 19, 2017).
15 For illustration, Japan, with a population of 127m, registered 395 homicides in 2011. See www.unodc.org/documents/gsh/pdfs/Chapter_1.pdf (accessed March 19, 2017).
16 Rosenfeld, "Obama Launches Gun Control Plans".
17 Michael Dimmock, "How America Changed During Barack Obama's Presidency", *Pew Research Center* at www.pewresearch.org/2017/01/10/how-america-changed-during-barack-obamas-presidency/ (accessed March 19, 2017).
18 See Pamela Haag, *The Gunning of America: Business and the Making of American Gun Culture* (New York: Basic Books, 2016).

appeared, a fairly simple machine that seems to animate discussion. In particular, many ask whether guns have any legitimate purpose. In the past, discussions about gun controls usually involved specific, suspect populations, such as slaves, African Americans, or immigrants. The discussion today is overwhelmingly about whether any private citizens have legitimate purposes for possessing firearms.[19]

There is a tendency – particularly in academic circles where few have personal experience of using guns of any variety – to see all firearms as one. In reality, different types of firearms perform very different functions. For civilians, rifles are used primarily for hunting (although so-called assault weapons are not particularly useful for hunting) but may also be used for protection in the home. Shotguns are generally used for hunting birds but can be deadly weapons when used against persons in close proximity. Rarely are either used in the commission of crimes. In 2014, according to the Federal Bureau of Investigation (FBI), out of a total of 8,124 murders using firearms, 262 murders were committed using rifles (including assault weapons) and 248 by shotgun. Handguns were used in nearly all other cases. Yet while they are the commonest weapon used in homicides in the United States, less than 0.5 per cent of them have ever been used in any homicide. So their primary purpose is as protection or security.[20]

Today's discussion is overwhelmingly concerned with legitimate and illegitimate *uses* of the gun. Many of the chapters in this book deal with self-protection. Is self-protection better served by individuals being able to arm themselves against potential attackers or by firearms being more widely restricted? Do more guns equal more violence? Or does mere possession of a gun dissuade others from doing us harm? One of the striking differences that historians might notice is the individuation of self-defense. There are few, if any, arguments to match those made in the 1960s by the Black Panthers that African Americans needed to defend themselves against the police or groups like the Ku Klux Klan. Absent, too, is the Cold War imperative of collective defense against invasion. The concept of the *posse comitatus*, of a collective, armed group of civilians who might be called upon in the event of riot or disorder, is today held to be suspicious in and of itself, tainted by associations with far-right groups. The founding fathers would hardly recognize the discussion today.

With this book, we hope to broaden the discussion and challenge the entrenched positions of both those who favor and those who resist gun controls. The book explicitly attempts to avoid the increasingly bitter cultural wall being built between Democrats, generally favorable to restrictions on gun ownership, and Republicans, generally opposed to any attempt to redraft the Amendment. Instead, its authors – whose own positions on the Second Amendment represent different sides of the debate – maintain that reasoned debate and open dialogue make real progress possible even in this most vexed of issues. It also aspires to move beyond the emotional and partisan appeals of politicians whenever they engage with the gun control issue. With luck, this book will signal the beginning of a new, more nuanced approach to a key element of one of the United States' founding documents.

The book's concept began with two principles. First, there is a rational discussion to be had between supporters of Second Amendment rights and those who favor more restrictions

19 Few, if any, question the need for police officers to wield guns. See Chapter 6, page 96.
20 In 2009, Americans owned 114 million handguns, 110 million rifles, and 86 million shotguns. William J. Krouse, *Gun Control Legislation* (Congressional Research Service, 2012), 8 at https://fas.org/sgp/crs/misc/RL32842.pdf (accessed March 19, 2017). If a different handgun were used for every handgun murder over the past fifty years, and we overestimated homicides at 10,000 per year, it would be less than half of 1 per cent.

on firearms. With more understanding, good will, rational discussion, and a willingness to deeply analyze the issues, the problems dividing Republicans and Democrats might be solved. We hope the book is infused with our own optimism about the possibility of resolving the issue through debate. If the book is able to be part of such a process, it has fulfilled our expectations.

Second, balance is absolutely necessary. The two editors began the project with differing viewpoints on whether more gun controls are desirable or not; we end with, if not utterly changed perspectives, more nuanced positions. The chapters and their authors reflect our contention that any progress in this question will only occur with free and open discussion. It is worth quoting John Stuart Mill at length on the issue:

> He who knows only his own side of the case knows little of that. . . . [I]f he is equally unable to refute the reasons on the opposite side, if he does not so much as know what they are, he has no ground for preferring either opinion. . . . Nor is it enough that he should hear the opinions of adversaries from his own teachers, presented as they state them, and accompanied by what they offer as refutations. He must be able to hear them from persons who actually believe them . . . he must know them in their most plausible and persuasive form.[21]

The chapters that follow are written by 'persons who actually believe' their arguments, which have been put 'in their most plausible and persuasive form.' If the chapters vary in their polemical level, they all add to the reader's understanding and thus his or her ground for preferring either opinion.

How have we broadened the discussion? What follows is diverse range of topics written by a similarly diverse range of authors. Normally, Americans themselves argue about their own Second Amendment as the rest of the world looks on. But this book includes European as well as American experts. Often, when awful shooting incidents in the United States merit international attention, Europeans respond with wagging fingers and sad shaking of heads. 'What did you expect with so many guns?' they ask. Yet, in this volume, several of the European-based authors are sympathetic to what has been called 'gun culture.' Moreover, it has been made an international issue in that the right to self-defense predates the United States and is, of course, relevant everywhere. Another sense by which the issue has become international is in the export of many of the terms of the discussion by the United Nations and by those, like Newt Gingrich, who have expressed a wish to export the Second Amendment itself.

The chapters in *The Second Amendment and Gun Control* are framed by two debates. The opening debate involves two of the most prominent academic analysts of the Second Amendment. Saul Cornell and Joyce Malcolm use the 2008 *District of Columbia v. Heller* and the 2010 *McDonald v. City of Chicago* Supreme Court decisions to investigate the historical roots of the current debate on the Second Amendment. Drawing on his reading of the grand sweep of American history, Cornell argues that myths of the American past dominate current interpretations of the Second Amendment and calls for an approach to gun ownership that is more rooted in the facts than an idealized vision of American history. Malcolm, by contrast, argues that the right to self-defense is the basis not only of a historic justification of gun ownership, but the reason it should not be restricted today. Drawing on

21 John Stuart Mill and Stefan Collini, ed., *On Liberty* (Cambridge: Cambridge University Press, 2003), 38.

British and American history, Malcolm focuses on the implications that gun control has on individuals' need to protect themselves. Their conclusions differ, but Cornell and Malcolm combine to demonstrate the depth and complexity of the debate over the Second Amendment, both in a national and international context.

How has American 'gun culture' evolved in relation to discussion of the Second Amendment? In a surprising revision to what is normally a male-dominated discussion, Karen Jones challenges conventional American history by demonstrating how armed western women wielded firearms for their own purposes on the frontier. Weaving factual and fictional accounts of the exploits of Martha Canary (better known as Calamity Jane) and discussing the sharpshooting achievements of Annie Oakley, Jones complicates our understanding both of women's roles on the frontier and in American popular culture. Their displays of acuity with firearms in various 'Wild West' shows presented a sharp challenge to the masculine hegemony of the American West (in both practical and symbolic guises). As Jones points out, '*who* carries the gun makes a fundamental difference to how they are received.'

Emma Horrex also trains a gendered lens on gun ownership, focusing on filmic representation of Chicana girl gangs and their ambivalent relationships to firearms. She critiques the stereotypical vision of female gang members through analysis of several key films that depict gang warfare, concluding that Allison Anders's *Mi Vida Loca* (1994) is a powerful source for understanding the cultural anxiety surrounding ethnic minorities and guns. The theme of self-protection, something that arises in so many chapters of this book, is raised in a direct way at the beginning of the film. The female gangsters seek to protect themselves and their children from rival gangs, using guns to do so. Anders's humanizing of these women, then, is an important contribution to the ongoing debate over the Second Amendment and gun use in California, with its specific ethnic contexts. Together, Jones and Horrex revise existing narratives about guns, feminizing their representation and indicating the various different uses of firearms employed by women.

Simon Wendt and Rebecca Rössling also challenge existing perceptions of who wields firearms and for what purpose. Focusing on armed self-defense by African American citizens, Wendt and Rössling observe that white assumptions of African American criminality and inattention to African American human rights are explanatory factors in the development of self-defense groups in black communities across time and space in the United States. Extending discussion of armed self-defense from the 1960s to the 1970s, they raise some surprising points about black use of self-defense to justify shooting policemen and others. Their specific concern is the cases of Hayward Brown and Larry Davis, two black men who were charged with murder after defending themselves with deadly force against local police officers and whose cases complicate our understanding of the relationship between guns and race in the United States.

Kevin Yuill and Firmin Debrabander discuss the implications of an armed citizenry for the polity. Yuill traces the place of the virtuous, armed citizen in history and his abrupt disappearance in the 1970s, replaced by the 'cramped little risk-fearing man' personified, in some ways, by Donald Trump. The issue of insecurity, Yuill argues, is crucial for understanding both sides of the discussion of the Second Amendment. The transformation of the image of the gun owner in the American mind, from the virtuous citizen to the 'gun nut,' has increasingly come to dominate gun control discourse, a development that Yuill suggests has major implications for civic trust and social cohesion. As he states, 'Entrusting fellow citizens with potentially lethal power is an act of faith in one's fellows.' In contrast to Yuill, Debrabander interprets the presence of guns themselves as the root of this civic insecurity. From a philosophical perspective, Debrabander argues that the most worrisome aspect of American gun culture, and the expansive agenda of the gun rights movement, is the threat to rule of law. Delving into philosophical discussions of rule of law, Debrabander suggests that conservative small-government gun rights advocates need to take heed if they are to square the compromises to rule of law that their support for gun ownership requires with their quest to minimize governmental interference in citizens' lives.

Bringing the discussion up to the present, Emma Long discusses the way the rule of law operates at a more concrete level in a section that examines the implications of recent Supreme Court decisions for the gun control discussion. Whereas the few previous Supreme Court cases that deal with the Second Amendment, such as *Cruikshank* and *Presser*, dealt with organizations and firearms (although the 1938 *Miller* decision upheld a law restricting sawed-off shotguns, ruling that the weapon in question could not be used for military purposes), the 2008 ruling in *District of Columbia v. Heller* held for the first time that the Second Amendment protects an ***individual*** right to bear arms. Long notes, however, the that judicial originalism, which many felt triumphed with *Heller*, is undermined by subsequent historical debate, inconsistencies within *Heller* itself, and the alternative approach offered in a dissent by Justice Breyer. The final two chapters move beyond American borders, investigating the international consequences of the Second Amendment debate. *The Second Amendment and Gun Control* closes, as it opened, with a hotly contested debate about the control of firearms. One of the interesting developments of the debate surrounding the Second Amendment occurring in the twenty-first century follows the United Nations' (UN's) involvement in restricting small arms and light weapons. Some in the United States reacted against the prohibition of civilian possession of arms proposed by the UN committee. As Peter Squires demonstrates, the Republican politician Newt Gingrich some used the opportunity to argue that the Second Amendment was 'for all mankind,' implicitly transforming the defense of gun ownership from one that encompasses hunting and sports shooting to one that is centered on self-defense. For Squires, this is another example of American cultural imperialism that threatens to weaponize areas of the globe hitherto untouched by such a corrosive debate.

Arguing explicitly against Squires, David Kopel makes the opposite case, arguing that self-defense is a fundamental human right that is becoming increasingly recognized around the globe. He states that, of the available tools for self-defense, firearms are the most effective and thus global citizens should have access to some type of firearm to defend their homes, within a reasonable regulatory environment. Kopel agrees that imposing all of the Second Amendment doctrines on other nations would be inappropriate due to many differences in culture and political structure, but that improving legal protections for the fundamental human right of self-defense would be in keeping with a long-established and nearly universal tradition of all nations and peoples.

These closing chapters echo themes that run throughout the book, placing them in context, uncovering what lies behind the thinking on either side of the debate. The Second Amendment, gun control, and self-defense animate deep philosophical debates that run across time and space. In embracing a scholarly approach to the many questions surrounding these issues, these closing chapters, along with previous chapters, encourage readers to think deeply about the Second Amendment and the rights of humans to own guns, and perhaps to think again about their own assumptions and prejudices. The collection makes no grand claims about providing a practical solution to these vexing issues, but instead aims simply to probe more deeply into the debate and hopefully to prompt further consideration of the Second Amendment in the twenty-first century.

1 Constitutional mythology and the future of Second Amendment jurisprudence after *Heller*

Saul Cornell

In *District of Columbia v. Heller*, the Supreme Court reinterpreted the meaning of the "right of the people to keep and bear arms" as an individual right to possess a weapon for self-defense outside of the context of service in a well-regulated militia.[1] Although Justice Scalia's majority opinion surveyed a variety of historical materials in *Heller*, his approach to history was decidedly ahistorical.[2] Furthermore, although originalists insist that the Second Amendment's meaning was frozen at the Founding moment, the right to keep and bear arms does not stand outside of history and culture.[3] It shares with every aspect of the Bill of Rights a complex and dynamic history.

Among all the rights esteemed by Americans, the right to bear arms seems uniquely able to focus constitutional anxieties and aspirations at key moments in American history. In the eighteenth century, the dominant fear was collective self-defense and the dangers posed by a powerful British-style standing army controlled by the new federal government. Antebellum Americans grappled with the nation's first gun violence problem, a moment when the market revolution supplied cheap and reliable handguns for the first time. During Reconstruction, Republicans sought to protect the recently emancipated freedmen and later grappled with ways to respond to the armed terror campaign of paramilitary groups such as the Ku Klux Klan. In modern America, champions of gun rights are likely to fear the risk of home invasion or the specter of "Black Helicopters" coming to take away gun owners' weapons, while gun control advocates are more apt to fear the threat of mass public shootings. Each generation of Americans has debated the meaning of the right to bear arms in terms that reflect the fears, preoccupations, and hopes of their own time.[4]

1 554 U.S. 570 (2008).

2 The Court had last dealt with the Second Amendment in *United States v. Miller*, 307 U.S. 174 (1939), in which it ruled that since shotguns with barrels less than eighteen inches in length had no relationship to a well-regulated militia, the Second Amendment did not guarantee a right to keep and bear such firearms. For a good sampling of scholarly reactions to *Heller*, see Saul Cornell and Nathan Kozuskanich, *The Second Amendment on Trial: Critical Essays on District of Columbia V. Heller* (Amherst, MA: University of Massachusetts Press, 2013).

3 Lawrence B. Solum, "The Fixation Thesis: The Role of Historical Fact in Original Meaning", 91 *Notre Dame Law Review* 1 (2015). For critiques of this view, see Jonathan Gienapp, "Historicism and Holism: Failures of Originalist Translation", 84 *Fordham Law Review* 935 (2015). For legal critiques, see Hedi Kitrosser, "Interpretive Modesty", 104 *Georgetown Law Journal* 459 (2016); James E. Fleming, *Fidelity to Our Imperfect Constitution: For Moral Readings and Against Originalism* (New York: Oxford University Press, 2015).

4 Saul Cornell, *A Well Regulated Militia: The Founding Fathers and the Origins of Gun Control in America* (New York: Oxford University Press, 2006).

Judges are not immune to the cultural anxieties and historical myths that have shaped American culture. History plays many roles in modern constitutional adjudication, but relatively little attention has been devoted to way historical myths have shaped modern constitutional law.[5] To the extent that constitutional scholarship has investigated myths, the focus has been on distinguishing historical reality from the distortions wrought by ideology.[6] In the field of cultural history and American Studies, the term myth is usually used in a more expansive sense. For scholars of American culture, "myth represents ideology in narrative form."[7] Thus, rather than focus exclusively on the distorting impact of ideology, historical and cultural analysis provides a means for understanding why certain conceptions of the past have had such a powerful influence on American culture at particular historical moments, and why certain motifs, images, and genres have enjoyed such longevity over the course of American history.[8] Simply correcting factual errors associated with such myths does not address the deeper cultural and historical forces that make such myths so pervasive in American culture. One of the most important lessons to be gleaned from an American Studies analysis is that simply correcting errors one at a time is unlikely to have much of an impact on the public debate over guns. Nor will fashioning sophisticated alternative academic theories of the Second Amendment decisively change the public debate over this contentious aspect of American law and politics. To make sense to Americans, policy solutions have to fit a narrative that also makes sense. Correcting the errors spawned and nurtured by mythic histories of the American past are analogous to the problematic cultural frames and cognitions that have tainted debates about gun policy. If "more statistics" has seldom led to "more persuasion" in the great American gun debate, a similar problem confronts those seeking to change public discourse over the meaning of the Second Amendment in American culture and law.[9]

The genius of the gun rights movement has been their ability to frame a message that easily fits on a bumper sticker and can be reduced to a sound bites. By contrast, those who support sensible gun regulation have never been able to articulate a persuasive theory of the Second Amendment that makes sense to Americans and that fits into any of the familiar narratives that have dominated American history. To be sure, the nearly hegemonic language of rights talk in modern America makes discussion about rights much more palatable than calls for greater regulation.[10] The iconic image of guns, and the mythic history of America's frontier past, ideas that continue to inform American popular culture, generally supports a gun rights narrative, not a pro-regulation one. Still, the Founders were hardly modern libertarians, and even Dodge City, the quintessential western frontier town, was not a Hobbesian

5 Richard H. Fallon, Jr., "The Many and Varied Roles of History in Constitutional Adjudication", 90 *Notre Dame Law Review* 1753 (2015); Jack M. Balkin, "The New Originalism and the Uses of History", 82 *Fordham Law Review* 641, 657 (2013).

6 Sanford Levinson, "'Constitutional Myths' and 'Democratic Politics': Two Takes on the American Constitution", 49 *Tulsa Law Review* 377 (2013).

7 Richard Slotkin, *Gunfighter Nation: The Myth of the Frontier in Twentieth-Century America* (Norman, OK: Oklahoma University Press,1998), 6.

8 Lucy Maddox, ed., *Locating American Studies: The Evolution of a Discipline* (Baltimore, MD: Johns Hopkins University Press,1999).

9 Dan M. Kahan and Donald Braman, "More Statistics, Less Persuasion: A Cultural Theory of Gun-Risk Perceptions", 151 *University of Pennsylvania Law Review* 1291 (2003).

10 Mary Ann Glendon, *Rights Talk: The Impoverishment of Political Discourse* (New York: The Free Press, 1991); Joseph Blocher, "Gun Rights Talk", 94 *Boston University Law Review* 813–833 (2014).

state of nature. In fact, Dodge City boasted some of the most robust gun regulations in American history.[11]

It is well beyond the scope of this chapter to formulate and craft an alternative narrative, a more useable past that would make the history of regulation as central to American historical mythology as the image of the outlaw or gunslinger.[12] Still, a critical analysis of the constitutional mythologies perpetuated and exploited by gun rights culture and its champions is a necessary first step to creating new alternative historical narratives.

James Madison, Davy Crockett, and the right to hunt bears

The myth of the frontier is one of the most enduring in American history.[13] It has shaped captivity narratives in the colonial era, the dime novels of the nineteenth century, and it continues to inform American movies from the classic westerns of the 1940s to such recent Hollywood franchises as *Die Hard* and *Rambo*.[14] The frontier has also been packaged and used to market everything from cigarettes to cars, and it has been central to the selling of firearms for more than a century.[15] Given these realities, it is hardly surprising that during the oral argument in *Heller*, the most important gun case to reach the Supreme Court in recent memory, Justice Anthony Kennedy embraced the frontier myth with passion, informing the court that the Founders needed their guns to defend themselves against "hostile Indian tribes and outlaws, wolves and bears and grizzlies and things like that."[16] The fact that grizzly bears are indigenous to the western United States, not the eastern, and that few reported instances of bear attacks are evident in either the Philadelphia papers or the writings of the Second Amendment's chief architect, James Madison, seemed entirely irrelevant to Kennedy's mythic conception of early American history.[17] It may not be much of an exaggeration to say that Justice Anthony Kennedy's vote was ultimately won by Fess Parker, the star of Walt Disney's popular 1954 TV series *Davy Crockett*.

The same frontier myth has also informed other post-*Heller* gun decisions in *Moore v. Madigan* and *Peruta* v. *San Diego*. Both cases evoked "the familiar image" of an armed "eighteenth-century frontiersman . . . obtain[ing] supplies from the nearest trading post."[18] This folksy frontier image owes more to America's mythic past than it does to the actual history lived by most Americans in the Founding era. Discussions of the right to hunt were actually quite rare during the debate over the Constitution. If Justice Kennedy's account of the driving force behind the Second Amendment were accurate demands for such a right would have been made in virtually every state. Yet, the main example of such a demand, a text endlessly recycled by modern gun rights advocates as *The Anti-Federalist Dissent of the*

11 Robert R. Dykstra, *The Cattle Towns* (Lincoln, NE: University of Nebraska Press, 1983); Adam Winkler, *Gunfight* (New York: W. W. Norton and Co., 2011).

12 Slotkin, *Gunfighter Nation*.

13 Robert V. Hine and John Mack Faragher, *Frontiers: A Short History of the American West* (New Haven, CT: Yale University Press, 2007).

14 Slotkin, *Gunfighter Nation*.

15 Pamela Haag, *The Gunning of America: Business and the Making of American Gun Culture* (New York: Basic Books, 2016).

16 Transcript of oral argument, 8 at www.supremecourt.gov/oral_arguments/argument_transcripts/07-290.pdf.

17 See William G. Merkel, "*The District of Columbia v. Heller* and Antonin Scalia's Perverse Sense of Originalism", 13 *Lewis and Clark Law Review* 349–381 (2009).

18 *Moore v. Madigan*, 702 F.3d 933, 936 (7th Cir. 2012) and *Peruta v. Cty. of San Diego*, 742 F.3d 1144, 1155–60 (9th Cir. 2014), reh'g en banc granted, 781 F.3d 1106 (9th Cir. 2015).

Minority of Pennsylvania, did not even make it on to Madison's short list of possible amendments.[19] In *Heller*, Justice Scalia took this idiosyncratic Anti-Federalist text and through the alchemy of originalist method transformed it into a proxy for what the typical reader of the Constitution would have thought the Second Amendment meant in 1791. Although the Dissent was influential as a statement of a particular backcountry Anti-Federalist ideology, none of its authors sat in the First Congress that drafted the Second Amendment. Despite actively campaigning for seats in Congress on a platform that demanded amendments, these radical Anti-Federalists were decisively defeated in elections for Congress. Rather than represent the thoughts of the typical competent user of English as originalist theory demands, the Dissent represents the voice of backcountry radicals, an odd choice for the foundation for arguments about original meaning.[20] Of course, one of the many problems with constitutional originalism is that it assumes a model of consensus history that was abandoned by scholars in the humanities and social sciences decades ago. American Studies scholarship has been deeply informed by theories of meaning and interpretation that link communities of discourse to processes of contestation, a model that acknowledges that this process of contestation is itself a product of deeper ideological and social conflicts.[21]

One concept that has been explored in great detail by scholars in American Studies is the frontier. The bulk of the nation's population in the eighteenth century was clustered along the coast, not the frontier.[22] In 1790, the mean population center of the United States, a standard measure of population distribution, was situated somewhere between Baltimore and Philadelphia, not western Kentucky, northern Maine, or the Ohio valley. Nor is there any evidence that Founders such as George Mason or James Madison were thinking about the plight of this tiny percentage of the American people when they discussed the right to keep and bear arms. The exploits of Daniel Boone and Davy Crockett that were popularized during the Jacksonian era, shared little with the Enlightenment and the republican culture of the Founding era that gave rise to the Second Amendment.[23]

Another variant of the frontier myth informed a recent suit brought by the Rocky Mountain Gun Owners Group (RMGO), a group that describes itself as a no-compromise alternative to the NRA.[24] The suit challenged the state of Colorado's ban on high capacity magazines.[25] Essentially, the RMGO claimed that Colorado's history was shaped by its libertarian western heritage. In this mythic history, the West exists as a sparsely populated

19 Cornell, *A Well Regulated Militia*, *supra* note 5.

20 On the notion of fully informed reads and originalism, see Gary Lawson and Guy Seidman, "Originalism as a Legal Enterprise", *Constitutional Commentary* 23 (2006), 47. For a critique of the over-reliance of the Dissent of the Minority in modern Second Amendment debate, see Saul Cornell, "Conflict, Consensus & Constitutional Meaning: The Enduring Legacy of Charles Beard", *Constitutional Commentary* 29 (2013), 383.

21 Saul Cornell, "Meaning and Understanding in the History of Constitutional Ideas: The Intellectual History Alternative to Originalism", 82 *Fordham Law Review* 721 (2013). On American Studies, see Maddox, ed., *Locating American Studies.*

22 Historical geographers agree that the free white population of the United States in the era of the Second Amendment was primarily clustered along the eastern seaboad, not along the "frontier." See Michael R. Haines and Richard H. Steckel, *A Population History of North America* (New York: Cambridge University Press, 2000). See *Animated Mean Center of Population for the United States: 1790 to 2010*, U.S. Census Bureau at www.census.gov/geo/reference/centersofpop/animatedmean2010.html.

23 For a useful historical corrective to such views, Robert V. Hine and John Mack Faragher, *The American West: A New Interpretive History* (New Haven, CT: Yale University Press, 2000).

24 www.rmgo.org/.

25 *Rocky Mountain Gun Owners v. Hickenlooper*, 371 P. 3d 768 (Colo. App. 2016).

wilderness peopled by uncivilized tribal societies.[26] Its settlement occurs as a result of the rugged individualism of pioneers, mostly men, who conquered the natural world and its aboriginal peoples. In reality, the West has been inhabited for thousands of years and was peopled by individuals who belonged to a wide range of sophisticated societies with complex political structures. The exploration and settlement of the West by Europeans required the assistance of the powerful nation states of the Early Modern era, most notably Spain and France. After the emergence of the newly independent United States of America, the geopolitical realities of the West shifted, but it did not end the role of state actors who remained central to its history.[27] Rather than exist as some type of state of nature without government or law, the history of settlement of the West was closely tied to actions of the federal government. Stanford scholar Richard White, one of the America's most distinguished historians of the West, has persuasively argued that Americans living in the nineteenth-century America West were more directly impacted by the actions of the federal government, and far more likely to experience its power in their day-to-day lives than Americans living in any other region of the nation. "The American West," White writes, "more than any other section of the United States, is a creation not so much of individual or local efforts, but federal efforts."[28] Federal exploration of the West was indispensable to map the region and stabilize diplomatic relations with the region's Indian peoples. Although Americans were generally uncomfortable with the idea of a professional standing army in the early Republic, clinging to the idea of the militia despite its limits as an effective means of combating Europe's professional armies, America's small army was absolutely essential to the conquest of the West. Government involvement in the creation of the postal service and eventually government aid for development of a network of rail roads was absolutely vital in helping to integrate the region into the burgeoning national economy.[29] White captures the ideological function of the Frontier myth in modern American history. "In the imagination of modern America, the West has come to stand for independence, self-reliance, and individualism." The related set of images, tropes, and narratives that sustain this mythology have obscured the complex realities of western history, including the experience of westward migration and settlement. The notion of pioneers going it alone, leaving civilization behind and entering a vast wilderness where they constructed a new society free of the corruption and over-reaching hand of government, is both nostalgic and deeply deceptive. With the notable exception of such male-dominated extractive industries as mining and logging, most emigrants westward moved as part of family and kinship networks or in some cases as entire communities. The goal was not to abandon the culture they left behind, but rather to reproduce it in the West.[30]

Treatments of the West in both literature and art echoed these frontier themes. Popular fictional genres such as dime novels and the images produced by new graphic design techniques such as lithography, a technique exploited by the venerable firm of Currier and Ives, made images of hearty pioneers bringing progress and prosperity with them, readily available to Americans eager to learn about the West. From the epic landscape paintings

26 Slotkin, *Gunfighter Nation*
27 Hine and Faragher, *The Amerian West*, 475.
28 Richard White, *"It's Your Misfortune and None of My Own": A History of The American West* (Norman, OK: University of Oklahoma Press, 1991), 55.
29 *Supra* note 1.
30 Anders Stephanson, *Manifest Destiny: American Expansion and The Empire of Right* (New York: Hill and Wang, 1996).

of Albert Bierstadt to the iconic image of John Wayne and other Hollywood cowboys, Americans have been exposed to a steady stream of images of the West shaped by the Frontier myth.[31]

One obvious counter-example to the idea that the West was dominated by an extreme form of liberal individualism was the movement of religious and utopian communities westward. The most important of these movements, the great Mormon migration westward was not driven by radical individualism, but by religious communitarianism. Mormons were impelled to settle in the West because of persecution in the East and Midwest. The survival of Mormon communities in Utah was absolutely dependent on their ability to act collectively and cooperatively to further their common goals.[32]

The transfer of Anglo-American law to the West

One of the most important routes west, the Oregon Trail, was arduous, but it provided a well-charted path westward for those willing to undertake the difficult journey. Western migration was generally an orderly process of settlement in which individuals, families, and communities travelled west together.[33] What did this process mean for the transfer of legal ideas? As the distinguished legal historian John Reid has shown in great detail:

> If there was any part of the western frontier where we might not expect to find Eastern law, it should be the overland trail, the place where there was no legal machinery and individuals told themselves: "There is no law."[34]

Yet, Reid documents that the contrary was the case. "There was not only law, it was law hardly distinguishable from the law emigrants thought they were leaving behind."[35] Not only did settlers bring the law with them on the trek, but once settlers arrived in parts of the West and established stable communities, they recreated the pre-existing legal order based on well-established principles of Anglo-American jurisprudence. Apart from religious and secular utopians, few communities experimented with any radical alternatives, libertarian or communitarian.

The history Reid uncovered is itself revealing about the role of guns in American society. He documents that there were relatively high levels of gun ownership among these settlers, a fact that seems unremarkable, particularly given the sensationalized stories of Indian attacks that circulated in the press. In reality, few pioneers died as a result of Indian raids. Illness and accident were far more likely causes of death on the trail. What was surprising is how often western migrants were injured in firearms accidents. Although settlers had acquired guns, many had minimal knowledge of how to handle guns safely. Once again, the role of guns in American society in the West was far more complex than Hollywood images suggest.[36]

31 Clyde A. Milner II et al., *The Oxford History of the American West* (New York: Oxford University Press,1994), 134, 676–696, 707–729, 794–795.
32 White, *"It's Your Misfortune and None of My Own"*, *supra* note 1.
33 Hine and Faragher, *The American West*, 362–373, 401–430.
34 John Phillip Reid, *Law For the Elephant: Property and Social Behavior on the Overland Trail* (San Marino, CA: Huntington Library, 1997).
35 Ibid., 359–360.
36 John Phillip Reid, *Policing the Elephant: Crime, Punishment, and Social Behavior on the Overland Trail* (San Marino: Huntington Library Press, 1997).

Images of Western violence have helped sell novels and movies for as long as these genres have existed. Accounts of the adventures of Davy Crockett, the traveling exhibitions of Kit Carson and Buffalo Bill Cody, and Hollywood westerns have created images of the West dominated by bandits, outlaws, and gun fighters.[37] There is a lively debate among scholars about how violent the West really was when compared to other regions of America.[38] Although the debate over rates of violence in the West is ongoing among scholars, there is broad agreement on a range of issues about the historical reality of violence in the West. The most violent communities in the West were those in which large numbers of young men lived under economically exploitive conditions. Mining towns, logging camps, and cow towns experienced far higher rates of violence than cities, towns, and stable agricultural communities. How much of this was a function of the West, and how much was function of the absence of traditional institutions, an unbalanced gender ratio, and skewed age distribution of the population is the subject of much academic debate. Still, there is also a general consensus that westerners were eager to impose order on these more violent communities and enacted some of the most stringent regulations of firearms in American history to accomplish this goal. In contrast to the South, where a tradition of permissive open carry of firearms emerged in some places in the antebellum era, in the post-Civil War West, many communities enacted broad bans on public carry.[39]

The early modern language of liberty: rights and obligations

One of the biggest problems with modern legal discussions of the Second Amendment is the difficulty of translating the early modern language of rights into terms that make sense to contemporary Americans.[40] In modern America, rights are typically seen as power-checking mechanism or "trumps," strong claims against government interference. In the early modern Anglo-American world, including colonial America, rights were often seen as a means for meeting civic obligations.[41] Although much has been made about the

37 Slotkin, *Gunfighter Nation*, *supra* note 27.

38 The debate over homicide rates turns on questions about statistical methodologies and small populations. See Robert R. Dykstra, "Quantifying the Wild West: The Problematic Statistics of Frontier Violence", 40 *Western Historical Quarterly* 321 (2009). For the contrary view, see Randolph Roth, *American Homicide* (Cambridge, MA: Harvard University Press, 2009).

39 Dodge City's ban on public carry required individuals to check their firearms before entering town; see Adam Winkler, *Gunfight: The Battle Over the Right to Bear Arms in America* (New York: W.W. Norton & Company, 2011). On restrictions in the "Wild West," see Dodge City, Kan., Ordinance No. 16, § XI (Sept. 22, 1876) and 1876 Wyo. Comp. Laws 52, § 1 (prohibiting anyone from "bear[ing] upon his person, concealed or openly, any fire arm or other deadly weapon, within the limits of any city, town or village."). Localities in Colorado enacted similarly restrictive measures, see Pueblo Colorado, Ordinances, Section Six, Art. II Chap 8 ("If any person other than a law officer shall carry upon his person any loaded pistol, or other deadly weapon, he shall upon conviction be fined not less than fifteen nor more than fifty dollars for each offense, and in addition thereto forfeit to the city any weapon found on his person.") On southern exceptionalism and traditions of open carry, see Saul Cornell, "The Right to Carry Firearms Outside the Home: Separating Historical Myths From Historical Realities", *Fordham Urban Law Journal* 39 (2012), 1695–1726 at note 101.

40 Richard A. Primus, *The American Language of Rights* (New York: Cambridge University Press,1999) and Knud Haakonssen, *Natural Law and Moral Philosophy: From Grotius to the Scottish Enlightenment* (New York: Cambridge University Press,1996); Brian Tierney, "Historical Roots of Modern Rights: Before Locke and After", 3 *Ave Maria Law Review* 24 (2005); Quentin Skinner, *Liberty Before Liberalism* (New York: Cambridge University Press,1997) and Jud Campbell, "Republicanism and natural rights at the Founding", *Constitutional Commentary* 32 (2017), 85.

41 Kenneth Campbell, "Legal Rights", in Edward N. Zalta (ed.), *The Stanford Encyclopedia of Philosophy* (Fall 2013 Edition) at http://plato.stanford.edu/archives/fall2013/entries/legal-rights/.

pre-existing right of self-defense under English common law, far less attention has been devoted to the obligations imposed by common law.[42] Under common law, individuals had an obligation to assist agents of the crown in restoring order when summoned by justices of the peace or constables. In the first state constitutions, the right not to be forced to bear arms was typically coupled with the right to bear arms, to protect religious pacifists such as Quakers, Moravians, and Mennonites, from being forced to bear arms in violation of their religious scruples.[43] The notion that rights might carry civic obligations and impose duties on rights holders cuts against the modern liberal conception of rights. In modern legal theory, rights are typically understood to impose obligations on *others* who are bound to respect the claims of rights holders, not impose obligations on the holders of rights themselves.

Early modern conceptions of liberty, including those embedded in Anglo-American law, were shaped by conceptions of civic republicanism and natural law notions that no longer have a powerful hold on modern legal culture. In America, the modern rights revolution has largely been driven by conceptions of negative liberty, not the ideas of positive liberty that were so central to civic republicanism and natural law theories of the early modern era.[44]

Thus, it is easy to see how Judge Richard J. Leon could so easily misconstrue early American laws requiring colonists to carry guns to church as evidence for a broad public right to travel armed.[45] Leon averred that "in the Colonial Period, carrying arms publicly was not only permitted – it was often required!" The problem with Judge Leon's interpretation is that the law he cites did not assert a rights claim, but it imposed a legal duty on colonists and levied a fine on those who failed to meet this obligation to assist in the public defense of the colony. Relations between Virginians and Indians in the region were exceedingly tense in 1619, and the law enacted by the colony clearly expanded the scope of normal militia duties to require some colonists to bear arms during *mandatory* church attendance.[46] The 1619 law referenced by Leon only applied to the portion of the population able to bear arms, a subset of white men, so in the analogy to a modern-style universal rights, the claim is even more strained.

> ALL men that are fittinge to beare armes, shall bringe their pieces to the church uppon payne for every effence, if the default be in the master, to pay 2lb. of tobacco, to be disposed by the church-wardens, who shall levy it by distresse, and the servants shall be punished commander.

42 *District of Columbia v. Heller*, 554 U.S. 570 (2008).

43 Cornell, *A Well Regulated Militia*, Chaps. 1–2.

44 On the correlative connections between rights and duties in modern law, Leif Wenar, "Rights", in Edward N. Zalta (ed.), *The Stanford Encyclopedia of Philosophy* (Fall 2015 Edition) at https://plato.stanford.edu/archives/fall2015/entries/rights/.

45 Much of the legal scholarship that Leon relied on was in the genre of law office history or "history lite." On the limits of these approaches to the legal past, see Stephen A. Siegel, "How Many Critiques Must Historians Write", 45 *Tulsa Law Review* 823 (2009) and Martin S. Flaherty, "Can the Quill Be Mightier than the Uzi?: History 'Lite,' 'Law Office,' and Worse Meets the Second Amendment", 37 *Cardozo Law Review* 663 (2015).

46 William Walter Hening, Act XLV 1 *Statutes at Large* 1619 at 198 (1823). Judge Leon also neglects to note that at this moment in Virginia history, there was no separation of church and state. Early Virginia also penalized parents for not properly instructing children and apprentices in the catechism endorsed by the Church of England, Id., ACT VII. At 181–182. It also taxed colonists to support the established church and penalized those who failed to attend church, see Id., ACT XVI. At 184.

When read in context, the law demonstrates the extraordinary power of early colonial governments exercised over inhabitants, and it does not vindicate a strong liberty interest that might be claimed against government authority. In 1770, Georgia enacted a similar law that required all white men "liable to bear arms in the militia" to bring arms to church. The preamble of the Statute made clear that the purpose of the law was to promote the "necessary security and defense of this province from internal dangers and insurrections."[47] Rather than support the myth of lone colonists, gun in hand, fighting off threats, or the notion of an absent state with little power and no interest in regulating arms, these laws demonstrate that individual colonies acted aggressively to force colonists to arms themselves when public safety required it. Laws regulating firearms are as old as America itself, and these laws were absolutely essential to preserving ordered liberty. The power of the state to compel its subjects and later citizens to bear arms was considerable. Using such laws as historical evidence of a private right to carry arms without government interference literally turns history upside down.

Creating a new gun rights mythology: inventing a right to travel armed

In *Peruta* v. *San Diego*, Judge Diarmuid O'Scannlain endorsed a popular gun rights myth about the pre-existing English right to have arms. According to O'Scannlain, travel with arms was only a crime under English common law if one carried "uncommon, frightening weapons." By contrast, "wearing ordinary weapons in ordinary circumstances posed no problem."[48] In this instance, the mythic history O'Scannlain's invoked was not of ancient vintage, but had been carefully manufactured by gun rights advocates and their academic supporters over the last forty years.[49] English history provides scant support for such a libertarian vision of the past, but it is important to recall that mythic histories are ideological constructs that need not conform to the traditional rules of academic debate or standards of historical proof.[50]

A key element in this invented tradition of gun rights was a new ideological reading of the Statute of Northampton (1328) proffered by gun rights activist David Caplan. This anachronistic reading was picked up by other gun rights scholars, including Joyce Lee Malcolm and David Kopel.[51]

As a strictly textual matter, there is little in the Statute of Northampton to support a gun rights reading. The statute declared that all individuals, regardless of their station, were bound to "bring no force in affray of the peace, nor to go nor ride armed by night nor by

47 Robert George Watkins, *A Digest of the Laws of the State of Georgia* (Philadelphia: R. Aitken, 1800), 157.

48 *Peruta v. San Diego*, *supra* note 19.

49 The gun rights view is succinctly stated by Eugene Volokh, "The First and Second Amendments", 109 *Columbia Law Review Sidebar* 97, 101 (2009).

50 For a critique of the gun rights view, see Patrick Charles, "The Faces of the Second Amendment Outside of the Home, Take Two: How We Got Here and Why It Matters", 64 *Cleveland State Law Review* 373 (2016), especially 392–398. Charles traces this invented right to the writing of gun rights advocate David Caplan who in 1975 was hired by the Indiana Sportsmen's Council to produce a pro-gun report on the Second Amendment. Caplan revised the essay and published it as David I. Caplan, "Restoring the Balance: The Second Amendment Revisited", 5 *Fordham Urban Law Journal* 31 (1976).

51 Caplan's take on Englilsh common law was then picked up by Joyce Lee Malcolm, "The Right of the People to Keep and Bear Arms: The Common Law Tradition", 10 *Hastings Constitutional Law Quarterly* 285–314 (1983) and David Kopel, "It Isn't About Duck Hunting: The British Origins of the Right to Arms", 93 *Michigan Law Review* 1333–1362 (1995) a slightly fawning and uncritical review of Joyce Lee Malcolm's book, *To Keep and Bear Arms: The Origins of Anglo-American Right* (Cambridge, MA: Harvard University Press,1994).

day."[52] Given the obvious plain meaning of text of the statute, transforming it into a provision justifying a broad right to travel armed required a good deal of creativity on the part of gun rights champions, both within and outside of the academy. If one parses the text, it would be hard to dispute that it embodies both a set of categorical prohibitions on armed travel in public and acknowledge some context-dependent exemptions to this general prohibition. Although the statute categorically bans travel in fairs and markets, or before representatives of the King's Peace, it does recognize certain contextual exemptions. The most important of these exceptions was the legal obligation to lend assistance to the agents of the crown to put down riots and enforce the peace. By confusing the exceptions to the rule with the rule itself, gun rights advocates have effectively turned the historical reality on its head.[53]

It is important to recall that under common law rights, claims could be linked to civic obligations. One had a right to own weapons, so that one might meet an obligation to help maintain the peace. Thus, the most important recognized exceptions to the ban on armed travel were the "hue and cry," a form of community policing. When a justice of the peace or other agent of the Crown summoned individuals to help keep the peace, subjects were expected to turn up with whatever weapons they were legally entitled to own, and this was itself determined by social class.[54]

Although *Heller* cast the English Declaration of Rights (1688) as a gun rights provision, the text hardly supports such an interpretation. The Declaration of Rights affirmed: "That the subjects which are Protestants may have arms for their defence suitable to their conditions and as allowed by law." Few rights enshrined in the Declaration of Rights (1688) fit the modern theory of rights as trumps. The right to have arms was not universal, but was limited by religion and class. Parliament's authority over arms was not in any way limited by the Declaration of Rights. In fact, the formulation of the right reasserted Parliament's plenary power to legislate on matters pertaining to arms and when necessary restrict this right in a manner consistent with its broad and nearly unlimited powers to protect the peace and promote public safety. Indeed, when Parliament considered revising the Game Laws in 1693, it expressly considered and rejected a proposal to carve out an exception for keeping arms at home for reasons of self-defense. Not only did the House of Commons reject a proposal to expressly protect a right to keep guns in the home, but the House of Lords quashed the idea as too radical because it tended to "arm the mob."[55]

The 1688 Declaration of Rights did not restrict Parliament's broad authority over weapons nor did it provide a legal justification for challenging the property requirements for gun ownership found in the various game laws.[56] The game laws not only limited who might keep arms, but they also placed limits on who could travel armed. The exceptions to the

52 The Statute of Northampton 1328, 2 Edw. 3, c. 3 (Eng.); on the creation of a gun rights interpretation of the Statue, see Charles, The Faces of the Second Amendment Outside the Home, 393.

53 Malcolm, *To Keep and Bear Arms*.

54 The Statute of Winchester 1 Statutes of the Realm 26 1235–1377 (1275) not only set out the obligations of the "hue and cry," but it differentiated the type of weaponry subjects were required to own to meet this obligation based upon the amount of land they owned.

55 See Lois G. Schwoerer, "To Hold and Bear Arms: The English Perspective", in Carl T. Bogus (ed.), *The Second Amendment in Law and History: Historians and Constitutional Scholars on the Right to Bear Arms* (New York: New Press, 2000), 207, 207–221; Patrick J. Charles, "Arms for Their Defence – An Historical, Legal and Textual Analysis of the English Right to Have Arms and Whether the Second Amendment Should Be Incorporated in McDonald v. City of Chicago", 57 *The Cleveland* State *Law Review* 351, 403 (2009).

56 William Nelson, *The Laws of England Concerning the Game of Hunting, Hawking, Fishing And Fowling, & C. . . .* (London, E. Richardson and C. Lintot, 1727), 165–177.

broad prohibition only serve to underscore how limited the pre-existing right was in practice. Many eighteenth-century commentaries on the law also noted that aristocrats traveling with arms suitable to their condition or with armed retainers did not violate the statute of Northampton.[57] This was a class privilege, not a rights claim. Building on the historical misreading of gun rights advocates, who have interpreted this aristocratic privilege as a rights claim, Judge O'Scannlain reasoned that only terrifying behavior, not mere possession of a gun ran afoul of the prohibition on armed travel. This interpretation not only makes little historical sense, but it does not make any logical sense given the wording of the exemption. It would hardly have been necessary to carve out a specific class-based exemption for aristocrats if there had been a broad general right to travel armed in England.[58]

Evidence to contradict this mythic history of the right to carry is not hard to find if one look at the contemporaneous English sources in a systematic manner. One of the earliest mentions of the Statute of Northampton after the Glorious Revolution was in James Tyrrell, *Bibliotheca Politica*.[59] Tyrrell played a key role in popularizing Lockean theory in the era of the Glorious Revolution. A conservative Whig, Tyrrell set out to formulate a defense of 1688 that would blunt the radicalism of the Revolution, particularly the danger posed by popular violence. Although he conceded that there was a limited right "to take up Arms," such a right was only to be exercised as a last resort that might be invoked by the people "in their own Defense against illegal Violence." He further qualified the right by asserting that such a claim had to be exercised "in such manner as the law directs." Thus even in the most extreme examples of tyranny, where liberty itself was at stake, the resort to violence was itself constrained by law. The right to carry arms in public outside of such extraordinary circumstances was even more restricted, a point stressed by Tyrell in his invocation of the Statute of Northampton. It was a crime, he confidently asserted "to ride or go arm'd as may appear in the Statute of *Northampton*."[60]

Michael Dalton's widely reprinted justice of the peace manual went through multiple editions in the decades after 1688, and he echoed this limited view of the right to travel armed: "All such as shall go or ride armed (offensively) in Fairs, Markets, or elsewhere; or shall wear or carry any Guns, Dags or Pistols charged" could be arrested and brought "before the Justice of the Peace, and he may bind them to the Peace."[61] Rather than encourage individuals to arms themselves in response to such threats, English law required individuals to seek out a magistrate, justice of the peace, or constable and have the aggressor disarmed and placed under a peace bond.[62] J. P. Gent's *A New Guide for Constables* (1705) reminded readers that standard constables' oath required that he "arrest all such Persons as in your presence shall ride or go armed offensively, or commit or make any Riot, Affray or Breach of the Peace." The crime of going armed offensively, was a legally distinct offense, and all of the accounts distinguish it from a riot, affray, or breach of the peace. Gent's account is typical of this approach. Joseph Keble, author of another popular guide to the law, warned that if anyone

57 Saul Cornell, "The Right to Carry Firearms Outside the Home: Separating Historical Myths From Historical Realities", *Fordham Urban Law Journal* 39 (2012), 1695–1726 at note 101.
58 *Peruta v. San Diege, supra* note 19.
59 James Tyrell, *Bibliotheca Politica: Or an Enquiry into the Ancient Constitution of the English Government Both in Respect to the Just Extent of Regal Power, and the Rights and Liberties of the Subject* (London: R. Baldwin, 1694), 460. For a brief but lucid discussion of his importance, see the review essay, Tim Harris, "James II, The Glorious Revolution, and the Destiny of Britain", 51 *The Historical Journal* 763 (2008).
60 Tyrell, *Bibliotheca Politica, supra* note 60 at 460.
61 Michael Dalton, *The Country Justice* . . . (London: H. Lintot, 1728), 380.
62 William Hawkins, *Pleas of the Crown* (London: E. Richardson and C. Lintot, 1715).

was so "bold as to go or ride Armed, by night or day, in Fairs, Markets, or any other places," constables could disarm him and "commit him to the gaol."[63]

These prohibitions on armed travel were carried over to colonial America. Many of the popular English legal guides, most notably Dalton, were adapted and published in the colonies. One of the earliest American versions was published by North Carolina jurist, James Davis, who wrote in 1774:

> Justices of the Peace, upon their own View, or upon Complaint, may apprehend any Person who shall go or ride armed with unusual and offensive weapons, in an Affray, or among any great Concourse of the People, or who shall appear, so armed, before the King's Justices sitting in Court.[64]

Again, Davis separated out riding armed from the crime of affray. After the Revolution, a number of states, including North Carolina, Virginia, and Massachusetts, expressly adopted their own versions of the Statute of Northampton.[65] Virginia's statute also drew on the original English text, with one important change, noted by William Hennig, a leading lawyer in the state, who remarked that legislature introduced additional due process protections for those accused of violating the law. "The act of assembly of Virginia materially differs from the act of parliament" he wrote, "being more favorable to liberty." In Virginia, a justice of the peace could not seize arms and imprison an individual for more than a month. To impose a stiffer penalty required a jury verdict, a higher due process standard, and hence a greater safeguard for liberty.[66] Massachusetts opted for a different formulation of the crime drawn from prior English commentators. It forbade anyone who "shall ride or go armed offensively, to the fear or terror of the good citizens of this Commonwealth."[67] A New Jersey guide for constables interpreted the state's inherited common law restrictions in terms similar to language of the Massachusetts statute. It banned anyone from going "armed offensively." The author of this guide elaborated on what this meant by this noting the following:

> So a Justice of the Peace may, in his own discretion, require sureties for the peace from one who shall go or ride armed offensively to the terror of the people, though they he may not have threatened any person in particular, or committed any particular act of violence.[68]

63 J.P. Gent, *A New Guide for Constables, Head-Boroughs, Tythingmen, Churchwardens* (London: The Assigns of Richard and Edward Atkins, esq.,1705), 13. Joseph Keble, *An Assistance to Justices of the Peace, For the Easier Performance of Their Duty* (1689 W. Rawlins, S. Roycroft, and H. Sawbridge, assigns of Richard and Edward Atkins, Esq.), 147, 224.

64 See J. Davis, *The Office and Authority of a Justice of the Peace*, vol. 13 (NewbernNC: J. Davis 1774), 13. https://digital.lib.ecu.edu/text/16960/unusual%20and%20offensive%20weapons#hit1.

65 Francois Xavier Martin, *A Collection of Statutes of the Parliament of England in Force IN the State of North-Carolina* (Newbern, NC: The editor's press, 1792), 60–61 prohibiting individuals who ("go nor ride armed by night nor by day"); *A Collection of All Such Acts of the General Assembly of Virginia, of a Public and Permanent Nature, as Are Now in Force* 33 (Richmond, VA: Augustine Davis, 1794).

66 See William Waller Hening, *The New Virginia Justice Comprising the Office and Authority of a Justice of the Peace, in the Commonwealth of Virginia. Together With a Variety of Useful Precedents Adapted to the Laws Now in Force* (Richmond, VA: Johnson and Warner, 1810), 50.

67 2 *The Perpetual Laws, of the Commonwealth of Massachusetts, From the Establishment of Its Constitution to the Second Session of the General Court, in* 1798 259 (Worcester, MA: Isaiah Thomas, 1799) prohibiting individuals who ("shall ride or go armed offensively, to the fear or terror of the good citizens of this Commonwealth").

68 James Ewing, *A Treatise on the Office and Duty of the Justice of the Peace, Sheriff, Coroner, Constable . . .* (Trenton, NJ: James Oram, 1805).

The notion that American Revolution had brushed aside earlier limits on armed travel in public is not borne out by contemporary sources from the Founding era. To be sure, there were many situations in America where traveling armed was sanctioned by law. Traveling to muster or hunting in season on private lands or areas permitted by law posed no legal problem in America. Traveling to the local gunsmith or engaging in target practice in places allowed by law were also perfectly legal. The constitution protections afforded bearing arms in a well-regulated militia would have created something akin to a penumbra of protection for carrying those militia weapons on a variety of non-militia occasions. Similarly, the traditional English exemption for traveling armed in areas beyond the King's peace, areas outside of populous regions where one could not depend on the protection of the law, continued to enjoy a common law exemption to the general ban on armed carry. The key for evaluating the legality of traveling armed was both context dependent and exceedingly sensitive to the time, place, and manner in which one chose to arm themselves. In this sense, the scope of the right to travel armed in public in the early American republic fits neither the radical gun rights position or the most assertive modern gun control stance. The historical reality lies somewhere between these extremes. If modern American politics seems to offer only two positions – pro-gun or pro-regulation, the stance that best captures the early American view would likely be both pro-gun and pro-regulation. The two were inextricably linked together in Anglo-American law.

The origins of the right to carry: Southern exceptionalism and Northern regulation

The American Revolution did not freeze the meaning of the right to keep and bear arms. Nor did it permanently fix the scope of the right outside of the home. American law, particularly regarding the right to travel armed, evolved as society and technology changed.[69] In the antebellum South, two different models of arms bearing emerged, and each had profound consequences for the scope of government regulation of armed travel in public. A libertarian tradition developed in parts of the South that vindicated a robust right to travel armed in public. Bans on concealed weapons were permissible, but only if open carry was available. A different civic republican model emerged in other parts of the South. This alternative conception extended heightened protection to the uses of arms consistent with the militia purpose of state provisions on the right to bear arms (defined in broad terms), and treated other firearms as ordinary property subject to the full scope of the state's police powers. *Heller* treated the libertarian Southern tradition as dominant, but most nineteenth-century commentators viewed the rival civic republican approach as the dominant antebellum juridical model.[70]

Legal scholarship prior to *Heller* naturally focused considerable attention on antebellum case law, a fact reflected in Justice Scalia's majority opinion in *Heller,* which looked to this tradition to understand the scope of Second Amendment rights in the decades

69 For a brief overview of these changes, see Saul Cornell, "The Right to Bear Arms", in Mark Tushnet, Sanford Levinson, and Mark A. Graber (eds.), *The Oxford Handbook of the U.S. Constitution* (New York: Oxford University Press, 2015).

70 *District of Columbia v. Heller*, 554 U.S. 570 (2008). Gun rights scholar Michael P. O'Shea, "Modeling the Second Amendment Right to Carry Arms: Judicial Tradition and the Scope of 'Bearing Arms' for Self-Defense", 61 *American University Law Review* 585, 637 (2012), argues that the Heller forecloses any legal recourse to the view of the right to bear arms embodied in the Southern cases within this civic republican tradition.

after its adoption. The fact that this jurisprudential tradition was unique to the slave South, did not spark much scholarly interest at that time and accordingly did not receive any judicial notice in *Heller*. More recent scholarship by historians has not only helped contextualize the emergence of this Southern tradition, but it has also uncovered a regulatory tradition previously invisible because it was not contested and did not produce any case law. Ironically, Scalia's injunction to look more closely at the history of regulation for guidance has produced a much richer understanding of the early history of gun regulation and a plethora of new evidence that armed travel in public was limited outside of the slave South.

Among the most significant discoveries of this new body of historical scholarship is the importance of local and regional variation in the gun regulatory traditions that emerged after the American Revolution and the adoption of the Second Amendment. This profound legal localism and regionalism was effectively invisible to the *Heller* court, which erroneously assumed that the Southern tradition embodied in the extant case law was representative of broader American legal attitudes in the Founding era and early republic. In fact, the Southern libertarian tradition of permissive carry was exceptional and reflected the unique circumstances of the slave South. Outside of the slave South, a different, more restrictive tradition of public carry emerged in the decades after the Founding era, one consistent with the idea of a well-regulated society[71]

This tradition of well-regulated liberty was embodied in the variant of the Statute of Northampton Massachusetts enacted in 1795. Rather than drew on the text of the ancient statute itself, the Massachusetts legislature adopted a gloss on its text that had become popular in many of the justice of the peace manuals printed on both side of the Atlantic in the eighteenth century. In a society in which there was a dearth of legal texts, these popular legal guides played an even more important role in shaping ideas about the law. Massachusetts framed its prohibition on public carry in robust terms: it outlawed anyone who "shall ride or go armed offensively, to the fear or terror of the good citizens of this Commonwealth."[72] This particular gloss on the Statute of Northampton provided the foundation for an alternative regulatory model that was copied by many states in the decades to come.[73] Other justices of the peace manuals in New England lauded this approach. In contrast to the libertarian legal ideology adopted in parts of the slave-owning South, New England's model was far more communitarian: the preservation of the peace was of paramount importance, and the powers of the justice of the peace to enforce this were considerable. As one Connecticut justice of the peace manual made clear, the law not only prohibited breaches of the peace, but even an "inchoate breach" such as traveling "offensively armed" or with "an unusual number of attendants." In 1835, Massachusetts revised the 1795 law, bringing it in line with more recent case law outside of the South and the wider movement to codify the common law.[74] The new Massachusetts statute prohibited armed travel, but it recognized and defined with greater precision the contextual exceptions to the general prohibition on armed travel. The law allowed an exception for situations in which a person faced

71 William J. Novak, *The People's Welfare: Law and Regulation in Nineteenth Century America* (Chapel Hill, NC: University of North Carolina Press,1996).

72 2 *The Perpetual Laws*, 259 *supra* note 59.

73 See Elisha Hammond, *A Practical Treatise;* or *An Abridgement of the Law Appertaining to the Office of Justice of the Peace; and Also Relating to the Practice in Justices' Courts, in Civil and Criminal Matters, With Appropriate Forms of Practice* 184–186 (1841).

74 Robert Gordon, "The American Codification Movement", 36 *Vanderbilt Law Review* 451 (1983).

a reasonable and imminent threat. Building on the common law tradition and the earlier 1795 statute the new law declared:

> If any person shall go armed with a dirk, dagger, sword, pistol, or other offensive and dangerous weapon, without reasonable cause to fear an assault or other injury, or violence to his person, or to his family or property, he may on complaint of any person having reasonable cause to fear an injury, or breach of the peace, be required to find sureties for keeping the peace.[75]

The distinguished Massachusetts jurist Peter Oxenbridge Thacher summarized the import of the new law:

> In our own Commonwealth no person may go armed with a dirk, dagger, sword, pistol, or other offensive and dangerous weapon, without reasonable cause to apprehend an assault or violence to his person, family, or property.[76]

The new Massachusetts model was emulated by a number of states in the North and West. By the era of Reconstruction, it had even gained support in parts of the South.

Heller accepted the outdated consensus history model of American law. More recent scholarship has demonstrated considerable regional and local diversity regarding the regulation of firearms.[77] By the end of the nineteenth century, there was a range of legal regimes in place regarding firearms and public travel in America. In parts of the slave South, an expansive libertarian vision of the right to bear arms had taken hold. This development reflected the unique history of the South, particularly the institution of slavery.[78] In other parts of the South a more eighteenth-century-style civic republican conceptions of arms bearing and the right to travel endured. Only militia weapons enjoyed full constitutional protection under this model. The most popular approach, however, was the new Massachusetts model and its modification of the common law right to travel armed. In contrast to the slave South, the Massachusetts Model continued to place greater emphasis on the preservation of peace and viewed the right of armed travel in narrow terms. This new paradigm did make explicit an exception to the general prohibition in cases where there was a clear and imminent danger that justified arming oneself.[79] Finally, in parts of the West, the area most closely identified with a libertarian mythology, the most restrictive regulatory regime – complete bans on public carry – emerged in a number of localities.

When one reconstructs the full range of regulatory regimes in place for public carry in the nineteenth century, it becomes clear that the Southern model is exceptional, not representative. Developing a modern firearms jurisprudence from opinions issued by slave holding

75 See *Perpetual Laws*, *supra* note 69.

76 Peter Oxenbridge Thacher, *Two Charges to the Grand Jury of the County of Suffolk for the Commonwealth of Massachusetts, at the Opening of Terms of the Municipal Court of the City of Boston, on Monday, December 5th, A.D. 1836 and on Monday, March 13th, A.D. 27–28.*

77 Cornell, "Conflict, Consensus & Constitutional Meaning", *supra* note 21.

78 For a brief overview of these changes, see Saul Cornell, "The Right to Bear Arms", in Mark Tushnet, Mark A. Graber, and Sanford Levinson (eds.), *The Oxford Handbook of the U.S. Constitution* (New York: Oxford University Press, 2015), 739–759.

79 Eric M. Ruben and Saul Cornell, "Firearm Regionalism and Public Carry: Placing Southern Antebellum Case Law in Context", 125 *Yale Law Journal Forum* 121 (2015), www.yalelawjournal.org/forum/firearm-regionalism-and-public-carry.

Southern judges, who were among the most extreme voices in pre-civil war America, does not make much sense. Together with radical abolitionists, slave owners voiced an aggressive view of the scope of the right to carry arms in public. Although the expansive vision of the Second Amendment espoused by these radical groups are an important part of America's legal tradition, using this model as the foundation for a new post-*Heller* jurisprudence seems problematic on a variety of levels. The chaos and violence of Kansas in the 1850s ought to serve as a cautionary warning about following this path.[80]

Conclusion: mythic histories and the Second Amendment

Although it is hardly surprising that constitutional mythologies have exerted a strong influence on popular understandings of the Second Amendment, the power that these myths have over recent judicial opinions is a bit more surprising. One might have expected judges to be less prone to reason based on mythic histories, but in the case of guns, this is not the case. In particular, judges inclined toward an originalist interpretation of the Constitution have been especially prone to confuse historical myth and reality. Originalism seeks to invoke the authority of history, but it has thus far studiously avoided engaging with the complex methodological problems associated with historical interpretation. At least for judges, a more rigorous historical methodology is needed to help them navigate the complex historical issues that *Heller*'s framework imposes on judges. Separating historical myths from historical reality is a good starting point.

Three particular myths have had an especially pernicious role in obscuring the historical meaning of the Second Amendment. The myth of the frontier, one of the most powerful myths in American history, has led judges to confuse the world of Davy Crockett with the world of James Madison. The Second Amendment was not a product of the frontier, but a constitutional response to eighteenth-century Whig concerns about the danger posed by standing armies. A second myth that has distorted discussions of the Second Amendment is the notion that early America was essentially stateless and that gun regulation is a relatively recent development in American history and has largely been driven by an insidious racist agenda. It is important to distinguish between the long history of racially neutral gun regulation in America and the separate history of racial disarmament perpetuated in the plantation societies of the slave South and resurrected in the post-Reconstruction era South. Finally, the notion that the pre-existing English right to have arms included a broad right to travel armed, a myth of relatively recent vintage, one deliberately crafted by gun rights advocates eager to further a pro-gun agenda, is not supported by the historical record. The right to travel armed was always narrowly understood under English law apart from some well-delineated legal exceptions. There is little doubt that early American society was far better armed than England, and it is equally indisputable that the number of circumstances in which American citizens might legally use guns in public was greater than the more restrictive situation faced by English subjects. Yet, this historical reality is a far cry from the myths manufactured by Hollywood that continue to shape public ideas about guns in America history.

Leaving aside questions of jurisprudence, the larger cultural project of shaping a popular narrative for the Second Amendment that makes gun regulation seem as American as apple pie poses a number of problems for those eager to deal with America's gun violence

80 Cornell, *A Well Regulated Militia*, *supra* note 4.

problem. Exposing existing mythology is an important first step in developing a new narrative that can accommodate the complex history of gun ownership and gun regulation in American history. Fashioning compelling narratives poses a whole new range of challenges for those eager to promote gun safety. Although guns have played a prominent role in American society since the colonial era, guns have always been regulated. Developing a story that recognizes both dimensions of the American past poses great challenges, but it is essential to moving beyond the current impasse in the great American gun debate.

2 The Second Amendment right to self-defence

The core freedom in the new century

Joyce Lee Malcolm

Self-defence therefore, as it is justly called the primary law of nature, so it is not, neither can it be in fact, taken away by the law of society.

—William Blackstone, *Commentaries on the Laws of England*, vol. 3, p. 4.

Those who would give up essential Liberty, to purchase a little temporary Safety, deserve neither Liberty nor Safety.

—Benjamin Franklin, for Pennsylvania Assembly in its *Reply to the Governor*, Nov. 11, 1755

To William Blackstone, self-defence was not only "justly called the primary law of nature," but "is not, either can it be in fact, taken away by the law of society."[1] The great English jurist was writing in the late eighteenth century. Since the freedom to exercise any particular right alters over the years, it is useful to gauge its vitality from time to time. Happily, in England and America, most liberties have tended to expand. By contrast, America's Second Amendment recognizing the right of individuals to arms for self-defence, an English legacy, has been under attack in both countries, and while reaffirmed and robust in America, it is now practically extinct in England. This Anglo-American right was unusual from the first. Few governments trust their people with weapons. While all individual rights pose some risk to public safety, many people in Britain and some in America have come to distrust ordinary people with the right to be armed, arguing it is archaic, that public safety is best served if only government professionals have firearms. Society, we are told, will protect us.

Will it? Can it? No police force, however large, can protect everyone, or even any one of us all of the time. What goes unsaid is that the danger to individuals, banned from adequate means to defend themselves and their families, has been deemed necessary in the interest of the supposed greater good. This view prevails in England where, unlike America, rights are not embedded in a constitution and thus susceptible to limitations or even abolition.

1 William Blackstone, *Commentaries on the Laws of England*, 4 vols. (Oxford: Clarendon Press, 1765–1769), vol. 3, 4.

Firearms have been restricted in England since 1920,[2] and handguns owned by civilians were confiscated and banned in 1998.[3] In fact, almost any item useful for personal defence, even those not lethal, such as chemical sprays, are prohibited. In answer to the question, "Are there any legal self-defence products that I can buy?" the British website "Ask the Police," replied, "The only legal self-defence product at the moment is a rape alarm."[4] The police advisor added,

> accepting there is a lot of concern about street crime, we can try to clarify matters a little by putting forward the following points. You **must not** [emphasis in the original], get a product which is made or adapted to cause a person injury. Possession of such a product in public (and in private in certain circumstances)is against the law.

A spray with a bright dye is mentioned as an alternative to the rape whistle although with the caveat, "be aware that even a seemingly safe product, deliberately aimed and sprayed in someone's eyes, would become an offensive weapon because it would be used in a way that was intended to cause injury." If attacked while shopping, the victim should "shout 'fire' rather than 'help'. It tends to attract more attention." This reversal of the common law requirement to intervene is the result of years of government cautioning people not to intervene – that is, help – if they see a crime taking place. Instead, they are to call the police. Clearly those crafting these policies seem unconcerned that any individual attacked on the street is at risk for immediate and grave injury and should be entitled to an effective means to protect himself or herself. Using force for self-defence now is denounced as vigilantism, as taking the law into one's own hands.

In America, by contrast, the common law right to be armed for self-defence still stands and is, if anything, more robust than in the past. This is despite the argument raised in the 1960s and widely promoted, claiming the Second Amendment is not an individual right, but a "collective" right granted only to members of a state militia. This question of the amendment's core meaning was settled by two recent landmark Supreme Court decisions.[5] In 2008, in *District of Columbia v. Heller*, the Supreme Court overturned a handgun ban imposed on residents of Washington, DC, for more than twenty years, and affirmed the right of individuals to keep and bear those firearms "in common use for self-defense and other lawful purposes." Two years later, in *McDonald v. City of Chicago*, the Court incorporated that Second Amendment protection throughout the country, overturning Chicago's handgun ban and finding the right to be armed "fundamental to *our* scheme of ordered liberty and system of justice."

2 Firearms Control Act, 1920. The requirement of this statute that the police must verify the suitability of the individual to own a gun, and whether he has a good reason for owning it, has been subject to a series of classified directives from the Home Office. These have worked to restrict the reasons for owning a firearm, finally, in 1969, eliminating self-defence as a good reason. See Joyce Lee Malcolm, *Guns and Violence: The English Experience* (Cambridge, MA: Harvard University Press 2002), 155–156, 159–161, 171–172.

3 Firearms Act, 1997, Firearms Act, no. 2, 1997.

4 "Ask the Police" at www.askthe.police.uk/.

5 US Supreme Court, *District of Columbia v. Heller* (2008), US Supreme Court, *McDonald v. City of Chicago* (2010). The idea that the Second Amendment did not protect an individual right but was only a guarantee that states could have a militia was argued from the 1960s and became a common view in law schools. The question had never been decided by the Supreme Court. Both recent decisions found the core of the amendment is the right of individuals to have arms for personal defense.

In recent years, American states have been easing their requirements for law-abiding citizens wishing to carry a concealed weapon. In thirty states, citizens who meet basic requirements must be allowed that right to carry a weapon, while twelve additional states go even further, permitting anyone who legally owns a gun to carry it without further regulation.[6] Of the fifty states, only eight remain "may issue" states. These eight have discretionary carry, imposing serious restrictions upon anyone wishing to carry a gun. The decision is usually left to the local police to determine whether an applicant has a "good reason" to be armed and/or meets other requirements.[7] An applicant failing to satisfy the police is stripped of any right to carry a firearm outside the home.

There is no exact figure for the number of privately owned guns in America because there is no central registry. However, before a firearm can be purchased, the Federal Bureau of Investigation (FBI) requires a background check employing the National Instant Criminal Background Check System database, or NICS, to determine whether the applicant has committed a felony or has some other indicator he or she might endanger the public. These background checks show that the number of private firearms has risen dramatically in the past few years. Eight months in 2015 set a record with a final tally for the year of 23,141,970 applications.[8] In sum, more Americans, based on these numbers, have firearms than in past decades and are freer to keep and carry them.

With two dramatically different approaches to the right to bear arms, it is possible to address the central question of whether preserving the common law tradition of armed self-defence or disarming everyone resulted in more violent crime, less violent crimes, or had no noticeable impact. Having outlined this distinction, it is useful to take a closer look at each country's experience. Let's begin with the basic view of the right to self-defence, then examine the manner in which England and America have dealt with it, and finally explore the repercussions.

Blackstone's judgment that the right to self-defence has been the primary law of nature was a commonplace among philosophers and jurists from ancient times. In this case, Blackstone explained, the law "respects the passions of the human mind and . . . makes it lawful in him to do himself that immediate justice to which he is prompted by nature and which no prudential motives are strong enough to restrain." "The future process of law," he conceded, was "by no means an adequate remedy for injuries accompanied by force."[9] A century earlier, John Locke, in "An Essay Concerning the true original, extent, and end of Civil Government," put it this way:

> he who attempts to get another man into his absolute power does thereby put himself into a state of war with him; it being to be understood as a declaration of a design upon his life For I have reason to conclude that he who would get me into his power without my consent would use me as he pleased when he had got me there, and destroy me too when he had a fancy to it.[10]

6 These "constitutional carry" states are Alaska, Arizona, Arkansas, Idaho, Kansas, Maine, Mississippi, Missouri, New Hampshire, Vermont, West Virginia, Wyoming. Several other states are considering changing to constitutional carry this year.

7 These eight include California in the west and New York, Massachusetts, Rhode Island, Delaware, New Jersey, and Maryland on the east coast, and Hawaii. The number of shall-issue states has increased year by year, leaving only these eight as holdouts.

8 www.thetruthaboutguns.com/2016/01/dean-weingarten/2015-record-year-for-firearms-sales-and-nics-background-checks/.

9 Blackstone, *Commentaries*, vol. 3, 3–4.

10 John Locke, *An Essay Concerning the True, Original, Extent, and End of Civil Government* (1690), par. 11.

In 1689, when the supporters of William and Mary met to elevate the pair to the throne and draft a declaration of those "ancient and indubitable" rights James II had violated, they included the right of Protestant subjects "to have arms for their defence suitable to their condition and as allowed by law."[11] While the language limits the right to Protestant subjects, then some 90 per cent of the population, and allows social and legal limits, by the time of the American Revolution and early republic the English right had become more general. In 1780, the recorder of London explained, "The right of his majesty's Protestant subjects, to have arms for their own defence, and to use them for lawful purposes, is most clear and undeniable."[12] In 1820, in the case of the *King v. George Dewhurst and Others*, Justice Bailey addressed the question whether arms were "suitable to the condition of people in the ordinary class of life, and are they allowed by law."[13] He affirmed that

> a man has a clear right to arms to protect himself in his house. A man has a clear right to protect himself when he is going singly or in a small party upon the road where he is travelling or going for the ordinary purposes of business.

The judge did not limit the right to Protestants. His only caution was that you could not carry arms to a public meeting "if the number of arms which are so carried are calculated to produce terror and alarm."[14] This was the rule up until 1920. Firearms could be owned and carried as long as they weren't brandished so as to produce terror and alarm.

In 1920, in the wake of World War I and the Bolshevik revolution, the British government feared communist revolution would spread to Britain, and the thousands of soldiers returning from the trenches of a terrible war posed a threat to public safety. In response, Parliament passed the 1920 Firearms Control Act, which introduced a registration system. The purchaser of a firearm had to be approved by his local police commissioner as a fit person to own the weapon, and who had a good reason to have it.[15] Both criteria were highly subjective. Over the years, the Home Office, through a series of classified directives to the local police, narrowed the "good reason" requirement until, in 1969, they informed police throughout the realm that it was never a good reason to have a gun for self-defence or to protect large sums of money.[16] These ever more stringent standards including eliminating the right to be armed for self-defence were decided in secret. They were not debated in Parliament or made public at the time.

In 1997, after the Dunblane massacre of sixteen Scottish school children and their teacher by a man who, although known to the police as unstable, legally owned guns, an intense campaign succeeded in persuading the Conservative and then the Labour government to outlaw virtually all handguns.[17] Legally owned handguns were confiscated. Even amendments to exempt Britain's Olympic target-shooting team and handicapped shooters failed.[18]

11 An act for declaring the rights and liberties of the subject and settling the succession of the crown, 1689, 1 Will. & Mary, sess. 2, c.2.

12 William Blizard, *Desultory Reflection on Police: With an Essay on the Means of Preventing Crimes and Amendment Criminals* (London: Dilly, 1785), 59–60.

13 See Joyce Lee Malcolm, *To Keep and Bear Arms: The Origins of an Anglo-American Right* (Cambridge, MA: Harvard University Press, 1994), 166–168.

14 *The King vs George Dewhurst and Others*, John Macdonell, ed. *Reports of State Trials*, new series, vol. 1, 602.

15 Firearms Act, 10 & 11 Geo. V, c. 43 (1920). And see Malcolm, *To Keep and Bear Arms*, 144–150.

16 Malcolm, *To Keep and Bear Arms*, 155–156, 171–172.

17 The Firearms (Amendment) Act 1997 c.5, 205; Firearms Act (No. 2) 1997, 205.

18 See Malcolm, *Guns and Violence*, 203–205.

Not satisfied with curtailing the right to firearms, in 1953, during fears of juvenile violence, the government convinced Parliament to pass the Criminal Justice Act, a far more sweeping disarmament that the government admitted was "drastic." The act prohibited individuals carrying an offensive weapon in public.[19] Any item carried with the idea it could be used to protect the owner if attacked was considered an offensive weapon. Anyone found to be carrying an "offensive" weapon "without lawful authority or reasonable excuse" was guilty. Four objections were raised repeatedly in both houses of Parliament about the terms of the act:

> It created a new crime, hitherto unknown to the law.
> It gave new power in certain circumstances to arrest without a warrant a person in a public street.
> It was vague in some of its terms.
> It put the burden upon a person who might be innocent to stand in the dock and prove his innocence.

The government never explained why this reversal of centuries of common law was preferable to simply imposing a more severe penalty upon someone who committed a crime using a weapon. This approach was all the more remarkable since the use of firearms and other offensive weapons up to 1953 was negligible.[20] When questioned about the situation of an innocent person afraid for his or her safety who carried some means of protection, the attorney general, Sir Lionel Heald, replied that if "in a special case" someone "really has justification for carrying a weapon . . . he would be found to have a reasonable excuse" but insisted that "we ought not to mind discouraging members of the general public from going about with offensive weapons in their pockets, even for their own protection." He insisted, "It is the duty of society to protect them, and they should not have to do that . . . the argument of self-defence is one to which perhaps we should not attach too much weight."[21] Glanville Williams explains in his textbook on criminal law that Englishmen are not allowed to make a habit of carrying a weapon or other article for defence, because "the excuse could be used by thugs as well as by honest men."[22] Since its passage, English men and women have been arrested for carrying a sheath knife, a shotgun, a razor, a sandbag, a pickaxe handle, a stone, and a drum of pepper.[23]

In a 1976 essay in *Criminal Law Review* on the 1953 prohibitions, A. J. Ashworth asked:

> When the law is unable to provide adequate protection of an individual, might it not be permissible for him to carry a weapon in order to defend life and limb? In the scope of the defence of 'reasonable excuse,' we encounter an issue which is constitutionally as fundamental as the justifications for the offence itself. Public order is at stake, certainly. But so is individual liberty – in some cases, the very right to life.[24]

19 The Prevention of Crime Bill, 1&2 Eliz. II, c. 14 (1953) and see Malcolm, *Guns and Violence*, 173–180, 182–189, 253.
20 Fyfe in T.C. Hansard, ed., *The Parliamentary Debates From the Year 1803 to the Present Time*, February 26, 1953, 5th ser., 511: 2324, 2333, 2340, 2341–2342, 2354, 2364, 2375, 2383, 2394, 2408.
21 Hansard, ed., *The Parliamentary Debates From the Year 1803 to the Present Time*, February 26, 1953, 5th sers., 511: 2364, 2375, 2408.
22 Glanville Williams, *Textbook of Criminal Law*, 2nd ed. (London: Stephens and Sons, 1983), 508.
23 See Malcolm, *Guns and Violence*, 184–185.
24 A.J. Ashworth, "Liability for Carrying Offensive Weapons", *Criminal Law Review* (1976), 727.

Serious concerns about the act failed to shift the government ban on individuals carrying anything for self-defence. Further degrading the right to self-defence, potential victims are threatened they will be prosecuted if they harm an attacker more than a prosecutor deems reasonable. Reflecting on the denial of an individual's right to use deadly force in self-defence to kill an armed attacker even accidentally, Glanville Williams notes,

> for some reason that is not clear, the courts occasionally seem to regard the scandal of killing of a robber (or of a person who is feared to be a robber) as of greater moment than the safety of the robber's victim in respect of his person and property.[25]

This tilt against the law-abiding person's ability to defend himself coupled with the threat not to harm his assailant was not helped by passage of the Criminal Law Act of 1967.[26] That statute's aim was to overhaul criminal law by abolishing the old division of crimes into felonies and misdemeanours. In the process of drafting this complex legislation, the common law standard that in certain circumstances threatened persons had to retreat before resorting to deadly force was altered. The act simply authorized a person to use such force as "is reasonable in the circumstances" to prevent a crime or assist in the arrest of offenders or suspected offenders. While the change would seem to strengthen the right of anyone attacked to defend himself or herself, the opposite has been the case. Everything now turned on what constituted "reasonable" force against an attempt to commit a crime. Extreme force is not considered justifiable to protect property. The legal position as one authority explained, seems to be that the only thing someone threatened with robbery can do by way of defence is "to give the robber blows and *threaten* him with a weapon."[27] One scholar found it "unthinkable" that Parliament "should inadvertently have swept aside the ancient privilege of self-defence" and felt that had Parliament debated the subject "it is unlikely that members would have sanctioned it."[28]

In addition to eliminating guns for protection and forbidding carriage of anything for defence, the government also established a separate list of prohibited weapons. Alongside rocket launchers and machine guns, owning chemical sprays or an ornamental sword stick will subject you to ten years in prison.

Since "society," that is the government, insisted on a monopoly for protecting individuals, it had a moral responsibility to enhance police protection. In fact, it has been woefully derelict in this regard. Sympathy for offenders, doubts about the value of incarceration and economic factors have led to measures that made Britain less safe. Sentences for serious crimes were cut in half, and those under seventeen were only jailed in extraordinary circumstances. In 2009, 70 per cent of apprehended burglars avoided prison, according to British Ministry of Justice figures.[29] That same year, 20,000 young offenders were electronically tagged and sent home, a 40 per cent increase in the number of people tagged over three years. Furthermore, "cautions" were introduced for first offenders – the first time they are caught, that is – who confess to any of some sixty crimes ranging from assault and arson to sex with an underage girl.[30] Cautions save time and money. Cautions mean no jail time, no

25 Williams, *Textbook of Criminal Law*, 507, 504.
26 Criminal Law Act, c. 58 (1967).
27 Williams, *Textbook of Criminal Law*, 507.
28 Carol Harlow, "Self-Defence: Public Right or Private Privilege", *Criminal Law Review* 537–538 (1974).
29 See British Ministry of Justice figures for 2009 online.
30 Criminal Justice Act 2003, secs. 22–27. Although only more minor crimes were to be treated with cautions there has been evidence that serious crimes were also dealt with in this efficient manner.

fine, no community service, no court appearance. Police were meant to use cautions only for minor offences, but too often resort to them for serious crimes as well. In November 2014, the Conservative and Liberal Democrat government published a plan to replace cautions with a system that would require offenders to make some restitution for their offences, but the inappropriate use of cautions has continued.[31] The following spring, the Commons home affairs select committee was alarmed to find that "in order to save time" up to 30 per cent of cautions, warnings and fixed penalty fines, and nearly 50 per cent of these in London had been used inappropriately to deal with serious, rather than minor offences, and repeat rather than first-time offenders.[32]

What has the impact been on public safety? According to a 2001 study by King's College London's Centre for Defence Studies, within a decade of the confiscation and ban of legal handguns, crime with handguns rose nearly 40 per cent, and a decade after that, gun crime had doubled.[33] For the first time, some units of the English police routinely carry firearms. Economic concerns, not public safety, seem to be driving British policing. Instead of putting more policemen on the streets to protect residents, surveillance cameras have been installed. London has a smaller police force than Paris or New York City, but more surveillance cameras than any other city in the world. By 2007, there were some 10,000 cameras at a cost of 1.2 million pounds. Violent crime has been "fairly flat in recent years," but homicide and knife crime increased during this period.[34]

This is not the place to explore British law enforcement in detail. Suffice it to say that despite, or because of, the draconian laws against the ownership and carriage of weapons, the Home Office annual report for 2009 showed a 25 per cent increase in contact crimes, crimes involving assault and battery for example, over the previous year. London shootings, historically low, had almost doubled compared with the previous year, and victimization surveys showed Britain the most violent country in Europe.[35] This increase in crime came before the wave of riots in 2010 when wild gangs of youths burned homes, shops and cars, and beat anyone who tried to stop them. The BBC news reported that 25 per cent of the rioters arrested had more than ten previous offences and 75 per cent had a previous caution or conviction. Those with criminal records averaged fifteen offences.[36] The English people had little means to defend themselves. "They come to our shops," one man told the London *Daily Mail*, "and we fight them with sticks."[37]

It is difficult to compare crime rates in England and America since there are different definitions for different types of crimes.[38] Also, in the past, the British police have reported fewer of the crimes reported to them than American police.[39] Victimization surveys seem a more accurate means of comparison. In 2004 and 2005, Gallup conducted

31 See "Putting an End to 'Soft Option' Cautions", Press Release, November 1, 2014 at gov.uk.
32 Alan Travis, "30% of Police Cautions and Fines Used Inappropriately, Say MPs", *The Guardian*, March 5, 2015.
33 "Handgun Crime 'Up' Despite Ban", *BBC News online*, July 16, 2001 at http://news.bbc.co.uk/1/hi/uk/1440764.stm (accessed March 12, 2017).
34 www.ons.gov.uk/peoplepopulationandcommunity/crimeandjustice/bulletins/crimeinenglandandwales/yearendingsept2016#main-points (accessed March 12, 2017).
35 *Guardian*, January 1, 2010. Victimization surveys tend to be more accurate than official police figures as many people fail to report crimes and police tend to undercount crimes reported to them.
36 *BBC News*, September 15, 2011.
37 www.dailymail.co.uk/news/article-2023932/London-riots-2011-Theresa-May-rules-tough-action-vigilantes-defend-shops.html (accessed March 13, 2017).
38 See Malcolm, *Guns and Violence*, 227–230.
39 Ibid., 230–231.

a crime survey of people in the United States, Canada and Britain. When asked whether a particular crime happened to the respondents or to anyone in their households in the past year, 32 per cent of US respondents in the study mentioned some type of crime, as opposed to 33 per cent of Canadian and 36 per cent of British respondents. Asked about violent crime, 5 per cent each of the US and Canadian households have been victims of such crime, compared with 8 per cent of British households. Britons were also most likely to report they live near an area where they would be afraid to walk alone. They also had the least confidence in their police.[40]

After years of complaint, the British government has begun to modify the rules for self-defence. Previously, householders confronting an intruder could use "such force as is reasonable in the circumstances as he or she genuinely believed them to be for the purposes of self-defence, defence of another, defence of property, prevention of crime or lawful arrest." In 2008, this was modified to return to the common law right that those attacked were not under the duty to retreat, but notice was to be taken if they could have, nor were they guilty if the level of force turned out to be "disproportionate in those circumstances." The idea was to give householders greater latitude in desperate situations. However, these instructions left room for judicial discretion:

> The court will need to consider the personal circumstances of the householder and the threat (real or perceived) posed by the offender. There are no hard and fast rules about what types of force might be regarded as 'disproportionate' and 'grossly disproportionate.'

Although American Justice Oliver Wendell Holmes explained "Detached reflection cannot be demanded in the presence of an uplifted knife," this modified 2008 rule does seem to require detached reflection. An example used to illustrate the rule pointed out that hitting a fleeing intruder was an example of disproportionate force, hence a crime.

The government moved to ease the provision for self-defence again in the fall of 2012 by granting anyone using force against an intruder the right to use any degree of force that was not "grossly disproportionate." The vehement attacks against this in the media, branding it lynch law and vigilantism, demonstrate how difficult it is to get the governing class to change the status quo even slightly.[41] In April 2013, Parliament did pass a somewhat modified "Use of force in self-defence at place of residence." As the title indicates, this law applies only for householders defending themselves in their homes, not for street attacks. The law begins by claiming it is rare for householders to be confronted by intruders in their homes and even rarer for them to be arrested, prosecuted and convicted as a result of any force they used to protect themselves. If the situation were as rare as the government pretends of course, there would have been no insistence on easing restrictions on active self-defence. The English people are still a long way from retrieving their right to protect themselves. Blackstone would be dismayed.

In America, the right to keep and bear arms is protected in federal and state constitutional law, and although there are limits on what type of firearms a citizen can keep, especially in the few discretionary carry states, for the great majority of Americans, the right to armed

40 David W. Moore, "Crime Rate Lower in United States, Canada than in Britain", *Gallup*, February 8, 2006.

41 See for example Rosa Prince, *The Telegraph*, October 9, 2012; Miranda Ching, "Self-Defence Plans Invite Vigilantism", October 12, 2012.

self-defence remains robust. Stand your ground laws have ensured the right that anyone attacked in a public place does not have to retreat before resorting to deadly force. Florida passed the first such law in 2005. There are now twenty-three states with similar stand-your-ground laws. Other states have adopted laws similar to stand-your-ground laws, but these usually apply only to the home or business and are referred to as "castle laws," echoing the common law tenet that your home is your castle and your sanctuary: you do not have to retreat from your home.

Has the American Second Amendment right to individual and armed self-defence harmed public safety? Quite the opposite. The high point for murder rates in America occurred in the early 1990s. In 1993, it was 6.6 per 100,000. By 2011, after the number of privately owned guns had gone from approximately 192 million in 1994 to some 310 million fifteen years later, the murder rate had fallen to 3.2 per 100,000.[42]

The gun homicide rate in America is far higher, of course, than in England. There are several important points to note in this respect. First, this is a pattern that has persisted for hundreds of years. At present, up to 60 per cent of the American gun deaths are due to suicide.[43] If people are intent on committing suicide lack of a firearm will not deter them. The American suicide rate, for example, is about the same as Great Britain, Canada, Denmark, Switzerland and Iceland, and below that of France and Greenland. The Japanese, with the highest suicide rate in the world, more than twice the American rate, have exceedingly strict gun laws.[44] The availability of firearms does not seem to be a key factor. How one counts the homicide rate also matters. The American homicide rate is as high as possible because the FBI counts all suspicious deaths as murder regardless of whether later information about a case would reduce that number. By contrast, the British police massage down the murder rate by tracking each suspicious death and eliminating any ultimately assigned to another category.[45] More important, however, gun homicides in America today are overwhelmingly connected to gang violence, not to the millions of average citizens who own firearms. According to the Center for Disease Control, gang homicides accounted for some 80 per cent of gun homicides.[46]

Only a small percentage of the firearms in America are ever used in crime. They are used for legal purposes including self-defence. Violent crime in the United States and gun crime have been declining for more than twenty years. In January 2012, an article in the *Christian Science Monitor* pointed out that the last time the serious crime rate was that low, gasoline was 29 cents a gallon.[47] The gun ban for residents of Washington, DC, that was overturned

42 See D'vera Cohn, Paul Taylor, Mark Hugo Lopez, Catherine A. Gallagher, Kim Parker and Kevin T. Maass, "Gun Homicide Rate Down 49% Since 1993 Peak; Public Unaware", *Pew Research Center: Social & Demographic Trends*, May 7, 2013 at www.pewsocialtrends.org/2013/05/07/gun-homicide-rate-down-49-since-1993-peak-public-unaware/ (accessed March 12, 2017); "Reported Violent Crime Rate in the United States From 1990 to 2015", *Statista, The Statistics Portal* at www.statista.com/statistics/191219/reported-violent-crime-rate-in-the-usa-since-1990/ (accessed March 12, 2017).

43 See, for example, Dustin Hawkins, "Putting Gun Death Statistics in Perspective", March 2013 at http://info.org/articles-assdO3/gun-stats-perspective.htm.

44 Hawkins, "Putting Gun Deaths in Perspective".

45 Malcolm, *Guns and Violence*, 227–229.

46 Hawkins, "Putting Gun Deaths in Perspective", 43. And see comments by police in Kate Mather, "Killings in Los Angeles Jumped 27.5% so Far this Year", March 8, 2016; Josh Saul, "Why 2016 Has Been Chicago's Bloodiest Year in Almost Two Decades", *Newsweek*, December 15, 2016.

47 Daniel B. Wood, "US Crime Rate at Lowest Point in Decades", *Christian Science Monitor*, January 9, 2012. Also see Mark Guarino, "FBI Reports a Drop in Crime in 2013: Why the Rate Continues to Fall", *Christian Science Monitor*, February 19, 2014. The homicide rate in several large cites has risen sharply from 2015 to the present due to tensions between the minority populations and the police, which have resulted in police retreating from more active policing, such as stopping suspicious persons.

as unconstitutional in the case of *District of Columbia v. Heller* had not made the nation's capital a safer city. That law forbade residents from owning a handgun, unless purchased before the law took effect in 1976, while any long gun in the home had to be kept disassembled. It could not be assembled even if an intruder broke into the home nor could it be carried from one room to another within the home. In the more than twenty years since the ban had been instituted, Washington, DC, compared to forty-nine other cities had become more, not less dangerous. The second landmark gun rights case, *McDonald v. City of Chicago*, involved a virtually identical gun ban, but despite the ban, Chicago was and remains a very violent city. Banning residents from owning firearms only made them more vulnerable to those who were willing to violate the law to prey on their neighbours. Since the *Heller* case was concerned with the DC law, if the ruling on the meaning of the Second Amendment were to apply across the nation, it needed to be incorporated through the Fourteenth Amendment. In the *McDonald* case, the Supreme Court did just that. The *Heller* opinion explained that laws to prohibit felons and the dangerously mentally ill from owning firearms were constitutional as were long-standing prohibitions of weapons in sensitive places. These, along with changed rules in many states that restricted guns, are fitfully working their way through the courts.[48] There has been resistance to the Supreme Court protection for an individual right to both keep and carry a firearm, and the Supreme Court has been reluctant to rule on these cases, preferring to let lower courts decide how strictly the right is to be applied. Much now depends on a state by state working out of the scope of the right.

To return to the main question, is all this armed self-defence really necessary? Won't the police protect you? We have seen that the English people cannot rely on police protection, and common sense makes it clear no police force, even if better staffed and focused on protecting the public could not possibly do it. An American case, *Warren v. District of Columbia*, makes clear where duty and protection lie.[49] Three young women were attacked by two men who broke into their town house near the US Capitol. The police were called repeatedly for half an hour by two of the women before they too became victims. No policeman ever came. For 14 hours, the women were raped and brutalized. They later sued the Washington police. The appeals court judge, in finding against them explained: "It is a fundamental principle of American law that a government and its agents are under no general duty to provide public services such as police protection, to any individual citizen." Fortunately, Americans have a right to self-defence and the means to protect themselves.

The right to individual self-defence enshrined in the American Second Amendment, a legacy of traditional English common law is, as Blackstone and philosophers from antiquity to modern times recognized, the most basic of human rights. No modern government can substitute the instinctive impulse of individuals to protect themselves and their families. The judge in the 1886 case of *Boyd v. United States*, cited in 2014 in *Riley v. California*, nicely summed up the danger of degrading little by little a basic right like self-defence:

> It may be that it is the obnoxious thing in its mildest and least repulsive form; but illegitimate and unconstitutional practices get their first footing in that way, namely, by silent approaches and slight deviations from legal modes of procedure. This can only be obviated by adhering to the rule that constitutional provisions for the security

48 See for example Joyce Lee Malcolm, "Judicial Nullification Continues: Connecticut Judge Defies Law Prohibiting Suits Against Gun Manufacturers", *JURIST*, May 2, 2016.
49 *Warren v. District of Columbia*, 444 A. 201, DC Court of Appeals, 1981.

> of person and property should be liberally construed. A close and literal construction deprives them of half their efficacy, and leads to gradual depreciation of the right, as if it consisted more in sound than in substance. It is the duty of courts to be watchful for the constitutional rights of the citizen, and against any stealthy encroachments thereon. Their motto should be obsta principiis.[50]

Since Magna Carta, there has been a struggle to protect the rights of individuals from the pretensions of central authority. That struggle continues.

50 *Boyd v. United States*, 116 U.S. 616 (1886) at 635. *Cited Riley v. California* (2014).

3 Annie, get your gun

Women, performance and the western heroine

Karen Jones

The nineteenth-century western frontier represents an important theatre in historical justifications of the Second Amendment, not only in asserting the ubiquity of firearms in the trans-Mississippi region, but also in positioning them as practical and symbolic tools integral to the 'Winning of the West.' Inevitably, of course, the associations of frontier folklore with the 'right to bear arms' maintains a stridently masculine posture (think Davy Crockett or Clint Eastwood). However, where various scholars have critiqued the assumption that the West was rife with *High Noon* style gunplay, the issue of gender dynamics has been rather less explored. This chapter seeks to destabilise the conventional narrative of smoking guns and macho heroism in the construction of America's frontier mythology to explore how western women seized the agency of firearms for themselves. Such a conclusion raises inevitable questions about modern cultural attitudes towards firearms, gender and celebrity, as well as reasserting the fact that our historical relations with guns are messy, convoluted and resist binary definition. More specifically, I look here at two prominent characters (or firearms celebrities) in the 'winning of the West' – Martha Canary (Calamity Jane) and Annie Oakley – to examine how two women came to take on the mantle of gun-toting heroines and how their stage presence added colour and contest to the frontier story. Both pointed, firstly, to a tradition of firearms use among pioneer women for whom skill with a rifle promised security and sustenance in remote climes. Moreover (and this is the principal focus here), the gun became a critical prop in the theatrical routines of Oakley and Canary as they developed their own cultures of celebrity in the latter years of the 1800s. Here stood two "armed western women," to borrow the phraseology of Laura Browder, who were consciously performative. 'Calam' paraded on stage in 'America's national costume' of buckskin, armed with a shiny Winchester, while Annie Oakley wowed audience with her trick shot routines and incredible accuracy. Such displays of acuity with firearms paid heed to the iconic status of the gun in the entertainment landscape of the American frontier and also presented a sharp challenge to its assumed masculine hegemony. As competition shots and pistol-packing raconteurs, women participated in the development of a heady national mythology, and in the process, found empowerment and confidence in this swirling choreography of cordite. At the same time, as this chapter concludes, there were firm limits to how far society was willing to accept the gun-toting frontier heroine as a model for the new womanhood of the late nineteenth century.[1]

1 Laura Browder, *Her Best Shot: Women and Guns in America* (Chapel Hill: University of North Carolina Press, 2006), 75.

'Hisland' and the frontier theatre of the gun-toting hero

Perhaps the most iconic character of the American West remains the stoic masculine hero, whether that be a cowboy, outlaw or a lawman, clothed in the typical garb of the frontier (buckskin jacket, denim, boots, Stetson) and armed with a firearm (often a Colt 45 or Winchester rifle). Brandished by such historical figures as Billy the Kid, Wyatt Earp, Buffalo Bill Cody and Theodore Roosevelt, men who tamed the trans-Mississippi region on behalf of civilisation, firearms acted as practical agents of westward expansion and figurative crutches to embellish the reputation of the rugged individualist leading man. Meanwhile, as the frontier made its way from history to legend – through nineteenth-century dime novels to cinematic celluloid – the gun took to the stage as an eminently translatable and adaptable device of expressive portent. The Remington Arms Company produced lavishly illustrated calendars from the late 1800s that celebrated the wild allure of the West and the six-gun mystique simultaneously, while the first western, *The Great Train Robbery* (1903), ended with a striking scene in which a ruffian pointed his pistol at an audience that instantly switched from voyeur to participant in an armed frontier showdown. Accustomed to playing a supporting role in the hands of Hollywood's leading men – the likes of Gary Cooper, John Wayne or Clint Eastwood – in *Winchester '73* (1950), the gun even took top billing in a narrative that saw the firearm elevated from the 'Gun that won the West' to a character in its own right, passing from protagonist to protagonist in the style of the lone western stranger. Adventure and gunplay went hand in hand in the performance genealogy of the masculine frontier hero.[2]

The role of women in this noble parade – what Susan Armitage and Elizabeth Armitage have dubbed the "hisland" of traditional western folklore – was typically corralled in the guise of observers and so-called gentle tamers. As Elizabeth Custer put it in *Following the Guidon* (1890), the army officers (led by her husband, the General) galloped by with carbines glittering valiantly, while the women sat on a nearly hill and watched the performance through binoculars. Revisionist historiography has modified this view considerably, seeing women as active, resourceful and engaged agents in the pioneering process, but even here there remains a tendency to see 'the women's West' through a domestic lens, the assumption being that firearms (and their attendant subcultures of violence and aggressive/assertive frontiering) tended to be holstered by men. To Julie Roy Jeffrey, the West was a place (both physical and psychological) where women "tried to maintain the standards of domesticity . . . with which they had been familiar before emigration." Larry McMurtry

2 For guns, masculinity and frontier mythology, see Richard Slotkin's trilogy *The Fatal Environment: The Myth of the Frontier in the Age of Industrialization, 1800–1890* (New York: Atheneum, 1985); *Regeneration Through Violence: The Myth of the American Frontier, 1600–1800* (Middletown: Wesleyan University Press, 1973); *Gunfighter Nation: The Myth of the Frontier in Twentieth-Century America* (Norman: University of Oklahoma Press, 1998); *John Cawelti, The Six Gun Mystique* (Bowling Green, OH: Bowling Green State University Popular Press, 1984 [1970]); Charles G. *Worman*, Gunsmoke and *Saddle Leather: Firearms in the Nineteenth-Century American West* (Albuquerque: University of New Mexico Press, 2005); James Grossman, ed., *The Frontier in American Culture* (Berkeley: University of California Press, 1994); Richard Aquila, *Wanted Dead or Alive: The American West in Popular Culture* (Chicago: University of Illinois Press, 1998); Gail Bederman, *Manliness and Civilization: A Cultural History of Gender and Race in the United States, 1880–1917* (Chicago: University of Chicago Press, 1995); Henry Nash Smith, *Virgin Land: The American West as Symbol and Myth* (Cambridge: Harvard University Press, 1950).

was rather more direct: labelling the frontier West as an essentially (and instrumentally) masculine space.[3]

This was, however, only part of the picture. In fact, women proved themselves to be both enthusiastic and eminently capable actors on the armed frontier, deploying guns for the purposes of sport, subsistence, entertainment and empowerment. For independent women with means, travel and adventure brought real possibilities of stretching the limits of gender heterodoxy. Here, the gun proved an important resource in facilitating security and sport, a welcome bedfellow for life under canvas and a vector through which the animals of the West could be 'spoken' to. In *Impressions of a Tenderfoot during a Journey in Search of Sport in the Far West* (1890), the Duchess of Somerset expressed excitement at visiting the "unknown lands" of the Rockies and the promise of stalking game for "health, sport and pleasure." A testament to burgeoning interest in hunting and guns among elite women in the late 1800s, sporting publications such as *Outdoor Life* and *Forest & Stream* began to dedicate editorials to "the lady sportsman." Some women seemed to shy from the full force of a militarised encounter with the West – British tourist Isabella Bird, for instance, slept with a gun under her pillow but confessed that she could not "conceive of any circumstances in which I could feel it right to make any use of it" – but period accounts provide ample confirmation that women travellers carried guns, and many were not afraid to use them.[4]

Within the context of a frontier domestic economy, too, firearms were vital in securing food, scaring off wild animals and defending the homestead ethic from all comers, as in August Leimbach's famous *Madonna of the Prairie* (1928) statue that featured a 10-foot pioneer woman shielding her children and grasping a rifle to her thigh (worth noting here is the fact that Rebecca Boone was every bit a hunter as her husband Daniel). Montana émigré Evelyn Cameron displayed keen gun skills in shooting grouse for the pot, fending off coyotes and engaging in annual hunting trips from her ranch in the 1890s. An accomplished outdoorswoman, she complained bitterly of the greenhorn companions who took to the hunting trail with her and husband Ewen: "Having these kind of young men to take out spoils all our pleasure. Mr C's terribly green and too fond of his ease to care about hunting much." Such demonstrative affection for the game trail (Cameron noted on one occasion "To the woman with outdoor propensities and a taste for roughing it there is no life more congenial than that of the saddle and rifle, as it may still be lived in parts of the Western states") showed the limits of a gender taxonomy that reserved the gun for male use, but also marked her as something of a local novelty. Arriving at the MacQueen House Hotel, Miles City, Montana fresh from the game trail, Cameron was greeted by a curious array of onlookers who read her presence in performance terms. As she put it, "Mrs Malone introduced me in to [the] sitting room and said it was like talking to some character out of

3 Susan Armitage and Elizabeth Jameson, eds., *The Women's West* (Norman: University of Oklahoma Press, 1988); Elizabeth Custer, *Following the Guidon* (New York: Harper, 1890), 194–212; Julie Roy Jeffrey, *Frontier Women: The Trans-Mississippi West* (New York: Hill and Wang, 1979), 73; Larry McMurtry, *In a Narrow Grave: Essays on Texas* (Albuquerque. University of New Mexico Press, 1968), 44. See also: Glenda Riley, *The Female Frontier: A Comparative View of Women on the Prairie and the Plains* (Lawrence: University Press of Kansas, 1988); Deborah Homsher, *Women and Guns: Politics and the Culture of Firearms in America* (London: Routledge, 2015), 33.

4 Duchess of Somerset Susan Margaret McKinnon St. Maur, *Impressions of a Tenderfoot During a Journey in Search of Sport in the Far West* (London: J. Murray, 1890), vii; Our Lady Sportsmen, *Forest and Stream* 1 (January 15, 1874); Andrea L. Smalley, "'Our Lady Sportsmen': Gender Class, and Conservation in Sport Hunting Magazines", 1873–1920, *Journal of the Gilded Age and Progressive Era* 4 (October 2005), 377; Isabella Bird, *A Lady's Life in the Rocky Mountains* (Norman: University of Oklahoma Press, 1960 [1879]), 52.

a book talking to me! The hunting trip seems to make them think the woman who hunts a wonder." Such reaction said something about the embedded theatrical codes of the hunt as well as pointing to the ways in which class, racial and regional identities helped smooth the course of armed femininity.[5]

Far from recoiling from their use, lady adventurers and pioneer women found in the gun a routine object of utility and a powerful tool of identification and enablement. In that sense, they were made of the same stuff as Richard Slotkin's independent and well-armed masculine heroes who championed the democratic coda of the every(wo)man frontier. Furthermore, in the landscape of frontier performance that played out on stage, script and screen in the nineteenth and twentieth centuries, women (as well as men) could be found twirling pistols and cocking rifles. On one level, the popularity of the frontier 'wild woman' in western folklore offered up a simple story of harmless whimsy, a world turned upside down that was designed to titillate the audience or offer a wistful nod to unruly and riotous frontier days long since passed. As the same time, however, the heroines of frontier theatre deserve further scrutiny, particularly in terms of the way that their routines pointed both to the transgression of gender orthodoxy and to the limits placed on that heretical behaviour. As Rosemarie Bank points out, "Performers complicate unitary readings and performance resists binary interpretations." Two of the most famous gun-toting celebrities of the West are under discussion here. More commonly known for her ***nom de plume*** Calamity Jane, Martha Canary trod the boards as a buckskin-clad raconteur who highlighted the 'wild woman' as a key character in the staging of the West in national folklore and spoke to the importance of the gun as a marker of western identity. Equally important as a female gunslinger was Annie Oakley, staple of Bill Cody's Wild West show, model of feminine deportment and trick shooter extraordinaire.[6]

Calamity Jane and the contestation of masculine hegemony

Born in Princeton, Missouri in 1852, Martha Jane Canary left for the Montana goldfields with her family in 1864. In her eight-page autobiography, *Life and Adventures of Calamity Jane, By Herself* (1896), she presented the journey west as equal parts adventure and exhilaration, professing her developing skills as a "fearless rider" and a good shot. The ability to command a horse, wield a gun and revel in an audacious frontier of all-action combat represented the essential prerequisites for the aspiring masculine frontier hero. Importantly, these were all firmly claimed and proclaimed by Canary as she (and others) crafted her performance repertoire as 'Calamity Jane: Heroine of the Plains.' As she put it: "the greater portion of my time was spent in hunting along with the men and hunters of the party, in fact I was at all times with the men when there was excitement and adventure to be had."[7]

Through the 1860s and 1870s, the young Martha Canary maintained a nomadic and somewhat feral existence, wandering between forts, mining towns and railroad camps and

5 Evelyn Cameron, Diary for 1895. Box 1, folder 5: Diaries 1895–6, Evelyn J. and Ewen S. Cameron Papers, MC226, Montana Historical Society, Helena, Montana (hereafter cited as MHS); Evelyn Cameron, Diary for 1893 & Diary for 1894. Box 1, folder 4: Diaries, 1893–1894, MC226, MHS; Evelyn Cameron, Diary for 1898; Evelyn Cameron, "'The Cowgirl' in Montana", *Country Life* (16 June 1914); Judith Halberstam, *Female Masculinity* (Durham: Duke University Press, 1998), 58; Evelyn Cameron, "A Woman's Big Game Hunting", *New York Sun*, 4 November 1900.

6 Rosemarie Bank, "Representing History: Performing the Columbia Exposition", in J. Reinelt (ed.), *Critical Theory and Performance* (Ann Arbor: University of Michigan Press, 1992), 598.

7 Martha Canary Burke, *Life and Adventures of Calamity Jane, By Herself* (n.p., 1896).

working in various capacities as a muleskinner, construction worker and teamster. Eyewitness Jesse Brown remembered her "dressed in a buckskin with two Colts six shooters on a belt . . . [she was] about the toughest looking human that I ever saw." An association with the US Army also began in these years, described by Canary as one of scouting glory and military feats, but in reality, her experience was more likely as an itinerant cook, teamster, laundress, prostitute, comic foil and 'camp-follower.' Canary was certainly inhabiting a territory far from usual normative female gender domesticity and, as such, began to earn notoriety for her drinking exploits, masculine affectations and dress, and, of course, rifle skills. General Dodge labelled her a "regimental mascot" and "a queer combination" of cook, nurse and adventurer, while medical officer Valentine McGillycuddy recalled her appearance on the parade ground wearing spurs, chaps and a sombrero as well as her exploits on the Black Hills Expedition of 1875 (from which she was barred, though she sneaked along dressed as a cavalryman).[8]

When Calamity Jane arrived in Deadwood on a wagon train from Fort Laramie in summer 1876, the *Black Hills Pioneer* proclaimed that "'Calamity Jane' has arrived" – an indication of her growing status as a regional celebrity and of the critical placement of Deadwood as a literal stage on which she enacted a grand recital of armed frontier swagger. Wearing the customary suit of the western hero – fringed buckskin – and clutching a rifle in performative style, Martha Canary demonstrated a keen grasp of the mythological potency of the frontier and the central place of firearms in that landscape of armed amusement. That Calamity Jane, the 'wildcat' of the plains was riding shotgun with another of the West's most notable celebrities, Wild Bill Hickok, advanced the gravitas of the occasion. Palpably aware of the theatrical trappings of the mining town (resonant with a sense of the drama and energy of frontier days) and keen to declare their arrival in Deadwood to all comers, the group "rode the entire length of Main Street mounted on good horses and clad in complete suits of buckskin" before pitching their tents. Thereafter, Canary could be found in various hostelries, enlivening the bar with her tales of adventure and gunplay, howling at the top of her voice and firing off her pistols when the mood took her and taking various jobs (including a stint as a dance-hall girl at the Gem Saloon, which meant she had to borrow money for skirts and dresses from Joseph 'White Eye' Anderson. As Canary put it, "I can't do business in these old buckskins"). The presence of the gun was instrumental to her emerging cult of celebrity – as one account in the *Anaconda Standard* related, when heckled by two young fellows at the bar, she drew pistols and "made them dance." One onlooker smiled at the ensemble and was offered a drink by Canary. The editorial surmised, "The command was made good with a wicked-looking gun."[9]

Calamity Jane's reputation as 'armed heroine of the plains' gained wider dissemination in the 1870s courtesy of western popular literature. Deadwood's locally notorious western character thus made the leap from regional interest to object of national literary attention.

8 Jesse Brown quoted in Richard Etulain, *The Life and Legends of Calamity Jane* (Norman: University of Oklahoma Press, 2014), 47; McGillycuddy quoted in Candy Moulton, ed., *Valentine T. McGillycuddy: Army Surgeon, Agent to the Sioux* (Norman: University of Oklahoma Press, 2011), 48; Dodge quoted in Glenda Riley and Richard Etulain, eds., *By Grit and Grace: Eleven Women Who Shaped the American West* (Golden: Fulcrum, 1997), 80. For the life of Martha Canary, also see James McLaird, *Calamity Jane: The Woman and the Legend* (Norman: University of Oklahoma Press, 2005).

9 *Black Hills Pioneer*, July 15, 1876; Richard Hughes, *Pioneer Years in the Black Hills*, ed. Agnes Wright Spring (Glendale, CA: Arthur H. Clark Company, 1957), 159–161; William Secrest, *I Buried Hickok: The Memoirs of White Eye Anderson* (College Station, TX: Creative Publishing, 1980), 102, 93–95; *Anaconda Standard*, 27 April 1902.

In Horatio Maguire's small pamphlet *The Black Hills and American Wonderland* (1877), she was presented as a "dare-devil boy . . . giving as good an imitation of a Sioux war-whoop as a feminine voice is capable of" while his *The Coming Empire* (1878), conveyed images of Canary in her signature buckskin, pistols held aloft in triumphant pose. In the lurid landscape of the dime novel, too, Calamity Jane cut quite a presence as the 'female scout.' She appeared in more than twenty works penned by prolific dime novelist Edward Wheeler and was a recurring character in his *Deadwood Dick* series. Here, Calamity Jane swaggered across the pages of salacious print copy, smoking cigars, swearing like a trooper and using her firearms as devices both explosive and expressive. Cast as "a boyish figure . . . dressed in a carefully tanned costume of buckskin," she offered a cross-dressing foil (and often *deus ex machina*) to the sometimes-hapless-sometimes-heroic Deadwood Dick, saving him from all manner of fixes. An energetic burst of reverie, Jane packed a pistol and a boisterous vernacular, as she noted in one story: "I'm as big a gun among the men as any of 'em." And yet, Wheeler's Calamity defies a simplistic reading – she was certainly flamboyant in her performative oration of what Judith Halberstam has described as "female masculinity" – yet much less heretical underneath. According to Wheeler, it was not 'normal' for a woman to behave in such a fashion, and he found it necessary, firstly, to explain Calamity's ways as the result of a failed romantic tryst, and secondly, to reveal her ultimate wish to settle down with Deadwood Dick and play dutiful wife. In that sense, Wheeler's dime novels presented a similar story of a 'tomboy' conforming to domesticity as the musical *Calamity Jane* (1953) – Doris Day's portrayal of 'Calam' being the most famous articulation of the character to date.[10]

Martha Canary left Deadwood to roam the plains in her usual nomadic fashion, but returned to old stomping grounds in October 1895. It had been fifteen years since the mining town had been graced with her presence – a period which had seen the fulsome creation of Calamity Jane as a frontier heroine with national purchase. Old-timers revelled in her return as a remnant of the frontier days of yore – relishing in her as an embodiment of a wild life long since replaced by a sense of settled decorum. The Rapid City *Journal* spoke for many when it hailed her as "the prickly cactus symbol of the pioneer days at the heart of their depravity." Local business interests, meanwhile, saw firm monetary benefits to stoking the fires of frontier celebrity, as did Canary herself. Accordingly, she sat in full buckskin costume, grasping a trusty rifle, at H. R. Locke's photographic studio in 1895 and touted the postcards at the gateway to Yellowstone National Park (among other places) to eager tourists wishing to purchase a memento. Her cult status was further elevated the following year, when Canary took to the stage, presenting 'Calamity Jane: The Famous Woman Scout of the Wild West' before enthralled audiences to the Kohl and Middleton dime museum tour. Again, the provenance of the gun was evident, as Calamity gesticulated with a shiny new Winchester rifle (and threatened punters with it when they questioned the veracity of her tales). Copies of her new ghost written autobiographical pamphlet, *Life and Adventures of Calamity Jane*, offered a rip-roaring tour of her frontier escapades, including her apprehension of Wild Bill Hickok's killer, Jack McCall, with a meat cleaver (she had left her guns at home on that occasion). The autobiography was almost entirely fictitious, but that did not serve to blunt its popularity. In the estimation of the *Daily Times* it was, "one of the most interesting and thrilling stories of western life ever put in type." The public *believed*

10 Horatio Maguire, *The Black Hills and American Wonderland* (Chicago: Donnelley, Lloyd & Co., 1877), 304; Horatio Maguire, *The Coming Empire* (Sioux City, IA: Watkins & Smead, 1878); Edward Wheeler, *Deadwood Dick: Prince of the Road* (New York: M. J. Ivers, 1877); Edward Wheeler, *Deadwood Dick on Deck, or Calamity Jane, the Heroine of Whoop-Up* (New York: M. J. Ivers, 1878).

in Calamity Jane as a credible western witness and natural storyteller and that was all that seemed to matter. As Captain Jack Crawford put it,

> She never saw service in any capacity under either General Crook or General Miles. She never saw a lynching and never was in an Indian fight. She was simply a notorious character, dissolute and devilish, but possessed a generous streak which made her popular.[11]

When Martha Canary died in South Dakota on 1 August 1903, the *Princeton Press* celebrated her as "one of the most picturesque and daring characters that has ever roamed the Western plains." Eulogies effused on her unruly and untameable qualities, her undeniably *western*-ness and her pistol-packing skills. In *Adventures with Indians and Game* (1903), hunter William Allen remembered meeting her near Custer City, apprehending "a white woman riding towards us at full gallop" with "daring intrepidity . . . rapidity of movement and . . . deadly skill with firearms." Firmly grasping the mantle of frontier heroics, Calamity Jane articulated a decisive challenge to the hegemony of the masculine western hero, claiming his attributes (in dress, use of firearms technology and performed gestures), while at the same time destabilising his assumed authority by emulation and mimicry. When she trod the boards at Frederick T. Cummins' Pan-Indian Exposition in 1901, the Buffalo *Morning Express* waxed lyrical about "the heroine who wears a hero's garb" and the Chicago *Inter Ocean* regaled its readers with details of the "most interesting woman" who "wears buckskin trousers and is not afraid of a mouse." By way of riposte, Canary castigated the "new women" of Chicago who were "way behind the times" and promised, in suitably theatrical tone, to give them a demonstration of a *real* western woman by riding city streets "astride her broncho" armed with a rifle in pursuit of lurking urban coyotes. Such an articulation suggested not only an attention to the changing sociological landscape of twentieth-century womanhood, but also a performed discourse that renegotiated the definitions of feminine taxonomy by playful juxtapositions of urban/rural and old-fashioned/modern in the idea of a 'new' woman. Moreover, in common with other frontier celebrities – Buffalo Bill Cody most notably – Martha Canary used dramatic performance to tap into the *fin-de-siecle* appetite for western adventure and eyewitness testimonials and create a niche as a celebrity 'wild woman.' Authenticity came from various things – a credible frontier aspect in gait and garb, historical reference, links to known western figures, and, of course, the possession of (and familiarity with) firearms. Early biographer J. Leonard Jennewein put it succinctly when he recalled her "flair . . . exuberance . . . [and] native sense of showmanship."[12]

At the same time, however, Calamity Jane never achieved recognition beyond that of a flamboyant eccentric. Skill with firearms could only take her so far. As Judith Halberstam points out, the masculinity of the white male (what she calls "epic masculinity") carries with not only a sense of performed gestures and tools, but also embedded codes of power, legitimacy and privilege. This Canary did not have. She may have tested the limits of

11 *Rapid City Journal*, 20 January 1896; *Black Hills Daily Times*, 5 October 1895; Jack Crawford quoted in William B. Secrest, "The Calamities of Calamity Jane", 2010 at www.historynet.com/the-calamities-of-calamity-jane.htm.

12 *Princeton Press*, 13 August 1908; William Allen, *Adventures With Indians and Game, or Twenty Years in the Rocky Mountains* (Chicago: A. W. Bowen, 1903), 32–34; Buffalo *Morning Express*, 4 August 1901; *Chicago Inter Ocean*, 28 January 1896; J. Leonard Jennewein, *Calamity Jane of the Western Trails* (Rapid City, SD: West Books, 1953), 6.

cross-dressing performance and won plaudits for her "grotesque wildness," but society was not yet willing to test the limits of gender normativity. Underneath the performance routine of the armed western heroine was the tragic tale of a social pariah, a disenfranchised woman trying to make ends meet in the West and struggling to find a place of physical and sexual identification. Her personal life was disastrous – a string of failed relationships, problems with alcohol dependency – compounded by endemic poverty. In her final years, Canary lived a hand-to-mouth existence, grabbing the odd booking at a dime museum and touting a postcard or two, but her room for manoeuvre was increasingly curtailed as the West eased into an era of post-frontier respectability. As an armed heroine, she enthralled audiences with tales of sharpshooting, but society seemed less willing to endorse social deviance, hard-drinking and trigger-itch when it took place off the stage and in the new civil society of the trans-Mississippi. As the *Sioux Valley News* reported on 22 January 1903:

> Do you remember Calamity Jane? It is not the Calamity Jane of today . . . that you want to remember. She of today is old and poverty-stricken and wretched. The country has outgrown her, and her occupation is gone. When, to put it very plain and ugly, she gets drunk, she tries to shoot up the town in good old frontier style. But that sort of thing has been outgrown with a lot of other things.

As a performing 'wild woman,' Calamity Jane had guaranteed her place in frontier folklore, but she was expected to shuffle off the stage with decorum rather than gunfire and gumption when the time was right. Fame was not the same thing as social acceptability for a rough and ready woman living an unorthodox existence. As Richard Etulain notes, Calamity Jane never seemed "to bridge the gap between experience and performance."[13]

Annie Oakley – genteel gunslinger

Like Martha Canary, the early years of Phoebe Ann Moses (later Annie Oakley) remain shrouded in mystery. A generalised past as an 'ordinary pioneer girl' seemed a crucial part of the genealogy of both performing heroines. We do know that her parents were Quakers, and she was born in Darke County, Ohio, in August 1860 into a life of rural poverty. In a story that was recited many times over in commemorative pamphlets and on the show-ground circuit, the eight-year-old Annie described how, following the death of her father, she gingerly took his Kentucky rifle from its hallowed position over the fireplace to wage war on the local rodent population. Following this youthful foray into the world of firearms, the teenage Annie worked as a market hunter, fetching game for a local grocery and hotels in Cincinnati (a project of some success, as she managed to repay the loan on the farmstead). Reflecting on these times, she mused, "I guess the love of a gun must have been born in me." As such, this autobiographical testament both established her credentials as a grounded backwoodswoman and set up a teleological arc that took her naturally to a life of armed performance.[14]

The next snapshot moment in the story of how Phoebe Ann Moses became Annie Oakley takes us to the competitive rifle shooting circuit of the Midwest. It was here, at the

13 Halberstam, *Female Masculinity*, 2; Dora Dufran, *Lowdown on Calamity Jane* (Deadwood: Helen Rezatto, 1981), 16–17; *Sioux Valley News*, 22 January 1903; Etulain and Riley, *By Grit and Grace*, 88.

14 *Nashville Barrier*, 28 March 1891; *The Rifle Queen: Annie Oakley* (London: General Publishing Co., 1884), 3. Oakley recounted her autobiography in *The Story of My Life* (n.p.: NEA Service, 1926).

Greenville showgrounds outside Cincinnati, that a timid Ohio farm girl took on acclaimed marksman and trick shot Frank Butler in a shooting competition. The story is quite possibly embellished – at the very least, corroborative evidence suggests it took place in 1881 and not in 1875 as Butler claimed – but it serves to attest to the power of performance in creating the mythology of Annie Oakley as an armed heroine. The story goes that Frank Butler (who worked with partner Sam Baughman on the travelling show circuit as "champion sharp-shooters and most illustrious dead-shots . . . the sportsmen's famous hunter heroes") was invited to compete in an impromptu shooting match by local hotelier Jack Frost. Figuring this was an easy way to win some money and show off his gun skills, Butler obliged, only to find himself beaten by a 4' 11" young woman who had never competed out of a trap before. Frank and Annie married a year later and travelled together on the vaudeville circuit. It was only when Butler's then partner, John Graham, became ill, that Annie found her chance to step from supporting role to leading star – standing in for Graham and winning audience hearts. By the time of the 1882 spring season, she had adopted Annie Oakley as her stage name (like Calamity Jane, there are competing stories as to why she assumed her *nom de plume*) and two years later was performing as one of the "champion rifle shots" in an energetic firearms showcase for the Sells Brothers Circus that combined marks(wo)manship, horse-riding feats and whimsical tricks performed by the pair's pet poodle George. That same year, at a show in St Paul, Minnesota, she crossed paths with Sitting Bull, who dubbed her 'Little Sure Shot,' a reference to her slight demeanour and firearms skills that were invoked throughout her career.[15]

Wild West showman extraordinaire William 'Buffalo Bill' Cody was not keen to take on the 'Great Far West Rifle Shots' (the name under which Oakley and Butler were performing) when he saw them perform in New Orleans. As he pointed out to collaborator Nate Salsbury, his Wild West show already had its fair share of shooting acts. However, when top-billing performer Captain Bogardus left the troupe in 1885, he decided to give Oakley a trial. This was a pivotal moment in her celebrity arc, as from here on in it was Annie who took centre stage (with Frank Butler consigned to the role of manager). Ever the perfectionist, she lost no time in preparation, including hosting an exhibition event in Cincinnati in which she shot 4,772 out of 5,000 balls in nine hours (such feats of 'extreme' marks(wo)manship in terms of accuracy and endurance were a key aspect of the competitive rifle shooting circuit). The entertainment appeal of an armed western woman was not lost on Salsbury, who after watching Oakley's mesmerising practice for Cody's inaugural show in Louisville Kentucky hired her on a full-time basis and commissioned lithograph posters to the tune of $7,000 illustrating *Little Sure Shot*, demonstrating her rifle skills and dressed in a sombrero, well-tailored long skirt and embroidered jacket.

Annie Oakley's homespun take on the armed western woman proved a remarkable success. She played with Cody's show for some sixteen seasons, traversing the theatrical territory from novelty act to "peerless lady wing shot", one of the biggest stars. The London *Evening News* regarded her as "the most interesting item on Buffalo Bill's programme." Cultivating a sense of gun-slinging gentility, Oakley greeted the audience with giggles, kisses and a sense of petite domesticity that contrasted sharply with what her routine promised: acts of daredevil shooting skill from all angles, sitting, standing, on horseback and while riding a bicycle. When the show began, Butler and other cowboy performers from the

15 The billing for Butler and Baughman appeared in the Sells Brothers Circus Courier, 1881. Reprinted in Isabelle S. Sayers, *Annie Oakley and Buffalo Bill's Wild West* (New York: Dover Publications, 1981); *Pittsburgh Despatch*, 4 February 1903.

troupe set the scene – bringing in props and furnishing a table with an array of firearms – before Oakley eased into her act, starting with easier feats and slowly building tension among onlookers as she shot balls in the air and hit targets from traps. Press agent Dexter Fellows recalled how "the first few shots brought forth a few screams of fright from the women, but they were soon lost in round after round of applause." As the pace and energy of the display picked up, the routine became more technical and decidedly more theatrical. Oakley shot holes in playing cards, knocked burning cigarette's from her husband's mouth, and, in her signature move, successfully hit targets shooting backwards and looking through a small mirror as a sight. She pouted dramatically on missing a shot (a rare occurrence) and ended her routine with a girlish leg kick. Such acuity with firearms was remarkable. As was her sense of performance savvy.[16]

An armed western woman (although critics might reasonably point to the need to preface her claims to a western identity with a 'mid'), Annie Oakley presented a visible and demonstrative challenge to the hegemony of the frontier hero and his exclusive command over firearms. Her performance heresy was all in the act – the guns did the talking as she took the lead before a series of male 'props' (including the future Kaiser Wilhelm II) – and ventured a strident riposte to the assumed superiority of men in the realm of competitive trick shooting. Oakley was, arguably, a better technical shot than Cody, who chose to avoid outright 'duels' with his leading lady shooter (notably at a proposed three-way competition at the Wimbledon shooting club during the London tour of 1887 with stars Oakley and Lillian Smith, 'the California huntress'). Played out before packed auditoriums, Oakley acted out a visible story of empowerment through action, trespassing on masculine territory with well-placed aim. As the popular pamphlet *The Rifle Queen* effused: "with natural ability and a little encouragement . . . courage and perseverance" some women "can do what any man can do." Her routine inspired a generation of women to enter the world of competitive sports, particularly rodeo, while as a role model she ventured fresh possibilities for the new womanhood of the late nineteenth century. In personal testimony, Oakley herself expressed delight at being part of a movement to extend women's spheres of influence, being "the first white woman to stand and travel with what society then might have thought impossible." She also attributed a formative role to the gun – not only as an enabling tool of her own celebrity, but also as an object of security (and thereby gender equalisation) in the hands of the independent woman. As she put it, "to the woman living in the lonely farmhouse, and for the business woman returning home late at night from work, the knowledge of how to use a pistol is a Godsend." Outside the showground, Oakley paraded a sense of patriotic duty in offering for service in the Spanish American War fifty 'lady sharp-shooters' carved in her image; a striking companion, had President McKinley accepted them, to Theodore Roosevelt's regiment of Rough Riders.[17]

Perhaps inevitably, a number of latter-day biographers tracked Oakley's story through a feminist gaze, notably Courtney Cooper's *Annie Oakley: Woman at Arms* (1927). At the same time, however, Annie Oakley carefully holstered her guns within a conservative veil of domesticated assurance. She was resolutely feminine in her airs, a dressmaker and homemaker, who assured her audience with her girlish charms and adherence to the

16 *London Evening News*, 10 May 1884; Dexter Fellows and Andrew Freeman, *The Way to the Big Show* (New York: Viking, 1936), 73; "The Woman Rifle Expert", *World*, 8 January 1888.

17 *Rifle Queen*, 3; "Rifle Expert Talks of Women and Firearms", *Cincinnati Times*, c.1904; *Annie Oakley Scrapbooks* (Cody, WY: Buffalo Bill Historical Center); Sayers, Annie Oakley and Buffalo Bill's Wild West, 19.

conformist upholstery of riding sidesaddle. As Laura Browder observes, the typical armed western woman was often "skilled at using firearms, yet not violent, exotically different in her western attire, yet emphatically white and domestic." This is where the performance routines of Annie Oakley and Calamity Jane diverged. Oakley's act was astonishing in its accuracy – and certainly demonstrated an instrumental skill with firearms not read as archetypally feminine – but it was not dangerous in its routine or embedded hetero-normative codes. She did not fend off stampeding bison herds, marauding grizzlies or whirling Lakota warriors as Bill Cody did. Nor did she perform an alternative reading of masculinity in the fashion of Canary's bristling persona. As circus performer Fred Stone observed, "It was always amusing to watch people who were meeting her for the first time. They expected to see a big masculine blustering sort of person and then the woman with the quiet voice took them by surprise." As such, Oakley's 'woman at arms' may have been daring in its execution, but it did not present a contest to the boundaries of customary gender behaviour (in other words, Annie may have been shooting at Frank, but her aim was not to hit him). As Tracey Davis notes, "there is an implicit questioning of order in this design but not a radical agenda for reordering." Visitors to her show tent thus found Annie sewing clothes, making tea or baking. Strewn around the tent were the material fixings of masculine frontier heroism (skins, trophies, rifles), but also domestic adornments in the form of cushions, throws and ornaments. It was, according to actress Amy Leslie, "a bower of comfort and taste." Both inside and outside the arena, then, Oakley was consistent in her casting as a Victorian lady (she insisted on being called Mrs Graham off stage and spoke out against female suffrage). Moral domesticity seemed an integral part of her self-identification and comprised an essential pillar of her celebrity success. Fiercely protective of her wholesome public image (she contested fifty-five libel suits against Hearst newspapers, including one 1903 headline which provocatively claimed "Famous Woman Crack Shot . . . Steals to Secure Cocaine," a crime actually attributed to one Maude Fontanella, who had taken to calling herself 'Any Oakley'), Oakley proved highly astute in her navigation of the connected worlds of the professional and the personal. As historian Virginia Scharff notes, "She was one of the first American celebrities who was really branding herself, and she was very shrewd about her own marketing."[18]

Women and guns: contested readings of performance on the armed frontier

The gun-toting recitals of Calamity Jane and Annie Oakley presented a story of grand incendiary entertainment and paid heed to the heady days of the vanishing frontier and popular interest in its raconteur eyewitnesses. More than just spectacle or whimsy, the performances of these 'armed western women' raised the spectre of an alternative reading of frontier experience and a destabilisation of the position of the masculine hero through a theatrical practice that centred on skills with firearms. Typically read as a profound agent only in the hands of the swaggering masculine hero, the experiences of Martha Canary and

18 Courtney Ryley Cooper, *Annie Oakley: Woman at Arms* (London: Hurst & Blackett, 1927); Browder, *Her Best Shot*, 75; Tracey C. Davis, "Shotgun Wedlock: Annie Oakley's Power Politics in the Wild West", in Lawrence Senelick (ed.), *Gender and Performance: The Presentation of Difference in the Performing Arts* (Hanover, New Hampshire: University Press of New England, 1992), 153–154; *Chicago Daily News*, 5 May 1893; Fred Stone quoted in Sayers, *Annie Oakley*, 85; Jess Righthand, "How Annie Oakley, 'Princess of the West,' Preserved her Ladylike Reputation", *Smithsonian Magazine*, 11 August 2010.

Phoebe Ann Moses illuminated the ways in which women used guns as both practical and figurative tools to claim power, agency and voice in the late nineteenth-century West. Using the cloak of frontier mythology, both women trespassed into territory conventionally seen as male – parodying, emulating and successfully competing against masculine protagonists. They both earned celebrity and (at least on first glance) seemed to be able to publicly assimilate and assemble the performance coda of the everyman frontier hero. That both were 'ordinary' women from rural backgrounds whose ethnicity was white was also important: as such, they were acceptable heirs to the 'armed western woman' mantle and thus within the reasonable heretical parameters of entertainment staple. The legacy of these firearms celebrities was significant, not only in contesting the monolithic image of the masculine frontier hero, but in informing modern perceptions about gender, gun culture and the Second Amendment (most notably in arguments about preserving a democratic defence of personal rights that is both owned and holstered by women). There is, however, a further layer to this tale. Annie Oakley and Calamity Jane may have claimed a slice of America's frontier gun culture for their own, but that did not mean the same as blanket acceptability. There were firm limits as to how far society was willing to countenance the armed western woman when she presented a challenge to normative behaviour. As such, the divergent fortunes of Annie and Calamity pay heed to a convoluted narrative of acceptability and otherness on (and of) the frontier as well as a choreography of the gun that complicated binary or simplistic readings of performance repertoire. As the other contributions in this volume note: *who* carries the gun makes a fundamental difference to how they are received. In the cases of Calamity Jane and Annie Oakley, even while the crowd roared and the gunpowder cracked, the re-negotiation of gender boundaries was not up for discussion. The leading man may not have got the best lines or, indeed, the best shot. However, there were limits to the life afforded the armed frontier heroine beyond the confines of the stage.

4 "A gun is a gun in anyone's hand"

Shooting the gang girl in *Mi Vida Loca*

Emma Horrex

In October 2015, the same year that the white supremacist Dylann Roof purchased a gun and shot dead nine African Americans in downtown Charleston (South Carolina), the National Rifle Association (NRA) released a video narrated by its executive vice president and CEO, Wayne LaPierre. In that video – in which Roof received no mention – LaPierre informed viewers of the "urgent need" to incarcerate the "criminal gangbanger" (a term he used four times in the four minute and fifty-one second feature) of (multi-racial) Chicago in order to "stop violent crime," rather than disarm the "good" farm dwellers of (the largely white) Nebraska and Oklahoma.[1] One month later and throughout his presidential campaign, the NRA-endorsed Donald Trump maintained such racialized, and encompassed gendered, rhetoric into his speeches, including a reference to "bad guys" with guns.[2] Trump insists, "We have gangs roaming the street and in many cases they're illegally here, illegal immigrants, and they have guns and they shoot people."[3]

Furthering the racialization of gun use, in a distinctly different manner, Democratic candidate Hillary Clinton established her campaign "Mothers of the Movement" (2016), which in part sought to advocate stricter gun laws and highlight ongoing gun violence amongst and against racially marginalised communities. For such efforts, and the fear that "If she [Clinton] gets to pick her judges, nothing you can do, folks," Trump seemingly invited the use of the Second Amendment against his opponent: "Although the Second Amendment people – maybe there is, I don't know."[4] Remarks made by, and the historical actions of, Trump have intensified national conversations surrounding gendered and racial inequalities during the ongoing civil rights struggle. The shooting of unarmed minorities by police officers (where racial stereotypes are perceived to influence the shooter's decision to shoot) and attacks against minority communities (including the recent 2016 Pulse nightclub shooting of LGBT and Latino people in Orlando, Florida) prompts debate surrounding the Second Amendment and its relationship to minority groups today, but also historically. Returning to the early 1990s in this chapter, a time in which police brutality against racial minorities similarly exacerbated racial tensions, contributing to gun-loaded

1 NRATV, "Wayne LaPierre: How to Stop Violent Crime", *YouTube*, October 27, 2015 at www.youtube.com/watch?v=-3zZr_Qbuaw (accessed March 03, 2017).

2 Donald Trump in Opposing Views, "Trump: 'Nobody Had Guns But The Bad Guys, Nobody'", *YouTube*, 16 November 2015 at www.youtube.com/watch?v=9k3ylw6ChnU (accessed March 03, 2017).

3 Donald Trump quoted in Daniella Diaz, "Trump: We Have to Take the Guns Away From 'Bad People'", *CNN* [Online], 27 September 2016 at http://edition.cnn.com/2016/09/26/politics/donald-trump-guns-presidential-debate-cnn/ (accessed March 03, 2017).

4 Donald Trump in The Associated Press, "Trump and Clinton on the Second Amendment", *New York Times*, 10 August 2016 at https://nyti.ms/2kyoAuh (accessed March 03, 2017).

protests and cinematic discourses – which often refused to perpetuate simplistic renderings of male "gangbangers" as simply shooters – fuses today's poignant conversations concerning gender, race, and guns, together.

Throughout the late 1980s and early 1990s, deprived inner-city neighbourhoods of Los Angeles (LA) were under fire. In a city literally surrounded by gun manufacturers that were preoccupied with sales figures rather than safety features (dubbed the "Ring of Fire" companies), inexpensive firearms were readily available on the urban streets.[5] At the same time, contemporary street gang membership (often medicalized in the same way as the "epidemic" of "gun culture") and gun violence, particularly amongst young non-white males, soared throughout disadvantaged areas such as Compton and East LA. Alongside the rise in gang activity, which surged in LA County from approximately 40,000 members in 1984 to 103,500 by March 1992, the proportion of gang-related homicides involving firearms increased from 71 per cent in 1979 to 95 per cent in 1994.[6] For Jeffrey Fagan and Deanna Wilkinson, the greater rate of violence within inner-city communities reflects the growing availability of firearms to gang members.[7] However, street gang membership and gun use emerged against a backdrop of systemic racial injustice, police brutality, and declining welfare. Rising gun use amongst gangs and young black and brown males must therefore be understood partly as a result of Reagan's deregulation of guns (including the Firearm Owners Protection Act 1986) and partially as a result of a combination of factors: a lack of viable employment opportunities, the alternative drugs economy, and the necessity to protect trade and turf with weapons.[8]

Much like sociological gang scholars' approaches to the proliferation of gang participation and firearm use within the late twentieth century, black cultural producers widely debated the topic in terms of (black) masculinity. Conveying and capitalising on the plights of the young black male, routinely racially profiled and segregated both socially and geographically, LA-based gangsta rap artists lived-up to and gave fuel to the media construction of the young, armed and dangerous black male. In 1988, N.W.A., self-promoted as "The World's Most Dangerous Group," came out of Compton literally loaded and armed.[9] Translating gangsta sensibilities to screen, images of guns pervaded the "ghetto action movie" (a term popularised by cultural scholar S. Craig Watkins) of the early 1990s.[10] Forming part of the ghetto action movie cycle, John Singleton's *Boyz n the Hood* (*Boyz*, 1991) opens with the

5 For a more detailed discussion of the "Ring of Fire" companies, see Nicholas Freudenberg, *Lethal But Legal: Corporations, Consumption, and Protecting Public Health* (New York: Oxford University Press, 2014), 48–54.

6 A reported 450 gangs across the county in 1984 increased to 942 by March 1992. Divided into groups, Paula McKibbin found that 452 of these gangs in 1992 were Latino, 299 Black and 191 classified as "Other," including Asian and white groups. See Paula Marie McKibbin, *Citizens' Handbook of California Street Gangs: 1992* (Sacramento: Center for Research, McGeorge School of Law, 1992); H.R. Hutson, D. Anglin, and D.N.J.K. Spears, "The Epidemic of Gang-related Homicides in Los Angeles County From 1979 through 1994", 274(13) *The Journal of the American Medical Association* 1031–1036 (1995).

7 Deanna L. Wilkinson and Jeffrey Fagan, "Role of Firearms in Violence 'Scripts': The Dynamics of Gun Events Among Adolescent Males", 59(1) *Law and Contemporary Problems* 55–89 (1996).

8 Statistics must be handled with a degree of vigilance; there is a general lack of accurate reporting regarding contemporary street gang activity which is problematised further due to varying notions of what actually defines "the gang." What is clear, however, is that (reported) gang activity and episodes of violence within LA by young black and Latino males rocketed in the late 1980s and early 1990s.

9 Consider for example, N.W.A.'s single "Straight Outta Compton." *Straight Outta Compton* (Ruthless/Priority, 1988). Words and music by O'Shea Jackson, Lorenzo Patterson, Eric Wright, and Andre Young.

10 S. Craig Watkins, *Representing: Hip Hop Culture and the Production of Black Cinema* (Chicago: University of Chicago Press, 1998).

sound of gunshots and images of walls penetrated by bullets in South Central LA.[11] Providing an opportunity for lucrative popular consumption that has dominated commercial and critical interest, the film industry extended this fascination with gang and gun culture in the early 1990s to include Mexican-American males, for example, *American Me* (1992).[12] Women, however, continued to remain on the margins of the cinematic ghettos and barrios, frequently assuming the dichotomous position of either "hoes" and "bitches" or conversely mothers or girlfriends often victimised by the loss of a son or boyfriend to male-on-male gun violence.[13]

This narrative trope, the death of a male lead, continues in *Mi Vida Loca* (which translates as "My Crazy Life"), a 1994 film written and directed by Allison Anders.[14] Leader of the Echo Park homeboys of East LA, Chicano Ernesto (Jacob Vargas) is shot dead, leaving behind homegirls and best friends Sad Girl (Angel Aviles) and Mousie (Seidy Lopez) who both have children to him. The film plainly narrates the "standard" gang tale – that a deprived urban neighbourhood has been disproportionally affected by cheap firearms, resulting in escalating firearms-related homicides and gun-related violence. Ernesto, however, is shot dead by a white female and it is the Chicana homegirls who are left to take up arms in the film's conclusion. Cinematically shot in a style that Anders herself terms as "romantic realism," *Mi Vida Loca's* treatment of the gun departs significantly from the ghetto action movies that had gone before.[15] Despite placing guns in the hands of the girls and deconstructing the gun as a symbol loaded only with phallic connotations, this chapter illustrates how Anders's problematic handling of firearms also serves to reinforce traditional gender dynamics. Much like the racialized males of the ghetto action movies that pulled the trigger previously, the homegirls are restricted in their right to self-defence as defined by the Second Amendment due to the illegality of their firearm use and marginal status in terms of class and race. Marginalised further by their gender, the homegirls' gun use, while not celebrated as an expression of liberation, is justified by Anders to a greater degree than the gun use enacted by their male counterparts, largely to compensate for their transgression of socially and cinematically defined roles of girls with guns. When this justification is not achievable, girls are placed against one another: the "good" girls with guns and the "bad" girls with guns. While this is relatively familiar ground in male Hollywood, Anders reveals that girl gang gun use is far from monolithic.

As the first feature film to deconstruct images of Chicana gang members as simple appendages to the male gang, *Mi Vida Loca* continues to garner academic attention over 20 years since its release, particularly from a Chicana/o and/or feminist perspective.[16] Up to this point however, there remains a lack of detailed analysis surrounding the complexities of Anders's depiction of female gun use which offers a far more convoluted handling of firearms than the traditional male ghetto action movie. To thoroughly understand Anders's representation of the role of young non-white women in relation to firearms, I take a Cultural Studies approach. This framework reveals how the filmic representation of guns is

11 *Boyz n the Hood* (John Singleton, Columbia Pictures, 1991).
12 *American Me* (Edward James Olmos, Universal Pictures, 1992).
13 *Boyz n the Hood* for example.
14 *Mi Vida Loca* (Allison Anders, Sony Pictures Classics, 1994).
15 Rosa Linda Fregoso, "Hanging Out with the Homegirls? Allison Anders's *Mi Vida Loca*", 21(3) *Cineaste* 37 (July 1995).
16 For a review of this scholarship, see Thea Pitman, "Allison Anders and the 'Racial "Authenticity" Membership-Test': Keeping Mi Vida Loca/My Crazy Life (1994) on the Borders of Chicano Cinema", 2 *iMex* 12–30 (July 2012).

informed by the social, political and historical context in which *Mi Vida Loca* was produced. The tensions inherent within Anders's "romantic realism" come into play most clearly when exploring girl gang gun use. However, to understand the representation of the girls, it is important to look at how the boys handle guns. This chapter thus begins with close textual analyses of the homeboys before turning to the homegirls, whose relationship with firearms both challenges and reinscribes prevailing attitudes to girls with guns.

Ernesto the "Bullet": male shooters in *Mi Vida Loca* and black and white gun use

To consider the extent to which guns retain their "maleness," this section examines the character of Ernesto and his relationship with the gun, illustrating a departure from the conventional ghetto action movie not simply by having girls pack weapons but in the handling of boys with guns. It is homeboy Ernesto who we first see holding a gun, but it is noteworthy that while Sad Girl and Mousie call Ernesto by his birth name, his gang name (or moniker), is Bullet. A phallic symbol of violence, Bullet contrasts greatly to the girls' feminised gang names, which are dictated and assigned by the boys: Whisper, Sad Girl, Baby Doll, Giggles, and Mousie. Mousie and Sad Girl's use of "Ernesto" instead of Bullet, however, disrupts the assumption that the girls are drawn to him simply because of an allure of danger.

Ghetto action movies had already started to challenge broader cultural perceptions of non-white male youth as simply dangerous, trigger-happy killers. Guns and their devastating consequences in the urban neighbourhood are aligned with political meaning in *Boyz*. Furious Styles (Laurence Fishburne) questions white capitalism and gentrification in the neighbourhood conveyed in a frequently cited passage that begins, "Why is it that there is a gun shop on almost every corner in this community?" Despite the politicisation of the gun establishing a political maturity amongst older black males, on the rare occasion that guns are in the hands of women in the contemporary street gang movie, gendered stereotypes are challenged to a certain degree but ultimately reinforced as women pay a price for firearm use.

In *New Jack City* (1991), Keisha (Vanessa A. Williams), a black female and competent shooter, is placed in a space previously reserved for black males.[17] Keisha's character is both feminised and masculinised: she wears delicate gold jewellery and yet the same white pant suit as her male counterparts. In defending her male employer, Nino, with gunfire, Keisha dies in a shoot-out at the hands of a man. Unlike one of the male characters, Keisha does not attempt to save a young girl caught in the crossfire. Ultimately Keisha's transgression of gendered expectations results in her death. In *Set It Off* (released in 1996, the same year that the production of ghetto action movies tapered off and the year Bill Clinton signed the Personal Responsibility and Work Opportunity Reconciliation Act, suggesting that welfare receivers had become too reliant on the state), the only character not avenging the racial profiling of black Americans by the state or reclaiming her children from social services is homosexual Cleo (Queen Latifah).[18] While the other (more reluctant) female firearm users agree to commit an armed bank robbery for personal and political reasons, Cleo shoots for both financial gain and pleasure. In film scholar Hilary Neroni's words, it is only Cleo, a "butch"

17 *New Jack City* (Mario Van Peebles, Warner Bros. Pictures, 1991).
18 *Set It Off* (F. Gary Gray, New Line Cinema, 1996).

lesbian who "dances around with her gun" who is "involved in gangsta street life that is often depicted as the environment within which they all live."[19] "Like her masculine counterparts and Keisha in *New Jack City*," media studies scholar Beretta E. Smith-Shomade writes, "she goes down fighting, like a man."[20] While both men and women are allowed a degree of political consciousness in relation to guns, women most willing to shoot in *New Jack City* and *Set it Off* are fatally gunned down. *Mi Vida Loca* moves beyond both these conventions as both the politicisation and masculinisation of the gun (and shooter) are complicated.

The first scene in Anders's movie that engages with the gun occurs when Ernesto and female gang member Whisper (Nelida Lopez, who was an actual Echo Park gang member) are discussing Ernesto's drugs business. As Ernesto talks about his illicit operation, he reveals his arousal when desperate female drugs clients seek their fix from him as he imitates their pleading:

> "Oh, Ernesto, please. I need it I had a bad day; I had a bad week; I'm stressed . . ." Hey if the chick's cute I might go easy, 'cause the next time she'll give me head for it. . . . But hey, I wouldn't fuck 'em. Not the white bitches . . . not the junkies, naw. But it gets me hard just to say, "all rato" ["later"].

Immediately after, Ernesto takes out his gun. Here, we are reminded how socioeconomic demands in the late 1980s contributed to the proliferation of the underground drugs economy in barrio environments but also extended beyond the racially marginalised. Anders also implicitly connects the gun with its phallocentric associations, reinforcing Ernesto's sexuality and masculinity. However, Ernesto reveals that the gun does not work; its only function is for "confidence."

This instantly serves to distance *Mi Vida Loca* from the traditional ghetto action movies in which the gun is in full working order: the opening scene of *Menace II Society* features an armed robbery leading to multiple deaths, setting up the violent trajectory for the rest of the film.[21] Additionally, Anders indicates how Ernesto exploits and depends on the visual threat of the gun to instil fear into white clients. Significantly, Anders reverses the historical power dynamic of white control of arms as a means of racial oppression.[22] Traditionally and historically both the gang and gun use has been linked with maleness and similarly they have held racialized dimensions. Distinctively, contemporary street gangs have been associated with the non-white male while gun ownership has historically been a white man's privilege. The Second Amendment right to bear arms refers to a "well-regulated militia;" an institution that historically composed of white men. Importantly, Sociologist France Winddance Twine reminds us that "while racial and ethnic minorities historically were denied the right to possess guns, during specific historical moments, white women have been encouraged to take up arms in the defence of white nation-building projects."[23] Despite attorney Alana Bassin's acknowledgement that women were negated in

19 Hilary Neroni, *Violent Woman, The: Femininity, Narrative, and Violence in Contemporary American Cinema* (Albany: State University of New York Press, 2005), 110.
20 Beretta E. Smith-Shomade, "'Rock-a-Bye, Baby!': Black Women Disrupting Gangs and Constructing Hip-Hop Gangsta Films", 42(2) *Cinema Journal* 36 (2003).
21 *Menace II Society* (The Hughes Brothers, New Line Cinema, 1993).
22 For a discussion of the racial politics of the Second Amendment, see Robert J. Cottrol and Raymond T. Diamond, "The Second Amendment: Toward an Afro-Americanist Reconsideration", 80 *Georgetown Law Journal* 309–361 (1991).
23 France Winddance Twine, *Girls With Guns: Firearms, Feminism, and Militarism* (New York and London: Routledge, 2013), 6.

the Second Amendment and its ratification, some (white) women have had greater access and permission to use guns than non-white males.[24]

Prior to the girls packing guns in *Mi Vida Loca*, Ernesto handles his non-functioning gun first. The first shot fired however is at the hands of one of the white "chicks" Ernesto sells drugs to. We see a correlation here with the broader historical and cinematic relationship of the gun with gender and race: the white female shooter precedes the non-white male who shoots before the racialized female. Before the non-white female could fire guns in Anders's film and *New Jack City*, the racialized male shooter had to exist previously in blaxploitation films of the 1970s. Black women did take up arms during this period of filmmaking but were often highly sexualised in film, *Coffy* (1973) being a prime example.[25] White women aiming fire came into both the critical and popular arena in full force in the late 1980s, particularly in Hollywood's characterisation of white female cops in films such as *Blue Steel* (1989).[26] In the media more generally, guns had already started to be challenged as a symbol of maleness by nationally circulated publications such as *Women & Guns.*

Women & Guns magazine debuted in the same year of *Blue Steel's* release and both the publication and the figure of the cinematic law enforcer served as a profitable platform for the discussion of gun ownership amongst women, predominately those of a white, middle-class background. Also in 1989, the advertisement of guns, for example Smith and Wesson's Lady Smith (a handgun designed for women and their handbags), deployed "feminist rhetoric to market guns to women as a 'niche' market."[27] The NRA placed emphasis on protection (relying on perceptions of women as victims) in a campaign with the slogan "Refuse to Be a Victim." Before this period of commercialisation, this notion of self-protection had already been well-circulated, as white markswoman Annie Oakley (1860–1926) reportedly "thought women should protect themselves, and a gun was the best way to do it."[28] As Oakley demonstrated, however, guns were not solely for protective purposes, they were equally employed for sport and entertainment purposes amongst white women. *Annie Oakley* (1935) brought to life the real gun-toting Oakley who far from the sexualised image of the armed woman in blaxploitation movies, "domesticated the gun" in Laura Browder's words.[29] But for the gun to become domesticated, it had to first be in the hands of (white) males, in genres such as the Western and as implicitly declared by the Second Amendment.

White men in the ghetto action movie (and less frequently, white women as seen in *South Central*, 1992) are gun-strapped cops, arresting youth simply for being black (see *Menace* for example).[30] The Second Amendment offers protection to the white police officers who perceive the young black male, armed or unarmed, as a threat or menace to society. Unprotected by the state and instead subjected to racial abuse, gun carrying for the young (black) male illustrates a self-entitlement to self-protection through the use of (illegal) weapons. By living outside the law and within white hierarchies of power, the Second Amendment is redundant to the young black male. The white police officers of *Menace* abuse their power, using a police baton to beat a young black male. There is no consequence of this police

24 Alana Bassin, "Why Packing a Pistol Perpetuates Patriarchy", 8(2) *Hastings Women's Law Journal* 351–363 (1997).
25 *Coffy* (Jack Hill, American International Pictures, 1973).
26 *Blue Steel* (Kathryn Bigelow, Metro-Goldwyn-Mayer, 1989).
27 Twine, *Girls With Guns*, 8.
28 Shirl Kasper, *Annie Oakley* (Norman: University of Oklahoma Press, 1992), 215.
29 Laura Browder, *Her Best Shot: Women and Guns in America* (Chapel Hill: University of North Carolina Press, 2009), 233.
30 *South Central* (Stephen Milburn Anderson, Warner Bros. Pictures, 1992).

brutality – a comment on the beating of Rodney King by the L.A.P.D in 1991 and the subsequent acquittal of the police officers involved. Yet ghetto action movies were also keen to illustrate that police brutality was not solely at the hands of white police officers. A racist black police officer in *Boyz* places a gun against protagonist, and unarmed, Tre's (Cuba Gooding Jr.) head revealing his misuse of power and firearms: "Oh think you tough, huh? Scared now, huh? I like that. That's why I took this job. I hate little motherfuckers like you. Little niggers like shit. I could blow your head off with this Smith and Wesson and you couldn't do shit." Classism and racism instilled within the black police officer rejects ideas of "blackness" as a unifying force. Ernesto's death at the hands of an armed white female drugs client further dismantles notions of race and class.

Shooting Ernesto dead, the white female performs the role that would have previously been occupied by a black or Latino male in the ghetto action movie and extends the use of firearms beyond that of the racially marginalised in what Susan Dever describes as a "symbolic reversal of media-hyped 'reality,' white girl kills brown boy."[31] Dismantling the fear of racialized crime during the early 1990s, the scene further distances itself from the convention of male-on-male violence featured in ghetto action movies. Ernesto's performance of hyper-masculinity undermined by his ill-equipped gun in the previous scene with Whisper is further illustrated as an "act." When confronted by the white female, Ernesto is without his weapon as Anders refuses to engage in what Murray Forman identifies as the "notion that urban youth are *always already* armed and dangerous."[32] Anders thus moves beyond the traditions of the ghetto action movie and the handling of the gun to a great extent. However, while Anders fractures the association between Ernesto's gun and his sexual prowess, guns continue to be linked to maleness in *Mi Vida Loca* most simply by the fact that in the gang, it is only the males that own firearms. The Echo Park homeboys are able to successfully shoot dead rival gang River Valley's leader El Duran (Jesse Borrego) due to the misunderstanding of the whereabouts of a truck. They have access to guns unlike the homegirls who must borrow firearms.

Girls, gangs, guns, and the sociologists

Statistically, firearms have and continue to be owned by a higher percentage of men than women.[33] However, scholarship (both sociological and film) pertaining to (white) female gun users has developed particularly since the time of *Mi Vida Loca's* production in line with the aftermath of Reagan's deregulation. Stange and Oyster note that "the extensive social-scientific literature on guns and their use almost invariably fails to take gender into

31 Susan Dever, *Celluloid Nationalism and Other Melodramas: From Post-Revolutionary Mexico to Fin de Siglo Mexamâerica* (Albany: SUNY Press, 2003), 146.

32 Murray Forman, "Getting the Gun: The Cinematic Representation of Handgun Acquisition", in Murray Pomerance and John Sakeris (eds.), *Bang Bang, Shoot Shoot!: Essays on Guns and Popular Culture* (Needham Heights: Simon & Schuster, 1999), 53.

33 While precise figures of firearm ownership are difficult to ascertain, made particularly problematic by a gender bias in gun literature and the nature of self-reports (Gallup Polls etc.), Smith and Smith found in their 1995 study that between 1980 and 1994, the pooled average of males owning a gun was 48.7 per cent, while amongst women gun ownership was 11.6 per cent. In September 2016, the *Guardian* (US) revealed in their "exclusively" obtained summary of a 2015 unpublished Harvard/Northeastern survey of the "most definitive portrait of US gun ownership in two decades," that "gun owners tended to be white, male, conservative, and live in rural areas." Tom Smith and Robert J. Smith, "Changes in Firearm Ownership in Women 1980–1994", 86 *Journal of Criminal Law and Criminology* 147 (1995); Lois Beckett, "Gun Inequality: US Study Charts Rise of Hardcore Super Owners", *Guardian*, 19 September 2016 [Online] at www.theguardian.com/us-news/2016/sep/19/us-gun-ownership-survey (accessed September 22, 2016).

account."[34] This "masculinist perspective on guns and gun use" has been challenged in contemporary scholarship, as a "small, but nevertheless significant, proportion of guns are in women's hands," not only in the home, but also the workplace, the recreational realm and on the streets.[35] Despite this, gangs and their relationship with guns are most frequently discussed in terms of (hyper)masculinity: the milieu of the gang has been recognised as encouraging hypermasculine qualities with "the gun metaphorically reinforcing both the power and sexuality of men."[36] Research carried out in the early 1990s, for example, aiming to examine the relationship between gun ownership, gun use, and gang membership omitted females from the study because according to Bjerregaard and Lizotte (1995), "girls rarely own guns, whether for sport or protection."[37] Although this notion is somewhat generalised, gang researchers did consistently find that girl gang members were less violent than their male counterparts in research conducted before the 1990s. However, to negate females completely from research concerning gangs and gun use fails to acknowledge that while perhaps not at the same "alarming" rate, there were girls in the gang, and in society more generally, carrying and using firearms.

This reality was not only projected but hyped significantly by media outlets throughout the 1990s. Television talk show programmes that translated the subculture of Latina and Black gang girls into mainstream discussion topics sought to take advantage of mainstream audiences' simultaneous attraction and repulsion surrounding female youth violence as girls admitted "we carry guns when we have to."[38] According to Meda Chesney-Lind and Katherine Irwin:

> the United States has always had "bad girls" and a collection of media eager to show their waywardness. In the 1960s and 1970s, American bad girls were female revolutionary figures such as Patti Hearst, Friedenke Krabbe, and Angela Davis who brandished guns and fought alongside their rebellious male counterparts.[39]

This popularization of female "badness," then, was certainly not a new phenomenon. However, the 1990s differed greatly in terms of arrest rates for juvenile girls; between 1994 and 2003 female arrests "generally increased more (or decreased less) than male arrests in most categories."[40] It must be noted, however, that the greatest increases for young females were for nonviolent drug crimes, including drug abuse violations, DUI's and disorderly conduct.

While youth violence was increasing in the barrios and ghettos of urban America in the early 1990s, these statistics do not simply equate to an "epidemic" of girl gang or female

34 Mary Zeiss Stange and Carol K. Oyster, *Gun Women: Firearms and Feminism in Contemporary America* (New York and London: New York University Press, 2000), 7.

35 Ibid.

36 Josephine Metcalf, *The Culture and Politics of Contemporary Street Gang Memoirs* (Jackson: University Press of Mississippi, 2012), 79.

37 Beth Bjerregaard and Alan Lizotte, "Gun Ownership and Gang Membership", 86(1) *Journal of Criminal Law and Criminology* (1995), 43.

38 A *Leeza* (NBC) television episode broadcast in the late 1990s with the subtitle "Girl Gangs: Badder than the Boys" featured a number of young non-white gang girls who discussed their gang activity; see Doneuemf, "Gangster Girls on a Talk Show Part 1 of 2", *YouTube*, July 10, 2009 at www.youtube.com/watch?v=xd4Cngl_Bfw (accessed December 21, 2015).

39 Meda Chesney-Lind and Katherine Irwin, "From Badness to Meanness: Popular constructions of Contemporary Girlhood", in Anita Harris (ed.), *All About the Girl: Culture, Power, and Identity* (New York: Routledge, 2004), 46.

40 Howard N. Snyder, *Juvenile Arrests 2003* (Washington, DC: Office of Juvenile Delinquency Prevention, August 2005), 8 at www.ncjrs.gov/pdffiles1/ojjdp/209735.pdf (accessed September 06, 2014).

youth violence more generally. Although offence statistics for overall crime increased, most violent crime committed by girls decreased between 1994 and 2003.[41] However, this reality became misplaced in the media hysteria. A combination of fact and fiction fuelled public interest in the aggressive non-white gang girl. Black and Latina girls were incarcerated more frequently than white girls compared to the previous decade, largely due to changing policies on youth crime as enforced by the Reagan Administration. The fictional notion that girls of colour had not only achieved equality with the homeboys through their (gun) violence, but were in-fact "badder than the boys" further contributed to the curiosity of the gang girl.

At the same time that Anders conveyed and capitalised on this distinct epoch of youth violence and the public fascination with Latina "bad girls" in its earliest stages, feminist criminology re-evaluated the role of the girl in the gang.[42] Significant development including Anne Campbell's *The Girls in the Gang* (1984) had already started to re-assess the critical failure of sociologists who previously identified the girls in the contemporary street gang as mere emulations of the boys. Although researchers continued to find that girls in the gang were not as aggressive as the boys, the former stereotype ascribed to them as mere support systems to their male counterparts, as "weapons carriers to the boys," began to be challenged as girls in the gang moved into sight and became talking points both cinematically and theoretically.[43] Sociologist Angela Stroud notes that sociological literature concerning gender and gun use has been male-centred.[44] Yet it is important to note that there has been an emergence in the last fifteen years or so of scholarship concerning the violent (white) woman in film and in particular, the role of the gun in filmic narratives of the early 1990s (films such as *Thelma and Louise* and *The Silence of the Lambs*).

This chapter aims to extend current scholarship pertaining to the cinematic gun holding female to include Anders's filmic representation of young Chicano women. Literature and film scholar Carol M. Dole recognises that "despite widespread support for strong images of women in the media, many mainstream film viewers and academic feminists alike have hesitated to celebrate cinematic women with guns, even those who uphold the law."[45]

The girls in *Mi Vida Loca* are law breakers unlike the female law enforcers of 1990s Hollywood. However, despite scholarship largely centring on the role of white female gun use in film (largely due to the fact that there are not as many non-white equivalents in mainstream film but in part because of the continued privileging of whiteness), Dole's contention is of significant importance. Guns play a central role in *Mi Vida Loca* yet female firearm use is similarly presented as non-celebratory and is instead layered with varying levels of justification. This complicates the boundaries between the perpetrator and the victim of gun violence.[46]

41 Ibid.
42 See for example, "Ann Campbell's Female Participation in Gangs", in Ron C. Huff (ed.), *Gangs in America* (Newbury Park and London: Sage, 1990), 163–182.
43 Bernard Williams, Jailbait: "The Story of Juvenile Delinquency", in Meda Chesney-Lind and John M. Hagerdorn (eds.), *Female Gangs in America: Essays on Girls, Gangs and Gender* (Chicago: Lakeview Press, 1999), 45.
44 For a review of the sociological literature pertaining to guns and masculinity, see Angela Stroud, "Good Guys With Guns: Hegemonic Masculinity and Concealed Handguns", 26(2) *Gender & Society* 216–238 (April 2012).
45 Carol M. Dole, "The Gun and the Badge: Hollywood and the Female Lawman", in Martha McCaughey and Neal King (eds.), *Reel Knockouts: Violent Women in Film* (Austin, TX: University of Texas Press, 2001), 79.
46 As philosophical theorist Vittorio Bufacchi informs us, "The terms 'Perpetrator' and 'Victim' are notoriously difficult to define, and therefore subject to controversy." Vittorio Bufacchi, *Violence and Social Justice* (Basingstoke: Palgrave Macmillan, 2007), 33.

Blind violence and evident religion

Operating within the "romantic realism" framework that Anders applies to her own style, justification for gang girl violence and gun use could be, and indeed has been, labelled in simplistic, melodramatic terms. For example, Leslie Felperin contends that the homegirls of Echo Park are "reared on cheap romance, and the religion of the gun."[47] However, this chapter shows that through religious imagery and by keeping violence off-screen, Anders reveals a more complicated relationship between racialized gang girl (gun) violence. Significantly, Anders departs from the signature element of the ghetto action genre not only by placing guns in the hands of girls, shifting the gendered dimensions of the cinematic lens, but primarily by keeping a significant amount of the violence off-screen. Viewers are not allowed to indulge in images of bodies penetrated by bullets (we never actually see bullets hit any of the victims, just the aftermath). *Menace*, which has been credited for the sideways gun grip (a technique which facilitates the framing of the gun pointers "menacing" face and weapon) and subsequent copycatting technique by criminals, and the ghetto action film cycle more generally, have been considered by film scholars as "uncompromisingly violent."[48] The contorting body of Caine (Tyrin Turner) whose body is fatally showered with bullets in the film's conclusion certainly underscores this as blood uncontrollably froths from his mouth. For Watkins, *Menace* "illustrates an important feature of change that marks the broader popular culture landscape, the intensification of violence in American film and television."[49] By comparison, *Mi Vida Loca* invites audiences to participate in an inquisitive trip down Echo Park Avenue without the bloodshed – or at least, not as much of it as viewers might expect.

When I asked Anders in an interview about the lack of on-screen violence in *Mi Vida Loca* (the film was Rated R by the MPAA) and the reasoning for keeping violence off-screen, she responded:

> I just think that violence ends the story, it ends the emotion. If you show a lot of graphic violence, then that's all that people are left with in my mind. Show the impact of it don't show the violence . . . it has a bigger impact. Everything is so violent these days . . . right down to the sound, it's an assault.[50]

Anders underscores ideas proposed by philosophical theorist Slavoj Žižek who, taking "sideways glances" at violence, proposes that "the overpowering horror of violent acts . . . inexorably function as a lure which prevents us from thinking."[51] Violence, then, distracts us. In resisting and subverting the expectations of creating a film set in East LA during a time in which Anders states "the girls I was working with, they were getting shot at and standing alongside people getting killed," refuses to indulge the viewer in violent episodes

47 Leslie Felperin, "*Mi Vida Loca* review", 5(4) *Sight and Sound* 48 (April 1995).
48 For a brief discussion of the impact of this "unorthodox grip" in *Menace,* see Brian Treanor, *Emplotting Virtue: A Narrative Approach to Environment Virtue and Ethics* (Albany: State University of New York Press, 2014), 181–182; Jonathan Munby, "From Gangsta to Gangster: The Hood Film's Criminal Allegiance with Hollywood", in J. Chapman et al. (eds.), *The New Film History: Sources, Methods, Approaches* (Basingstoke: Palgrave Macmillan, 2007), 166.
49 S. Craig Watkins, *Representing: Hip Hop Culture and The Production of Black Cinema* (Chicago and London: University of Chicago Press, 1998), 200.
50 Allison Anders, *Personal Interview* [Recorded Interview] March 22, 2015, 1 pm. Echo Park, Los Angeles.
51 Slavoj Žižek, *Violence: Six Sideways Reflections* (London: Profile, 2008), 3.

that were so regularly and intrinsically part of the ghetto action movies that had gone before.[52] Indeed, insistent that the film was about humanising the relationship between the homegirls and not about what Susan Dever terms the "media-embattled barrios," Anders reveals that unlike the black and Latino male filmmakers that had previously and exclusively presented the gang ridden streets, she did not want *Mi Vida Loca* to be a "genre" film.[53] Most evidently, this is achieved not only by the cinematography (the barrio streets are filled with sunlight) and episodic structure (the narrative is told in three vignettes), but undeniably through the lack of violent imagery.

For Anders *Mi Vida Loca* is melodrama: "I realized what I do is melodrama and that *Mi Vida Loca* was melodrama – Douglas Sirk in the barrio."[54] Keeping violence off-screen certainly operates within the romantic realist framework; violence is absent yet also present. But it also raises some important questions about violent filmic women and audiences. The primary question is whether there is a particular discomfort when watching non-white armed women who kill on screen. In the scene that follows Ernesto's gun handling with Whisper, Sad Girl and Mousie are preparing to come face-to-face with one another to settle their dispute concerning Sad Girl's betrayal of Mousie's friendship by sleeping and having a baby with Ernesto. Here, Anders includes religious imagery to illustrate Sad Girl's own discomfort with guns, reinscribing the gendered dynamics of firearms.

Prior to Sad Girl and Mousie's duel, Whisper tells Sad Girl "You're going to need lots of luck" and passes her a scapular, before handing over male gang member Snoopy's gun, thus the gun is linked to both religion and maleness. Discussing the acquisition of the handgun in *The Terminator* (1984), *Thelma and Louise* (1991), *Falling Down* (1992), *Juice* (1992), and *Strapped* (1993), Forman recognises that the ways in which guns "are acquired are frequently overlooked or ignored in the script," despite the importance of what the acquisition reveals.[55] Indeed, scholars have failed to analyse the acquisition scene in *Mi Vida Loca* where the scapular and the gun offer equal modes of male protection. Sad Girl must borrow a male-owned firearm, while the scapular is symbolic of devout Catholicism in which the worship of God requires the worship of a male. However, as the scene develops, it fails to support Felperin's contention that the women of Echo Park are "reared on cheap romance and the religion of the gun."[56] Sad Girl receives the gun while standing at the kitchen sink as Whisper passes the gun through the kitchen window from outside to inside. The gun transitions between the public sphere, the barrio streets (traditionally considered as a male site), and the private, domestic sphere (traditionally female). As the gun enters the home, the boundaries between the dangers of the street and the safety of the home become disrupted. However, Sad Girl's admission that she has "never shot nobody" as she tries to return the gun wrapped inside a kitchen tea-towel (domesticating the gun) to Whisper, indicates her reluctance to use the weapon. While she may engage in religious practices, Sad Girl's uncertainty about the necessity of the gun dismantles Felperin's statement. The fact that none of the girls have ownership of their own gun and have to protect themselves by male modes of protection continues to reinforce the gun as male.

52 Allison Anders quoted in Nellie Eden, "Lean Like A Chola", *Wonderland* [Online], 3 March 2015 at www.wonderlandmagazine.com/2015/03/lean-like-chola/ (accessed December 21, 2015).
53 Dever, *Celluloid Nationalism*, 127; Anders, *Personal Interview*.
54 Allison Anders quoted in Sheila Benson, "Girl Gangs Get Their Colors", 24(6) *Interview* 96 (June 1994); German filmmaker Douglas Sirk (1897–1987) was famed for his melodramatic cinema of 1950s Hollywood.
55 Forman, "Getting the Gun", 49.
56 Felperin, "*Mi Vida Loca* review", 48.

Friendship and female operations

In full melodramatic style, firearms are not as powerful as the friendship between Sad Girl and Mousie, but the reality is that guns are required for drugs operations: Bernard Harcourt confirms that "youths who sell drugs also often feel the need to carry firearms."[57] We see both romantic and realistic representations of firearms, but the gun continues to be aligned with maleness. Once Sad Girl and Mousie do have possession of guns (Ernesto gives Mousie his non-functioning gun), they are shown, just as the all-female gang The Lizzies are in Walter Hill's 1979 cult classic *The Warriors*, to be incapable of using them.[58] In a shoot-or-get-shot scenario, both Mousie and Sad Girl fail to pull the trigger on one another, and it is instead the off-screen sound of a distant gun shot that can be heard echoing through the park as Ernesto is shot dead. Discussing the use of guns within *Mi Vida Loca*, Anders stated during interview that the film "put the guns in the girls' hand. Put all the power in the girls' hands really."[59] Symbolically, the placing of the gun in the hands of those previously negated from screen is powerful, but Mousie holding Ernesto's non-operational gun suggests a false sense of power.

Interpreting this scene in light of Anders's comments, Sad Girl and Mousie's decision not to shoot each other suggests their friendship holds more power than the gun does in their hands. Sad Girl's narration underpins this: "We stood face to face at the logs, and all I ever knew about Mousie and all she ever knew about me flashed before our eyes. We had a serious past, her and me, and I guess that's why we couldn't do it." Whether loaded symbolically with phallic connotations or loaded physically with bullets, both girls recognise that the gun, an inanimate object so frequently imbued with such symbolic and physical power, is meaningless when compared to the bond between two homegirls. The gun has no emancipatory potential in either the kitchen or shoot-out scene; rather, it is the girls' resistance to firearm use that is celebrated here. In this sense, the power is in the girls' hands.

Despite reading the scene in this way, in which guns ironically draw truces, the episode underscores the problematic handling of the gun. Regardless of race, no female character is shown to have the complete capacity to successfully utilise a gun. The white female drugs client who shoots Ernesto dead also inadvertently injuries Whisper, physically disabling her and implicitly placing (young) women against one another. Welfare dependent and unable to afford hospital fees, Whisper is left using the aid of a walking stick. With Ernesto dead and unable to use money from his drugs business to provide for his two children, the girls are forced to start their own "operation."

The girls are unable to "count on the boys" who as Sad Girl reveals by the age of 21, are either "disabled, in prison or dead." As a subculture more generally they are also unable to rely on state protection. Sad Girl reveals:

> We have our own meetings now – our own operation and we defend our own neighbourhood. By the time my daughter grows up, Echo Park will belong to her, and she can be whatever she wants to be. The homegirls have learnt to pack weapons 'cause our operations have become more complicated.

57 Bernard E. Harcourt, *Language of the Gun: Youth, Crime, and Public Policy* (Chicago and London: University of Chicago Press, 2006), 83.
58 *The Warriors* (Walter Hill, Paramount Pictures, 1979).
59 Anders, *Personal Interview.*

The girls thus pack weapons as a means of attempting to take control of realms that were previously controlled by the boys. However, in her analysis of the film, Dever makes a perceptive statement underpinning the necessity of recognising that not all violence originates from the same source:

> We cannot assume, as gang films universally seem to do, that all violence in the barrio is the same, stemming from savage gang members killing each other. Taking life as it comes in post-Rodney King L.A. is a much more complex proposition; violence is everybody's domain.[60]

Although *Mi Vida Loca* highlights the "importance of separating individual from group behaviours," illustrated most clearly in the juxtaposing of the boys who in homeboy Sleepy's (Gabriel Gonzales) words "blasted" El Duran "for no good reason" and the girls who in Sad Girl's words "use weapons for love," Anders also makes a clear distinction between the type of acceptable violence that these young women exhibit.[61] That Sad Girl's closing narration pertaining to weapon use intersects with dialogue concerning her daughter illustrates this. The viewer is informed that violence not only stems from varying sources, but also suggests that violence, and primarily gun use, has varying degrees of legitimacy.

Shooting the innocent: the closing scene

The closing scene of *Mi Vida Loca* underscores the differences in legitimate girl gang gun use, while illustrating that gun use is far from monolithic amongst these young women. Sad Girl insists that the Echo Park girls are "safe and practical" in their gun use. However, Anders further conveys the inability of women to use weapons successfully. The rival River Valley girls accidentally shoot dead Big Sleepy's (Julian Reyes) daughter when attempting to shoot the younger homeboy Sleepy and avenge their leader (El Duran)'s death. In a scene reminiscent of the conclusion of *Menace*, a young child sat playing on a toy bicycle is caught up in a shooting. Yet in *Mi Vida Loca*, a young girl dies at the hands of a female gang member. The ending is distinctly different to the death of gang member Caine in *Menace* whose bullet-laden body acts as a shield enabling the survival of a young boy. "We do not," as Professor of psychology Wayne Wilson reminds us in his discussion of why consumers attach value judgments to murder (rather than accept murder as a deliberately negative act), "expect women to come out with guns blazing and display a willingness to murder in the same style and flourish compared to men."[62] Thus the killing of the child, and in Dever's words, the gun's "lethal potential" to "destroy the very things it purports to protect," renders the rival homegirls violence completely futile.[63]

Polly Wilding observes in her study of gendered violence in Brazil that "violent acts are rarely random, but are infused with meanings."[64] Indeed, feminist film scholar Karen Hollinger notes in her analysis of *Mi Vida Loca's* presentation of female friendship "that violence

60 Dever, *Celluloid Nationalism*, 146.
61 Ibid.
62 Wayne Wilson, *Good Murders and Bad Murders: A Consumer's Guide in the Age of Information* (Lanham: University Press of America, 1991), 3.
63 Dever, *Celluloid Nationalism*, 161.
64 Polly Wilding, *Negotiating Boundaries: Gender, Violence and Transformation in Brazil* (New York: Palgrave Macmillan, 2012), 77.

enacted by a woman is just as destructive as that perpetrated by a man."[65] However, the meaning behind the rival gang's gun use and the boys' blasting of El Duran is not associated with the protection and love of a child. The young victim is not presented as one who "deserves" to die, unlike characters such as Harlan, Thelma's attempted rapist, in *Thelma and Louise*.[66] Although the homeboys are mourning the loss of Ernesto when the shooting of El Duran occurs, their firearm use is incomparable to the use of guns with the aim of protecting the self and/or the child, rendering it ultimately "senseless" to those positioned outside the gang. In the final scene, the River Valley homegirls, rivals to the Echo Park members to which the viewers have now established an allegiance with, commit unjustifiable violence which continues to link female aggression, and the gun, to a man: "We watch the sequence," as Dever observes, "in near silence."[67] Although *Mi Vida Loca's* narrative "unfolds" in the words of Fregoso as a "sisterhood saga," the River Valley homegirls are placed against the Echo Park homegirls in this scene as they deviate from accepted modes of justifiable violence.[68]

Sad Girl and Mousie clutching hold of their children, and Whisper her walking stick, instead of guns as they leave the funeral of the young girl in the closing moments of the film suggests that these gang girls wield weapons to protect those weaker than themselves. Their firearm use is due to a necessity to protect, unlike the boys who exploit their ability to carry firearms to engage in violent competition which stems from a temporary loss of control. As Wilding remarks, "if acts of violence fall into particular categories, or are labelled in certain ways, as 'self-defence' as opposed to 'anger' for example, this can legitimise the actions of violent individuals."[69] This is clearly played out in *Mi Vida Loca* as well as mainstream cinematic discourses more generally. Discussing the "cinematic female law enforcers" of the 1990s, Dole reveals they always "wish to protect those weaker than themselves: never men, but always women or children, ideally female children."[70] The Echo Park homegirls fulfil this role.

The fact that the rival River Valley homegirls seek revenge for El Duran continues to link the gun to a male character yet moves beyond the boundaries of the girls in the gang seeking to protect only those who are younger and weaker than themselves. As Dever contends, "a gun is a gun in anyone's hands," but justification for gun use is variable.[71] The boys' hotheaded gun use and the rival homegirl's revenge killing for El Duran simply fuel the cycle of burials, conveyed as the girls and audience witness the third funeral of the film in its closing. Viewers can only speculate that the Echo Park homegirls might also contribute to an endless cycle of violence and funeral processions as they raise children around guns. For Forman, the "evolution" in *Thelma and Louise* from "gun-shy homebodies to gun-savvy, pistol packing mommas is consistent with women's capacity to adjust to new options, opportunities and circumstances as they ascend the social ladder."[72] This can also be recognised in *Mi Vida Loca*, as the girls seek new opportunities in the absence of men, and gun use is intrinsic to

65 Karen Hollinger, *In the Company of Women: Contemporary Female Friendship Films* (Minneapolis and London: University of Minnesota Press, 1998), 197.
66 *Thelma and Louise* (Ridley Scott, Metro-Goldwyn-Mayer, 1991).
67 Dever, *Celluloid Nationalism*, 161.
68 Rosa Linda Fregoso, *MeXicana Encounters: The Making of Social Identities on the Borderlands* (Berkeley and London: University of California Press, 2003), 99.
69 Wilding, *Negotiating Boundaries*, 77.
70 Dole, "The Gun and the Badge", 81.
71 Dever, *Celluloid Nationalism*, 161.
72 Forman, "Getting the Gun", 55.

this development. However, the Echo Park homegirls, as Timothy Shary indicates "do not enjoy the thrill of violence" as having weapons in close proximity of the children makes Sad Girl (in her own words) "nervous."[73] They arguably do not achieve the same confidence in gun handling as Thelma and Louise.

Sad Girl and Mousie's reluctance to use firearms in the earlier kitchen and shoot-out scene results in the rekindling of their friendship as they choose friendship over firearms and Ernesto. By comparison their decision to utilise guns at the end of the film is considered acceptable toughness by incorporating into the dialogue justification for their actions. Their willingness to protect their children, fulfilling the mother's traditional role as protector of her child, is juxtaposed against the irrational gun use of the rival homegirls who shoot dead the child (the ultimate symbol of innocence). As Wilding writes, "violence constructed as 'legitimate' produces less fear than acts committed by unruly actors, whose violence is viewed as unpredictable, disproportionate or indiscriminate."[74] The River Valley homegirls' shooting of the young girl diversifies the representation of gang girls and refuses to present a monolithic narrative of the roots of violence. At the same time, Anders illustrates that there is a necessity for the Echo Park homegirls to arm themselves against others that are willing to kill for a different kind of love, that of a man; something that Mousie and Sad Girl refused to resort to in their duel.

Anders contended in interview that the moviemakers of the ghetto action genre "were saddled with go to school and do right and everything will be OK" moralistic tales.[75] By comparison, Anders claims that she "didn't have to make proclamations or solve the problem."[76] *Mi Vida Loca's* conclusion concerning the use of guns certainly confirms this idea as the girls gather at the final funeral, and the soundtrack reveals "Girls It Ain't Easy."[77] Remaining on the margins of society, at a safe distance from mainstream social order, there is a degree of legitimacy in the girls' gun use, who, as the film's tagline reveals, must perform multiple identities as "Mothers. Warriors. Sisters. Survivors." Inserting the word "Warriors" alongside "Mothers" in the tagline provides further justification for their violence. The idea that warriors employ violence for noble, legitimate reasons translates to the Echo Park girls' gun use. As Marita Gronnvoll notes, "women warriors must operate within strict limitations if their violence is to be socially sanctioned."[78] Thus Anders is careful not to position the girls as mythic (masculine) warriors that are proud of their violent capabilities and firearm use.

In closing: renegotiating the gun

Placing the gun in the homegirls' hands renegotiates the phallocentric association of the gun in the gangsta narrative to some extent. However, guns do not equal freedom. Writing for *The Times* in 1993, the year that Anders's film was shown at Cannes film festival, film critic Kate Muir insists that "where once girls were often described by male gang members as "hos (whores) and bitches. . . . They have discovered that a gun means the end of

73 Timothy Shary, *Generation Multiplex: The Image of Youth in Contemporary American Cinema* (Austin, TX: University of Texas Press, 2002), 135.
74 Wilding, *Negotiating Boundaries*, 45.
75 Allison Anders, *Personal Interview*.
76 Ibid.
77 4 Corners, "Girl's It Ain't Easy", originally performed by Honey Cone, *Take Me With You* (Hot Wax, 1969) words and music by Ronald Dunbar and Edyth Wayne.
78 Marita Gronnvoll, *Media Representations of Gender and Torture Post-9/11* (London: Routledge, 2010), 123.

physical inequality."[79] For Muir, who only briefly considers *Mi Vida Loca* at the end of an article that explores the rise of gun-toting girls and girl gangs in the United States, "Equal opportunities have caught up with teenage violence in America."[80] Chesney-Lind and Irwin insist that,

> by arguing that girls were becoming as violent as the boys in the 1990s, the media suggested that Latina and African-American girls were being liberated from traditional gender norms and consequently participating in the violent gang world on equal footing with boys.[81]

As *Mi Vida Loca* reveals, suggestions such as Muir's are problematic. While Smith and Wesson aimed for females in the early 1990s, marketing firearms as "equalizers," guns in the hands of these gang girls do not simply equal liberation and equality neither in terms of gender nor political relations.

The pro-Chicano organisation the Brown Berets demanded in June 1968 "the right to keep and bear arms to defend our communities against racist police, as guaranteed under the Second Amendment of the United States Constitution."[82] Much like the Black Panthers, gun use for the Brown Berets was politically loaded.[83] Although the homegirls' and homeboys' right to bear arms is complicated due to their criminal and marginalised status, the girls exercise (yet ultimately fail to fulfil), their individual right to protect those weaker than themselves, in particular, their young children. However, defining the girls' gun use as political is problematic.

Mi Vida Loca as a film boasts political significance in its creation of space for the discussion of Chicana girl gang life and its challenging of media representations of its subjects. Anders's overall aim of "humanising" the homegirls is in itself political. Certainly, the homegirls recognise their marginalised position and ex-gang member Giggles' (Marlo Marron) desire to work can be identified as politically resistive in meaning, particularly when "numerous employers and unions in the past had purposely excluded Chicanos from employment except for the most menial tasks."[84] The role of these young women in relation to firearms also partially stems from the state's failure to protect gang members due to their criminal and marginalised status. Police presence occurs only to arrest these youth or after a fatal shooting. However, gun use for the characters themselves is limited in its political interest. Black cultural scholar Todd Boyd discusses how ghetto action movies such as *Menace* replaced the "political baggage" of *Boyz* with nihilism.[85] Moving away from the ghetto action genre, Anders replaces both the overtly political message and nihilism with romantic elements as Sad Girl declares "women don't use weapons to prove a point, women use weapons for love."

At the time of *Mi Vida Loca's* production, media outlets helped promote cultural anxiety surrounding the use of guns and the violent tendencies of non-white youth. Anders

79 Kate Muir, "Girls and the Hood", *The Times*, 3 August 1993, 12.
80 Ibid.
81 Chesney-Lind and Irwin, "From Badness to Meanness", 50–51.
82 No author, "Brown Berets: Serve, Observe and Protect", 13 *La Raza* 13 (7 June 1968).
83 I.F. Haney-López, *Racism on Trial: The Chicano Fight for Justice* (Cambridge: Belknap, 2003), 187.
84 Vernon M. Briggs, Jr., Walter Fogel, and Fred H. Schmidt, *The Chicano Worker* (Austin and London: University of Texas Press, 1979), 123.
85 Todd Boyd, *Am I Black Enough for You?: Popular Culture From the 'Hood and Beyond* (Bloomington: Indiana University Press, 1997), 102.

humanises the homegirls who are both victims and perpetrators of violence. Yet this humanisation is achieved, at least partially, by keeping violence off-screen. The film generated a relatively decent amount of revenue for a low-budget film, grossing just under $3.3million at the US box office.[86] Significantly, more recent girl gang films set in East LA featuring more violent Latina gang girls (for example, *Down for Life* [2010], which unlike *Mi Vida Loca* features well-established actors such as Danny Glover and rap artist Snoop Dogg) have been unsuccessful both financially and critically.[87]

The transgression of traditional feminine behaviour through the demonstration of violent capabilities and firearm use in *Mi Vida Loca* asks audiences to challenge notions of gendered categories. Simultaneously, viewers are offered justification and explanation for this behaviour: a protective function associated with motherhood, the loss of male figures, or more fleetingly social conditions. Anders is quick to rationalise girl gang gun use, but when this is not achievable, such as in the case of the River Valley homegirls, women are placed against women. Reflective of the reality of gang rivalry, particularly at the time of the film's production, this also leads to clear distinctions in the legitimacy of gun use. The protecting of the child mitigates girl gang violence to a certain extent, but ultimately, while firearms and gang membership might imbue a sense of protection for these marginalised homegirls, they do not equal freedom. The gun is a figurative tool loaded with meaning beyond its physicality, providing its handler with far greater function than a Second Amendment right to bear arms. This is particularly significant for those who were not included in, or envisioned to ever become a part of, the constitutional legislature. Today, the gun continues to be drawn upon in political campaigns, polarising opinions. For Trump, the (male and raced) "criminal gangbanger" of his America uses a gun as a deadly weapon and for the sole intent of shooting others dead, senselessly and violently. Like the gun debate more generally, there is a huge disparity between this rendering of the gangsta and Anders's cinematic representation of gang members who use guns for varying reasons, including its usage to negotiate minorities' access to resources during a period of intense socioeconomic struggle, or as a tool for safety, feeding the rhetoric of self-protection. In the same way in which the reading of the Second Amendment has generated different interpretations, the gun is a powerful symbol, and at times a deadly weapon, that carries different meaning and functions.

86 Although figures for *Mi Vida Loca's* budget are unavailable, according to IMDb box office figures, the movie grossed $3,269,420.

87 *Down for Life* (Alan Jacobs, B.D. Fox Independent, 2010).

5 "The thought of a black male with a weapon scares America"

African Americans, the Second Amendment, and the racial politics of armed self-defense in the civil rights era and beyond

Simon Wendt and Rebecca Rössling

"The thought of a black male with a weapon scares America," the African American gun owner Yafeuh Balogun told the *New York Times* in July 2016. "They automatically fear that we're seeking some form of vengeance. We're not seeking vengeance. We just want to protect our community and our homes."[1] In 2014, Balogun had founded the Huey P. Newton Gun Club in Dallas, Texas, as a response to what his organization calls "police terrorism" against non-white people.[2] Several widely publicized cases of unarmed black men who were shot and killed by white police officers since the Gun Club's founding probably confirmed the fears of Balogun and many other citizens of color across America. His conversation with the *New York Times* took place in the wake of a demonstration of African American activists against police brutality in Dallas, during which a black sniper killed several white police officers. Members of the Newton Gun Club – named in honor of the co-founder of the Black Panther Party – had escorted the demonstration, openly displaying their rifles, which initially led the police to mistake them for the sniper or his supporters.[3]

The Huey P. Newton Gun Club and its founder's comments hint at the striking continuities in the history of black gun ownership and black self-defense in the United States. It also testifies to the powerful legacy of the Black Power era, during which African American activists such as the Black Panther Party denounced and sought to counter police brutality against citizens of color and the racial stereotypes that were invoked to justify it. This chapter probes the complex history of African Americans' efforts to defend themselves and their communities against white attackers with gun violence, focusing on the civil rights and post-civil rights era. It argues that while the post-World War II era allowed an increasing number of black citizens to defend themselves successfully against racist attacks, African American defenders tended to be denounced as dangerous radicals or criminals, reflecting white America's entrenched fears of armed citizens of color. Especially in the aftermath of those confrontations that pitted black shooters against white police officers, racial stereotypes of black criminality undermined African Americans' argument that they, too, had a right to bear arms and to use them in self-defense. Examining the period 1945–1970, as well as hitherto ignored examples from the 1970s and 1980s, this article thus calls attention

1 John Eligon and Frances Robles, "Police Shootings Highlight Unease Among Black Gun Owners", *New York Times*, July 8, 2016, A16.
2 The Founding Dallas Council, "Political Framework" at http://hueypnewtongunclub.org.
3 Eligon and Robles, "Police Shootings Highlight Unease Among Black Gun Owners", A16.

to the complex racial dimensions of the Second Amendment and related notions of armed self-defense.[4] As Yafeuh Balogun's Huey P. Newton Gun Club reminds us, the legacy of these complexities is still with us today.

The history of African Americans and armed self-defense prior to World War II

The beginnings of black resistance to white oppression date back to the seventeenth century, when the first African slaves were brought to America's shores, although bondsmen and bondswomen were rarely able to use armed force to defend themselves against white violence prior to 1865. Instead, numerous slaves showed their opposition through such subtle forms of subversion as breaking tools or feigning illness, while many others simply tried to escape. Conspiracies and rebellions were the most militant form of slave resistance, but despite the initial success of some rebellions, most conspiracies were discovered before rebels of color were able to put their plans into action, and white retaliation was always swift and brutal. Compared with other slave societies, however, the United States experienced few and relatively small slave revolts. American slaves tended to be a minority and lived on smaller estates, most of which were closely watched and managed by their vigilant owners. Similarly important, the end of the slave trade in the United States in 1807 halted the importation of single African men, who had been at the forefront of almost all slave rebellions in the eighteenth century. U.S.-born slave men who had families tended to be less militant than native Africans, since they had more to lose. The lack of large natural refuges further diminished chances of success for American slave rebels. Although generally unsuccessful, slave conspiracies and rebellions did become symbols of hope for many nineteenth-century Abolitionists, whose activism contributed to the outbreak of the Civil War and the end of slavery in 1865.[5]

4 Black armed self-defense during the southern civil rights struggle has received enormous scholarly attention since the late 1990s. The post-1970 period, however, remains a historiographical lacuna. The most important studies include Charles E. Cobb, *This Nonviolent Stuff'll Get You Killed: How Guns Made the Civil Rights Movement Possible* (New York: Basic Books, 2014); Nicholas Johnson, *Negroes and the Gun: The Black Tradition of Arms* (Amherst, NY: Prometheus Books, 2014); Akinyele Omowale Umoja, *We Will Shoot Back: Armed Resistance in the Mississippi Freedom Movement* (New York: New York University Press, 2013); Simon Wendt, *The Spirit and the Shotgun: Armed Resistance and the Struggle for Civil Rights* (Gainesville: University Press of Florida, 2007); Christopher Strain, *Pure Fire: Armed Self-Defense as Activism in the Civil Rights Era* (Athens: University of Georgia Press, 2005); Lance E. Hill, *The Deacons for Defense: Armed Resistance and the Civil Rights Movement* (Chapel Hill: University of North Carolina Press, 2004); Timothy B. Tyson, *Radio Free Dixie: Robert F. Williams and the Roots of Black Power* (Chapel Hill: University of North Carolina Press, 1999).

5 On this history, see, for example, David F. Allmendin Jr., *Nat Turner and the Rising in Southampton County* (Baltimore: Johns Hopkins University Press, 2014); Larry Eugene Rivers, *Rebels and Runaways: Slave Resistance in Nineteenth-Century Florida* (Champaign: University of Illinois Press, 2012); Peter Charles Hoffer, *Cry Liberty: The Great Stono River Slave Rebellion of 1739* (New York: Oxford University Press, 2010); Kenneth S. Greenberg, *Nat Turner: A Slave Rebellion in History and Memory* (New York: Oxford University Press, 2003); W. C. Rucker, *The River Flows On: Black Resistance, Culture, and Identity Formation in Early America* (Baton Rouge: Louisiana State University Press, 2006); Douglas R. Egerton, *Gabriel's Rebellion: The Virginia Slave Conspiracies of 1800 and 1802* (Chapel Hill: University of North Carolina Press, 1993); M. L. Dillon, *Slavery Attacked: Southern Slaves and Their Allies, 1619–1865* (Baton Rouge: Louisiana State University Press, 1990); E. D. Genovese, *From Rebellion to Revolution: Afro-American Slave Revolts in the Making of the Modern World* (Baton Rouge: Louisiana State University Press, 1979); Herbert Aptheker, *American Negro Slave Revolts* (New York: Columbia University Press, 1943).

The Union's victory opened a new chapter in the history of black self-defense in the United States. Faced with an upsurge of anti-black violence after the end of slavery, newly freed African Americans in the American South frequently resorted to armed force to protect themselves and their communities. Compared with similar efforts by black revolutionaries prior to the Civil War, black defensive efforts during the Reconstruction period were more widespread and more successful. While slaves had been prohibited from owning weapons, the Thirteenth and Fourteenth Amendments to the U.S. Constitution not only ended slavery and made African Americans citizens of the United States, but also allowed them to carry weapons. Across Dixie, African Americans purchased rifles, shotguns, and pistols, which they frequently used in confrontations with white attackers. Black Civil War veterans in particular were determined to fight back. In many parts of the South, former black Union soldiers formed paramilitary organizations to defend their communities against the Ku Klux Klan and other terrorist groups.[6]

In exercising and claiming the right to defend their lives and their families, black Americans observed a strong American tradition. In the eighteenth century, colonists had retained a form of self-defense that came out of the English common law tradition. Only when violent attacks forced defenders to retreat "to the wall" could they legitimately kill in self-defense. By the end of the nineteenth century, this tradition had been transformed into what Richard Maxwell Brown has called the principle of "no duty to retreat." As a result of this transformation, Americans' reluctance to kill in self-defense while holding their ground had dwindled. The attacker's death not only became legally justifiable, armed self-defense also turned into a symbol of manliness and courage.[7]

Among white Southerners, however, black citizens who adhered to the principle of "no duty to retreat" conjured up deep-seated fears of violent black insurrections, since they reminded them of pre-Civil War slave rebellions. The so-called Black Codes that many southern state legislatures passed after the war were one attempt to eliminate this perceived threat. While these new laws were primarily intended to maintain a cheap black labor force on white cotton plantations, they also impeded African Americans' ability to defend themselves by restricting black gun ownership. For example, the Louisiana code of 1866 prohibited blacks from carrying firearms without the written permission of their employer, while Mississippi's code went even further, barring blacks entirely from owning guns. Some scholars have suggested that former Confederate states sought to continue such restrictions after the repeal of the black codes in 1867 by passing concealed weapons laws. Yet the implementation of such regulations proved difficult. Since legal restrictions on blacks' ability to bear arms tended to be unsuccessful, most white Southerners continued to rely on extralegal violence to suppress black militancy. As during the aftermath of slave revolts

6 Some of the most important studies on this particular aspect include Daniel R. Weinfeld, *The Jackson County War: Reconstruction and Resistance in Post-Civil War Florida* (Tuscaloosa: University of Alabama Press, 2012); Charles Lane, *The Day Freedom Died: The Colfax Massacre, the Supreme Court, and the Betrayal of Reconstruction* (New York: Henry Holt, 2008); James G. Hollandsworth, *An Absolute Massacre: The New Orleans Race Riot of July 30, 1866* (Baton Rouge: Louisiana State University Press, 2001); Robert J. Cottrol and Raymond T. Diamond, "'Never Intended to Be Applied to the White Population': Firearms, Regulation, and Racial Disparity – The Redeemed South's Legacy to National Jurisprudence", 70(3) *Chicago-Kent Law Review* 1307–1335 (1995); George C. Wright, *Racial Violence in Kentucky, 1865–1940* (Baton Rouge: Louisiana State University Press, 1990); Eric Foner, *Reconstruction: America's Unfinished Journey, 1863–1877* (New York: Harper and Row, 1988); Herbert Shapiro, *White Violence and Black Response: From Reconstruction to Montgomery* (Amherst: University of Massachusetts Press, 1988).

7 Richard Maxwell Brown, *No Duty to Retreat: Violence and Values in American History and Society* (New York: Oxford University Press, 1991), 5, 20.

and conspiracies, rumors of resistance were frequently sufficient reason for self-proclaimed white vigilantes to indiscriminately search the homes of African Americans and to take away their weapons.[8]

Ultimately, white supremacists' numerical and military superiority, as well as the federal government's reluctance to come to the aid of embattled freedmen, made black resistance a dangerous venture that tended to bring about brutal reprisals and could not halt the advent of segregation and disfranchisement in the late nineteenth century. Racist violence also continued. During the 1880s and 1890s, lynching emerged as a new form of racial terror to confine African Americans to second-class citizenship. When African Americans joined together, they were sometimes able to repel white mobs. More often, however, black militant resistance provoked rather than deterred racist aggression. Those blacks who took up arms to confront exploitative employers, white lynch mobs, or abusive police officers almost always faced swift retaliation against themselves and their communities.[9]

In the first two decades of the twentieth century, a number of black activists and ordinary citizens of color practiced and publicly advocated armed self-defense against racist terrorism in the North and the South. In the aftermath of World War I, for instance, when race riots broke out in Houston, Chicago, Washington, DC, and numerous other American cities, a number of combat-experienced black veterans joined together to protect black neighborhoods. Black nationalist leaders such as Marcus Garvey and Cecil Briggs applauded such examples of black militancy and urged their followers to confront white aggression in the same manner.[10] During the 1920s, many African American intellectuals hailed the advent of what they called a "New Negro," a black man who refused to be intimidated by racist violence, and sometimes, as in the case of the black physician Ossian Sweet, who in 1926 was acquitted after having killed a member of a white mob that had attacked his home in Detroit, New Negro assertiveness was victorious.[11] But as

8 See Cottrol and Diamond, "'Never Intended to Be Applied to the White Population,'" 1307–1335; Robert J. Cottrol and Raymond T. Diamond, "The Second Amendment: Toward an Afro-American Reconsideration", 80 *Georgetown Law Journal* 309–361 (1991); Dan T. Carter, "The Anatomy of Fear: The Christmas Day Insurrection Scare of 1865", 42 *Journal of Southern History* 345–364 (August 1967); Edmund L. Drago, "Militancy and Black Women in Reconstruction Georgia", 1 *Journal of American Culture* 838–844 (Winter 1978).

9 See Christopher Waldrep, *African Americans Confront Lynching: Strategies of Resistance From the Civil War to the Civil Rights Era* (Lanham, MD: Rowman & Littlefield, 2008); W. Fitzhugh Brundage, "The Darien 'Insurrection' of 1899: Black Protest During the Nadir of Race Relations", 74(2) *Georgia Historical Quarterly* 234–253 (1990); Neil R. McMillen, *Dark Journey: Black Mississippians in the Age of Jim Crow* (Urbana: University of Illinois Press, 1990), 225–226; Leon F. Litwack, *Been in the Storm So Long: The Aftermath of Slavery* (New York: Knopf, 1979), 427–428; Kevin Yuill, "'Better Die Fighting Against Injustice Than to Die Like a dog': African-Americans and Guns", in Karen Jones, Giacomo Macola, and David Welch (eds.), *A Cultural History of Firearms in an Age of Empire* (Burlington, VT: Ashgate, 2013), 211–230.

10 David F. Krugler, *1919, The Year of Racial Violence: How African Americans Fought Back* (New York: Cambridge University Press, 2015); Steven A. Reich, "Soldiers of Democracy: Black Texans, and the Fight for Citizenship, 1917–21", 82 *Journal of American History* 1478–1504 (March 1996); Robert V. Haynes, *A Night of Violence: The Houston Riot of 1917* (Baton Rouge: Louisiana State University Press, 1976); Theodore G. Vincent, *Black Power and the Garvey Movement* (New York: Ramparts Press, 1971), 75–77; Mark Solomon, *The Cry Was Unity: Communists and African Americans, 1917–36* (Jackson: University Press of Mississippi, 1998), 9–14.

11 On the Sweet case, see Kevin Boyle, *Arch of Justice: A Saga of Race, Civil Rights, and Murder in the Jazz Age* (New York: Henry Holt, 2004); Kenneth G. Weinberg, *A Man's Home, A Man's Castle* (New York: McCall Publishing Company, 1971).

in the case of resistance to lynching, self-defense could also trigger anti-black violence. In 1921 in Tulsa, Oklahoma, for example, white residents invaded and destroyed the city's black neighborhood after African Americans had attempted to protect a young black man from a lynch mob.[12]

Despite such horrific incidents as the Tulsa riot, black militant resistance continued in the 1930s and 1940s. During the Great Depression, some southern black sharecroppers and tenants relied on armed protection to safeguard the meetings of a nascent union movement. Other African Americans opted to shoot it out with white sheriffs and their deputies rather than submit to unwarranted arrests.[13] World War II further politicized and radicalized black citizens, many of whom refused to acquiesce to white violence. African American soldiers frequently rose up against their mistreatment. Black civilians fought back when attacked by whites during urban race riots. Between 1941 and 1943, hundreds of racial clashes erupted in cities across the country. As in the case of slave rebellions in antebellum America, black unrest fueled rumors among white Southerners that African Americans were plotting armed uprisings after the war. Such revolts never occurred, but numerous black veterans used their guns to defend themselves when confronted by racist attackers upon their return to the United States. In 1946, for example, in Columbia, Tennessee, several hundred veterans of color guarded the city's black neighborhood, ready to repel a rumored white attack. Yet armed resistance to white violence continued to be risky, especially in the Deep South, where Jim Crow remained firmly in place. In Columbia, white policemen overwhelmed the black defenders, destroyed black homes and businesses, and arrested hundreds of African Americans. Only with the help of the National Association for the Advancement of Colored People (NAACP) did the indicted defenders of black Columbia eventually regain their freedom.[14] Although World War II helped trigger social and political developments that would contribute to the emergence of the civil rights movement in the 1950s, African Americans' determination to "stand their ground" when confronted with white attacks was fraught with danger. Swedish scholar Gunnar Myrdal's assessment of the efficacy of black armed resistance in his famous 1944 study *An American Dilemma* spoke to the experience of generations of African Americans. "There is little that Negroes can do to protect themselves, even where they are the majority of the population," Myrdal concluded. "They can, of course, strike back but they know that that means a more violent retaliation, often in an organized form and with danger to other Negroes."[15]

12 See Scott Ellsworth, *Death in a Promised Land: The Tulsa Race Riot of 1921* (Baton Rouge: Louisiana University Press, 1982).

13 Adam Fairclough, *Race and Democracy: The Civil Rights Movement in Louisiana, 1915–1972* (Athens: University of Georgia Press, 1995), 26–28; Greta de Jong, *A Different Day: African American Struggles for Justice in Rural Louisiana, 1900–1970* (Chapel Hill: University of North Carolina Press, 2002), 58; Leon F. Litwack, *Trouble in Mind: Black Southerners in the Age of Jim Crow* (New York: Knopf, 1999), 424–425; Robin D. G. Kelly, *Hammer and Hoe: Alabama Communists During the Great Depression* (Chapel Hill: University of North Carolina Press, 1990), 44–45.

14 Ann V. Collins, *All Hell Broke Loose: American Race Riots From the Progressive Era Through World War II* (Santa Barbara, CA: Praeger, 2012); Harvard Sitkoff, "Racial Militancy and Interracial Violence in the Second World War", 58(3) *Journal of American History* 661–681 (1971); Gail Williams O'Brien, *The Color of the Law: Race, Violence, and Justice in the Post-World War II South* (Chapel Hill: University of North Carolina Press, 1999).

15 Gunnar Myrdal, *An American Dilemma: The Negro Problem and Modern Democracy* (reprint, 1944; New York: Harper and Row, 1962), 559.

Armed self-defense during the civil rights and Black Power era

During the southern civil rights struggle of the 1950s and 1960s, white supremacists again launched a reign of terror to stop the black quest for social and political change, but African Americans organized for armed self-defense on an unprecedented level to confront racist violence. Even Martin Luther King Jr., who later became the most ardent advocate of Gandhian nonviolence, accepted armed protection in the early days of the famous Montgomery Bus Boycott, which successfully desegregated the city's bus lines in 1956. After the Montgomery movement, NAACP activist Robert F. Williams emerged as a prominent proponent of what he called "armed self-reliance." In 1957, the black military veteran founded a black self-defense organization in Monroe, North Carolina, to protect the local freedom movement against the revived Ku Klux Klan. Two years later, he engaged in a debate with Martin Luther King on the merits of armed resistance and nonviolence. That same year blacks in Birmingham, Alabama, founded the "Civil Rights Guards" to prevent dynamite attacks against the church of local civil rights leader Rev. Fred Shuttlesworth, while armed men in Little Rock, Arkansas, formed a "volunteer guard committee" to protect the home of NAACP leader Daisy Bates, who fought for an end to racial segregation in public education.[16]

After these early attempts to protect the southern freedom movement with guns, numerous well-organized black self-defense groups emerged during the first half of the 1960s, when civil rights activists' massive nonviolent demonstrations and voter registration drives in the region faced racist violence on a daily basis. Confronted with the federal government's reluctance to provide protection against the Ku Klux Klan and other white terrorists, numerous African Americans resolved to rely on their own protection. Nonviolence remained the driving force behind the civil rights movement and helped its members win their most important victories, but peaceful protest was frequently complemented by self-defense. In the summer of 1964, for example, black military veterans in Tuscaloosa, Alabama, organized a highly sophisticated defense squad, which guarded African American activists and their white allies. During the Freedom Summer project of 1964, which was initiated by the Student Nonviolent Coordinating Committee (SNCC), a number of black Mississippians formed similar groups to repel segregationist attacks.[17] That same year, blacks in Jonesboro, Louisiana, formed the Deacons for Defense and Justice (DDJ), a defense group that patrolled black neighborhoods with guns, provided armed escorts for white and black activists, and guarded the offices of the Congress of Racial Equality (CORE). In 1965, African American activists formed another DDJ group in Bogalusa, Louisiana, achieving nationwide notoriety after shootouts with the Ku Klux Klan.[18] The armed actions of the Deacons and other black self-defense groups during the first half of the 1960s helped local freedom movements survive in the face of white violence, bolstered the morale of civil rights

16 Adam Fairclough, *To Redeem the Soul of America: The Southern Christian Leadership Conference and Martin Luther King, Jr.* (Athens: University of Georgia Press, 1987), 25; Tyson, *Radio Free Dixie*, 80–83; Robert F. Williams, *Negroes With Guns* (New York: Marzani & Munsell, 1962); Andrew M. Manis, *A Fire You Can't Put Out: The Civil Rights Life of Birmingham's Revered Fred Shuttlesworth* (Tuscaloosa: University of Alabama Press, 1999), 110, 117–118; Glen T. Eskew, *But for Birmingham: The Local and National Movements in the Civil Rights Struggle* (Chapel Hill: University of North Carolina Press, 1997), 141; Daisy Bates, *The Long Shadow of Little Rock: A Memoir* (New York: David McKay Company, 1962), 111.

17 See Wendt, *The Spirit and the Shotgun*, 42–65, 100–130.

18 See Lance Hill, *The Deacons for Defense*.

activists, instilled pride in black protectors, and sometimes served as an additional means of coercion in negotiations with southern white authorities. At the same time, they generated frequent and heated debates about the legitimacy of armed self-defense among nonviolent activists, although most of the black and white civil rights organizers who worked in the Deep South eventually came to accept it as a pragmatic necessity.[19]

What is particularly striking about the various incidents involving black armed self-defense in the southern civil rights struggle of the 1950s and 1960s is the fact that they triggered fewer brutal repercussions than had been the case in the pre-World War II period. Prior to the 1950s, white vigilantes, police, and state militia frequently disarmed entire black communities with impunity, but after 1950, this practice stopped. Southern law enforcement officers certainly harassed and tried to intimidate armed activists such as the Tuscaloosa defense organization or the Deacons for Defense, but they did not attempt to disarm these groups, let alone the black communities they protected. Given the scarcity of sources that might explain this change, we can only speculate as to why white authorities' reactions remained so subdued in the civil rights era. One explanation could be the specter of federal intervention on behalf of blacks, echoing the deep-seated trauma of federal occupation in the aftermath of the Civil War. Southern governors might also have feared a small-scale race war if they disarmed groups like the Deacons for Defense and Justice with force. But on a more general level, it is conceivable that white Americans' steadfast commitment to the Second Amendment and the right to self-defense might ultimately have been stronger than their fear of a race war, since gun restrictions would have affected both black and white Americans. The fact that a few of those southern blacks who had killed white attackers during the 1950s and 1960s were acquitted in court lends credence to such an interpretation.[20] White Southerners might thus have grudgingly accepted black citizens' right to self-defense because they felt that refusing to do so would have restricted their own constitutional rights. More thorough historical research will be necessary to explain more fully this surprising phenomenon. By 1968, however, when the civil rights movement had gained important legislative victories and federal authorities finally began to take seriously their responsibility to protect African American citizens, most southern self-defense groups had already disbanded or were in the process of doing so. Only in Mississippi, as Akinyele Umoja has demonstrated, did a few black defense organizations remain active beyond 1970.[21]

While the use of defensive gun violence seemed no longer necessary in the eyes of most southern black activists after 1965, armed self-defense took on new significance in the emerging Black Power movement as part of its multi-layered ideology of black liberation, which revolved around black pride, black nationalism, Pan-Africanism, radical internationalism, and black political power.[22] Black Power activists' insistence on the vital role of self-defense

19 Wendt, *Spirit and the Shotgun*, 1–2, 29–32, 124–130, 132–136, 194–196.

20 See, for example, Lowell M. Limpus, "Trial in the South", *New York Times*, December 18, 1953, 38; "Klansman's Killer Freed in Alabama", *New York Times*, June 1, 1960, 33; "White Man Invading Negro Home is Slain", *New York Times*, September 7, 1962, 30; "Negro Woman Cleared in Night Rider Slaying", *New York Times*, September 9, 1962, 53.

21 Umoja, *We Will Shoot Back*, 211–252.

22 On the Black Power movement's history and multi-layered agenda, see, for example, Peniel E. Joseph, *Waiting 'Til the Midnight Hour: A Narrative History of Black Power in America* (New York: Henry Holt, 2006); Peniel E. Joseph, ed., *The Black Power Movement: Rethinking the Civil Rights-Black Power Era* (New York: Routledge, 2006); James Edward Smethurst, *The Black Arts Movement: Literary Nationalism in the 1960s and 1970s* (Chapel Hill: University of North Carolina Press, 2005); Jeffrey O.G. Ogbar, *Black Power: Radical Politics and African American Identity* (Baltimore: John Hopkins University Press, 2004); Nikhil Pal Singh, *Black Is a Country: Race and the Unfinished Struggle for Democracy*

in the African American freedom struggle owed much to the widespread opposition to nonviolence among militant black activists, chief among them Malcolm X, who became the most prominent spokesman of the black nationalist Nation of Islam (NOI) in the 1960s. As early as 1961, Malcolm X lambasted Martin Luther King and his nonviolent philosophy, calling his ideas on peaceful protest ineffective and effeminate. While preaching the NOI's gospel of black pride, moral uplift, and economic self-reliance, the militant Muslim minister repeatedly insisted on blacks' right to self-defense and the necessity to form self-defense groups to repel white supremacist terror.[23] Malcolm's militant message had a tremendous impact on black militant activists who were dissatisfied with the nonviolent mainstream. Among the NOI leaders' earliest devotees were Maxwell Stanford and Donald Freeman, who in 1962 founded the Revolutionary Action Movement (RAM), an organization that planned to utilize mass action and armed resistance to create a revolutionary movement for racial change. Between 1962 and 1966, Malcolm's militant ideology and almost daily news reports about white supremacist violence in the South resolved an increasing number of African American activists to renounce nonviolence and to embrace armed self-defense. After the James Meredith March of 1966, during which SNCC activist Stokely Carmichael first voiced the slogan Black Power, traditionally nonviolent organizations such as SNCC and CORE officially embraced self-defense, regarding it as an integral part of the black freedom struggle.[24]

Even though armed self-defense took on new significance during the Black Power era, it came to play a very different role and underwent a process of radical reinterpretation. While southern civil rights activists had used armed force primarily to protect themselves and their communities against white terrorist attacks, Black Power organizations utilized it as a militant symbol that called attention to the grim reality of police brutality in black urban communities, served as a publicity and recruiting tool, and boosted male activists' masculinity, which white Americans had belittled for centuries.[25] The most prominent advocate of this new type of militant resistance was the Black Panther Party for Self-Defense (BPP), which was founded in Oakland, California, in 1966 and pioneered armed patrols in poor inner-city

(Cambridge, MA: Harvard University Press, 2004); Scot Brown, *Fighting for US: Maulena Karenga, the US Organization, and Black Cultural Nationalism* (New York: New York University Press, 2003); Robert O. Self, *American Babylon: Race and the Struggle for Postwar Oakland* (Princeton: Princeton University Press, 2003); Yohuru Williams, *Black Politics/White Power: Civil Rights, Black Power, and the Black Panthers in New Haven* (St. James, NY: Brandywine Press, 2000); Komozi Woodard, *A Nation Within a Nation: Amiri Baraka (LeRoi Jones) & Black Power Politics* (Chapel Hill: University of North Carolina Press, 1999). An earlier study that continues to provide a good overview but focuses on the movement's cultural dimensions is William L. Van Deburg, *New Day in Babylon: The Black Power Movement and American Culture, 1965–1975* (Chicago: University of Chicago Press, 1992).

23 On the life of Malcolm X, see Peter Louis Goldman, *The Death and Life of Malcolm X*, 2nd ed. (Urbana: University of Illinois Press, 1979); Eugene Wolfenstein, *The Victims of Democracy: Malcolm X and the Black Revolution* (Berkeley: University of California Press, 1981); James Cone, *Martin & Malcolm & America: A Dream or a Nightmare* (Maryknoll, NY: Orbis Books, 1991); Bruce Perry, *Malcolm: The Life of a Man Who Changed Black America* (New York: Station Hill, 1991); William W. Sales Jr., *From Civil Rights to Black Liberation: Malcolm X and the Organization of Afro-American Unity* (Boston: South End Press, 1994); Michael Eric Dyson, *Making Malcolm: The Myth and Meaning of Malcolm X* (New York: Oxford University Press, 1995); Manning Marable, *Malcolm X: A Life of Reinvention* (New York: Viking, 2011).

24 Wendt, *The Spirit and the Shotgun*, 169–170; 179–182.

25 On the gender dimensions of armed self-defense during the civil rights and Black Power movement, see Robyn C. Spencer, *The Revolution Has Come: Black Power, Gender, and the Black Panther Party in Oakland* (Durham: Duke University Press, 2016); Simon Wendt, "'They Finally Found Out that We Really Are Men': Violence, Non-Violence and Black Manhood in the Civil Rights Era", 19(3) *Gender & History* 543–564 (2007).

neighborhoods to observe and, if necessary, to confront white police officers who violated African Americans' constitutional rights.[26] Just as importantly, the BPP and other Black Power groups such as Ron Karenga's US organization – which used "us" as a reference to African Americans as opposed to "them," that is white people – or the Republic of New Africa radically reinterpreted traditional concepts of self-defense, making guns and the right to self-defense a central pillar of a revolutionary ideology that considered armed resistance an essential means of black liberation. Relying on the ideas of Malcolm X, anti-colonial theorist Frantz Fanon, and revolutionaries such as Che Guevara and Mao Tse Tung, the Panthers, Karenga, and others argued that race riots and revolutionary violence actually constituted a legitimate form of self-defense to counter racist oppression.[27] For blacks, as BPP co-founder Huey Newton argued in his memoirs,

> the only way to win freedom was to meet force with force. At bottom, this is a form of self-defense. Although that defense might at times take on characteristics of aggression, in the final analysis the people do not initiate; they simply respond to what has been inflicted upon them.[28]

Viewed from this perspective, armed self-defense and armed aggression became virtually indistinguishable.

During the hundreds of race riots that rocked U.S. cities between 1964 and 1968, the type of revolutionary violence that many Black Power activists envisioned was rare, but over the years, a number of armed confrontations between African American militants and white police did take place. On many occasions, shootouts were the result of white police officers' provocations and the efforts of the Federal Bureau of Investigation (FBI) to eliminate what they deemed a threat to national security. Beginning in 1967, the FBI used a sophisticated counterintelligence program named COINTELPRO to disrupt and to destroy the Black Panther Party and other black nationalist organizations that advocated armed self-defense. FBI agents infiltrated these organizations and attempted to fan animosities within black nationalist circles. On several occasions, the FBI even orchestrated deliberate assassinations of Black Panther Party members or aided the police to imprison party leaders on fabricated charges.[29] As a result, Black Panthers engaged in gun battles with police officers on several occasions. One of the most violent confrontations took place in New Orleans in September

26 On the Black Panther Party, see, for example, Spencer, *The Revolution Has Come*; Joshua Bloom and Waldo E. Martin Jr., *Black Against Empire: The History and Politics of the Black Panther Party* (Berkeley: University of California Press, 2013); Donna Jean Murch, *Living for the City: Migration, Education, and the Rise of the Black Panther Party in Oakland, California* (Chapel Hill: University of North Carolina Press, 2010); Paul Alkebulan, *Survival Pending Revolution: The History of the Black Panther Party* (Tuscaloosa: University of Alabama Press, 2007); Charles E. Jones, ed., *The Black Panther Party [Reconsidered]* (Baltimore: Black Classic Press, 1998).

27 Wendt, *The Spirit and the Shotgun*, 6–7. On Ron Karenga's US organization, see Scott Brown, *Fighting for US: Maulana Karenga, the US Organization, and Black Cultural Nationalism* (New York: New York University Press, 2003).

28 Huey P. Newton, *Revolutionary Suicide* (New York: Harcourt Brace Jovanovich, 1973), 111–112.

29 See Ward Churchill and Jim Vander Wall, *Agents of Repression: The FBI's Secret War Against the Black Panther Party and the American Indian Movement*, 2nd ed. (Brooklyn, NY: South End Press, 2001); Ward Churchill, "'To Disrupt, Discredit and Destroy': The FBI's Secret War Against the Black Panther Party", in *Liberation, Imagination, and the Black Panther Party: A New Look at the Panthers and Their Legacy*, ed. Kathleen Cleaver and George Katsiaficas (New York: Routledge, 2001), 78–117; Kenneth O'Reilly, *"Racial Matters": The FBI's Secret File on Black America, 1960–1972* (New York: Free Press, 1989).

1970. After what the *Chicago Tribune* described as "a massive gun battle" between the New Orleans BPP and police officers, one young black man lay dead, while three others had been wounded. Similar to the police in cities outside the South, the New Orleans police department interpreted the party's armed assertiveness as a direct challenge to white authority and as an imminent threat to America's social and political status quo. Yet, it became increasingly difficult for police officers to prove their assertions in court. After the raid, twelve Black Panthers were charged with attempting to kill police officers, but in 1971, a jury of ten blacks and two whites acquitted all defendants of the charges.[30]

Despite the acquittal of BPP members in New Orleans, such confrontations, which took place in both northern and southern cities, called attention to the dangers of Black Power activists' decision to make self-defense such a salient component of their activist agenda. Not only did it obscure the important social activism that many militant activists engaged in on a daily basis, but it also cemented Black Power groups' image as gun-wielding criminals who were believed to plot the destruction of white America. In the case of the Black Panther Party, the news media continued to focus on the organization's paramilitary character, ignoring the discrimination and abject poverty that Newton and Seale wanted to call attention to. The BPP's ten-point platform, for instance, named self-defense as only one of several of the organization's goals, including the demand for self-determination, full employment, decent housing, and education for the black community. Yet the American public paid little attention to the party's attempts to alleviate these dismal conditions through such strategies as free breakfast programs for school children or legal and medical assistance for poor African Americans.[31]

Especially in the case of the Black Panther Party, the symbolic use of the gun seriously hampered the organization's effectiveness. Huey P. Newton was one among very few militants who admitted that the BPP's self-defense stance became counter-productive in the face of white authorities' war against the Panthers. In his autobiography, Newton pointed out that the efforts of the FBI and the police to disrupt the activities of his Oakland-based organization had not started until the Panthers staged their infamous armed demonstration at the Sacramento Capitol in 1967. Chapters outside California also faced problems. By the mid-1970s, numerous incarcerations, as well as deliberate infiltrations by police informers, had weakened the Baltimore chapter considerably. In Philadelphia, for example, police officers raided the homes of party members and indicted Black Panthers on fabricated charges. By 1969, having become acutely aware of these problems, Newton and the BPP's other co-founder Bobby Seale deliberately toned down their militant rhetoric. A year earlier, they had already dropped the term self-defense from the group's original name (Black Panther Party for Self-Defense), but with their media image firmly in place, police harassment and government repression continued unabated.[32] As historian Curtis Austin has concluded in his study of the Oakland organization, it was primarily the BPP's "early emphasis on

30 "1 Black Slain, 3 Shot by Police", *Chicago Tribune*, September 16, 1970, 2. See also "Police Kill Negro and Hurt Three in Shootout", *Los Angeles Times*, September 15, 1970, 15; "Jurors Acquit 12 Panthers in New Orleans", *Los Angeles Times*, August 7, 1971, C14.

31 On the BPP's media image, see Jane Rhodes, *Framing the Black Panthers: The Spectacular Rise of a Black Power Icon* (New York: New Press, 2007).

32 Newton, *Revolutionary Suicide*, 149–150; Matthew J. Countryman, *Up South: Civil Rights and Black Power in Philadelphia* (Philadelphia: University of Pennsylvania Press, 2006), 288; John A. Courtwright, "Rhetoric of the Gun: An Analysis of the Rhetorical Modifications of the Black Panther Party", *Journal of Black Studies* 4, no. 3 (1974): 249–267.

self-defense" that "left it open to mischaracterization, infiltration, and devastation by local, state, and federal police forces."[33]

The type of armed defiance so aggressively displayed by the Black Panthers and similarly minded Black Power organizations, coupled with the violence that erupted during hundreds of race riots in 1967 and 1968, also triggered a new debate among white pundits and politicians over whether to restrict African Americans' right to bear arms, a discussion that stretched into the 1970s. In the case of the Panthers, California ended its open carry policy shortly after the organization had entered the state legislature in Sacramento with loaded weapons. In addition, numerous journalists and lawmakers called for stricter gun legislation to stop "lawless rioters" in American cities.[34] In response to such biased calls for gun control, a number of white liberal lawyers vehemently rejected such plans, arguing in the 1970s that gun control would impede the ability of minorities to defend themselves against racist attacks. Jonathan A. Weiss, for instance, who had worked for years in projects related to providing legal services for the poor in Washington, DC, and New York City, penned a passionate "Reply to Advocates of Gun-Control Law," which was published in the *Journal of Urban Law* in 1974. Drawing connections between the southern black freedom struggle's right to voice its protest against racist injustice and the right to bear arms, Weiss was of the opinion that "the second amendment" could "either manifest or lend assistance to an exercise of the first amendment rights. The possession of arms manifests a choice or a freedom of life style which is consistent with the democratic philosophy." Using civil rights activism in the South as an example, Weiss further explained:

> For instance, those who worked on voter registration in the South almost uniformly report that the possession of guns by Southern blacks gave them the necessary confidence to overcome the threats, harassment, burning crosses and sniper shots to which they were frequently subjected. In order to survive and to realize a measurable degree of personal dignity the Southern blacks needed the guns. As a protection, it made it easier to organize and to insist on the exercise of their constitutional rights to vote and speak.[35]

While the new restrictive legislation that Weiss opposed was never passed, the debate testifies to both the particular fears that black men who challenged white authorities with arms continued to conjure up among white Americans and the fact that the Second Amendment and the right to self-defense could become important assets in the African American freedom struggle. Although many Black Power activists sought to call attention to this important interrelationship of guns and freedom, the ambiguous interpretations of self-defense that the Black Panthers and other militant groups offered during the late 1960s and early 1970s obscured some of the Black Power movement's most important messages and contributed to the resentment and the subsequent misconceptions that burdened the movement and its legacy.

33 Curtis J. Austin, *Up Against the Wall: Violence in the Making and Unmaking of the Black Panther Party* (Fayetteville: University of Arkansas Press, 2006), xxii.
34 Wendt, *The Spirit and the Shotgun*, 193.
35 Jonathan A. Weiss, "A Reply to Advocates of Gun-Control Law", 52(3) *Journal of Urban Law* 583 (1974). For similar liberal critiques of restrictive gun legislation, see John R. Salter, Jr. and Don B. Kates, Jr., "The Necessity of Access to Firearms by Dissenters and Minorities Whom Government is Unwilling to Unable to Protect", in *Restricting Handguns: The Liberal Skeptics Speak Out*, ed. Donald B. Kates Jr. (Croton-On Hudson: North River Press, 1979), 186; Don B. Kates Jr. "Why a Civil Libertarian Opposes Gun Control", 3 *Civil Liberties Review* 25 (June–July 1976).

The politics of black armed self-defense in the 1970s and 1980s

While black self-defense efforts in the southern civil rights struggle and the Black Power movement have received enormous scholarly attention in recent years, historians have conducted surprisingly little research on black efforts to use gun violence to confront white attacks in non-movement settings. Neither have they examined the discourses surrounding such confrontations outside the South in the 1970s and 1980s.[36] In light of Black Power activists' angry indictments of police brutality in urban black communities, a closer look at two court cases in which suspected black criminals won acquittals by claiming the right to armed self-defense after engaging in shootouts with white police officers in 1972 and 1986, respectively, reveals much about the impact of the civil rights and Black Power movement on African Americans' ability to claim that right in court and the fundamentally different ways in which black and white citizens viewed black defenders. These two cases also call attention to the conspicuous continuities with regard to tenacious racial stereotypes about black crime during an era that was characterized by urban decline, housing segregation, rising crime rates, and the emergence of what pundits and scholars termed the black "underclass."[37]

The case of Hayward Brown, for example, testifies to the powerful impact of the Black Power movement on urban African Americans' confidence to assert their right to armed self-defense, while also showing how increasingly repressive police tactics against citizens of color in U.S. cities could trigger armed confrontations between white officers and poor inner-city blacks. In January 1971, city authorities in Detroit launched an approach to policing that groups such as the Black Panther Party had long tried to counter. Named Stop the Robberies, Enjoy Safe Streets (STRESS), the new program encouraged special undercover police officers to combat street crime by using excessive force against residents of the city's poor and mostly black neighborhoods. By September 1971, STRESS officers had arrested 1,400 persons and killed nine African Americans. Unsurprisingly, relations between the city's black population and the police, which had been extremely tense since the race riot of 1968, deteriorated further and created an explosive brew of frustration, fear, and anger.[38]

Amid this tense atmosphere, the eighteen-year old black high-school student Hayward Brown engaged in two shootouts with STRESS officers. Brown was a member of the Black Power group Sons of Malcolm X and had been deeply influenced by the slain Muslim minister's ideology. Malcolm's insistence that young black men's liberation hinged on their willingness to foreswear drugs and other addictions that adversely affected the black community impressed Brown. Together with two young allies, he decided in late 1972 to take actions against the drug dealers who sold heroin in their neighborhood. In early December 1972, the trio armed themselves and went to confront a well-known heroin dealer, hoping that their confrontational stance would convince him to leave the neighborhood. When the

36 For the most important studies on black self-defense during the civil rights and Black Power era, see footnote 4.

37 On these developments, see, for example, Thomas Sugrue, *The Origins of Urban Crisis: Race and Inequality in Postwar Detroit* (Princeton: Princeton University Press, 1996); Khalil Gibran Muhammad, *The Condemnation of Blackness: Race, Crime, and the Making of Modern Urban America* (Cambridge, MA: Harvard University Press, 2010); Douglass S. Massey, *American Apartheid: Segregation and the Making of the Urban Underclass* (Cambridge, MA: Harvard University Press, 1993).

38 Heather Ann Thompson, *Whose Detroit? Politics, Labor, and Race in a Modern American City* (Ithaca: Cornell University Press, 2001), 82, 147–149.

three activists shadowed the man, however, a car manned with several plainclothes STRESS officers followed them and eventually blocked their VW Beetle. Fearing for their lives and not knowing that they were confronted by police, Brown and his two companions fired at the armed officers who had drawn their guns, wounding several of them in the subsequent shootout. Unscathed, the three black men fled the scene and hid for several days, but were eventually detected and engaged in another fire fight with the police in late December, which left one officer dead and another one maimed. Brown, who was believed to be the shooter, yet again managed to escape but was eventually captured and charged with several counts of assault with intent to commit murder, as well as with first-degree murder. However, during the three trials that Hayward Brown faced in 1973, prosecutors were unable to convince the jurors, most of whom were black, that the African American teenager had actually been the shooter, and revelations about the illegal police tactics of STRESS officers further eroded the prosecution's case against Brown. Eventually, Brown was acquitted of all charges, which represented an important victory against police brutality in the eyes of many black Detroiters.[39]

Brown's case is instructive because it reveals much about the politics of black self-defense during an era that was characterized by Black Power activism, police brutality against African American citizens, as well as white Americans' fear of black crime and the civil rights movement's general impact on society. Kenneth Cockrel, Brown's black chief counsel, had argued from the very beginning that the decision of Brown and his two companions to use their guns had been an act of justifiable self-defense, since the three black men had feared for their lives.[40] Reflecting a growing confidence among African Americans that they, too, had a right to defend themselves if they felt that their lives were in danger, he stated during the trial:

> If I'm riding around in a car and some unidentified white males in civilian clothes jump out with .357 magnums, shotguns, every other kind of goddamn thing, if I feel my life to be in danger – and if I knew they were STRESS there's even more reason to be concerned about your life – I have every goddamn reason in the world to assert my right to self defense.[41]

Especially, black critics of STRESS, like Cockrel, accused the program's officers of harassing, intimidating, and murdering Detroit's black residents with impunity. Brown's actions were therefore believed to be a reasonable form of resistance rather than a malicious rebellion against white authorities, a line of reasoning that juries would have been unlikely to accept before the 1970s.[42]

Race largely determined observers' assessments of Brown, his actions, and the verdict. In the eyes of many African Americans, Hayward Brown became a heroic vigilante who had not only tried to rid the black community of crime, but who had courageously countered the extralegal attacks of a racist white police force.[43] Unsurprisingly, the Black Panther Party lauded the verdict, as well as Kenneth Cockrel's self-defense argument, calling attention to

39 Ibid., 149–153.
40 "Black Youth Tried in Shots at Police", *New York Times*, May 6, 1973, 84.
41 Quoted in Thompson, *Whose Detroit?*, 155.
42 "Tactics of an Elite Police Unit Election Issue in Detroit", *New York Times*, June 11, 1973, 30.
43 Dan Georgakas and Marvin Surkin, *Detroit: I do Mind Dying. A Study in Urban Rebellion* (Brooklyn, NY: South End Press, 1998), 171.

the dangers that urban blacks faced on an almost daily basis when encountering white police officers. The BPP's newspaper *Black Panther* opined in July 1973:

> Brother Haywood acted in self-defense because he was afraid of his life. One month after his capture two of his companions . . . were gunned down by pursuing police, proving the validity of his fears. We are not surprised with Attorney Cockrel's statement, "There has never been a conviction (in Detroit) of a White officer for a homicide against a Black man" – we know the reasons why.[44]

White conservatives, by contrast, argued that the Brown case showed how minority interests undermined law and order, suggesting that black judges and black jurors would not respect the letter of the law. Similarly, many white newspapers highlighted Hayward's criminal past and his purported drug addiction before and during the trial, utterly ignoring the self-defense argument made by his attorney. While many African Americans praised Brown as a heroic champion of black liberation, then, most white commentators evoked and thus helped to perpetuate entrenched stereotypes of black criminality, a portrayal that continued until Hayward Brown's death in 1984.[45]

In 1986, thirteen years after Hayward Brown's acquittal, a similar case in New York elevated an aspiring black rap artist and suspected drug dealer named Larry Davis to fame and notoriety, revealing that the racial politics of armed self-defense did allow for occasional black victories, but tended to be characterized by conspicuous continuities in the post-Black Power era. As in Brown's case, Davis was charged with attempted murder after wounding several members of a police unit who had attempted to arrest him at his sister's apartment in the Bronx, one of the city's poorest boroughs that was plagued by crime and drugs. In another echo from the past, Davis's legal counsel, the renowned white civil rights attorney William M. Kunstler, claimed that his client had acted in self-defense because he feared for his life. In fact, Kunstler argued, police had forced Davis to sell drugs for them and wanted to silence him because of his inside knowledge of their illegal activities. By contrast, the prosecution portrayed the young black man as a dangerous criminal who had resisted arrest. In 1988, after a four-month trial, a jury that was composed of ten African Americans and two Hispanic citizens acquitted him of the most serious charges of aggravated assault and attempted murder.[46]

44 "Hayward Brown Wins Third Acquittal", *The Black Panther*, July 28, 1973, 5.

45 Thompson, *Whose Detroit?*, 154; "Detroit Police Continues Manhunt; Suspects Freed", *Ludington Daily News*, January 3, 1973, 1; "STRESS Suspect Held After Wild Shootout", *Ludington Daily News*, January 12, 1973, 13; "Mom Delivers Emotional Appeal to Blacks", *Rome News Tribune*, March 1, 1973, 8; Lynda Ann Ewen, *Corporate Power and Urban Crisis in Detroit* (Princeton: Princeton University Press, 2015), 42; Billy Bowles, David Kushma, and Sandy Mcclure, "Police Hunt Slayers of '70s Nemesis,'" *Detroit Free Press*, June 15, 1984, 3A; Herb Boyd, "Blacks and the Police State: A Case Study of Detroit", *Black Scholar* 12, no. 1 (1981): 60; Joe T. Darden, Richard Child Hill, June Thomas, and Richard Thomas, *Detroit: Race and Uneven Development* (Philadelphia: Temple University Press, 1987), 26.

46 John T. McQuiston, "Six Police Officers Shot in Bronx While Trying to Make an Arrest", *New York Times*, November 20, 1986, 1; Robert McFadden, "Hunt for Police-Shooting Suspect Widens to At Least 5 Other Cities", *New York Times*, November 23, 1986, 1; "Task Force Hunts Suspect Who Shot 6 NYC Officers", *Bangor Daily News*, November 21, 1986, 63; "Rap Musician Eludes Police After Shooting", *Eugene Register Guard*, November 23, 1986, 32; "Nationwide Search on for N.Y. Gunman", *Gainesville Sun*, November 23, 1986, 7; "Suspect in Shooting Still at Large", *Herald Journal*, November 23, 1986, 2; Jim Sleeper, *The Closest of Strangers: Liberalism and the Politics of Race in New York* (New York: W. W. Norton & Company, 1990), 252; "Jury Acquits Man Charged With Killing Drug Dealers",

As in the case of Hayward Brown, Davis's Lawyer William Kunstler described in vivid detail how African Americans suffered from police brutality, stressing that they had every reason to be afraid when armed officers confronted them. Testimony from Davis's mother, who stated that police officers had threatened to kill her son in her presence, gave additional force to Kunstler's argument. The non-white jury, whose members were all residents of the Bronx and had firsthand knowledge of police intimidation, could therefore relate to the young defendant's situation. Instructed by the presiding judge to determine whether Davis's fear and his subsequent decision to use armed force to protect himself were reasonable from the young black man's point of view as well as when judged objectively from an outside perspective, the jury members later revealed that they deemed armed self-defense fully justified. "They came in to wipe him out," the jury's forewoman Cecilia Thompson later told the *New York Times*, adding: "The judge said to us, if we felt he was justified in defending himself, then it's automatically self-defense."[47]

Although Davis was convicted of unlawfully possessing a weapon, his acquittal on the grounds of self-defense was a stunning victory that drew much applause from African Americans. Even more so than Brown, Davis became a "folk hero" among many black New Yorkers, who regarded his use of armed force against the police as an audacious form of resistance against a corrupt and brutal police force.[48] Davis's lawyers also stressed the danger that urban blacks were confronted with when encountering the city's police and argued that they were fully justified in resorting to armed self-defense. Even two years after the trial, for instance, Lynne F. Stewart, who had been a member of Davis's legal team, continued to defend Davis, writing in a letter to the *New York Magazine* in August 1990: "my former client . . . defended himself against murderous police and not only lived to tell about it but was exonerated by a jury. Self-defense is a right guaranteed even to Third World youth confronted by homicidal cops."[49] While the *New York Times* was more cautious in its appraisal of the verdict's significance, its editors similarly acknowledged that African Americans were rightfully suspicious of white authorities' misconduct in their dealings with black New Yorkers. "It is easy to dismiss the verdict as an outrageous result of attempts to portray Mr. Davis as a 'folk hero,'" they wrote. "But it is equally reckless to deny the better explanation: The jury, predominantly black, was influenced by the police department's recent history of overreaction and misconduct."[50]

The prosecution and the New York Police Department did not hide their disappointment and sharply criticized the acquittal and Davis's supporters' elation. Bronx District Attorney Paul T. Gentile said: "Some people are trying to hold up Larry Davis as a role model or a hero. That is disgraceful."[51] Both Gentile and New York's police officers regarded Davis as a menace to society, an interpretation with which some journalists seemed to agree, since they had penned articles that portrayed the black man as a dangerous "killer" or highlighted

---

Schenectady Gazette, March 4, 1988, 18; "Man Acquitted in Police Shooting Case", *Free Lance Star*, November 21, 1988, 17.

47 Sam Howe Verhovek, "Davis Juror Defends Verdict and Ward Assails It", *New York Times*, November 22, 1988, 10.

48 William G. Blair, "Jury Bronx Acquits Larry Davis in Shooting of Six Police Officers", *New York Times*, November 21, 1988, 1; "The Message of the Davis Case", *New York Times*, November 25, 1988, 12; David J. Langum, *William M. Kunstler: The Most Hated Lawyer in America* (New York: New York University Press, 1999), 306.

49 Lynne F. Stewart, "New Frontier", *New York Magazine*, August 6, 1990, 5.

50 "The Message of the Davis Case", 12.

51 Quoted in Verhovek, "Davis Juror Defends Verdict and Ward Assails It", 10.

his criminal past.[52] After the verdict, more than 1,500 police officers staged a public demonstration to protest against what they considered a travesty of justice.[53] Police officers and conservative commentators would continue to repeat their excoriations throughout the 1990s and the early twentieth century. When Larry Davis was sent to prison in 1991 for murdering a rival drug dealer, some of them voiced satisfaction that justice had finally been served, and they did not hide their elation when Davis was stabbed to death by a fellow prisoner in 2008. Former New York mayor Ed Koch, for example, when asked about his death, tartly replied that there was a place reserved in hell for Davis.[54]

Ultimately, the Brown and Davis cases and their outcomes speak not only to the ambivalences of the racial politics of the Second Amendment and the right to self-defense in the 1970s and 1980s, but also to the long history of racial discrimination in jury selection in American courts. Throughout U.S. history, prosecutors and defense attorneys have used various means to systematically eliminate black jurors from juries. Just as importantly, the white or mostly white juries that are thus created tend to be biased toward African American defendants, especially toward those defendants who appear to be "stereotypically black." As a consequence, poor black citizens with a criminal record tend to receive harsher sentences or run the danger of being convicted in cases that would have resulted in acquittals had the defendant been white.[55] The Brown and Davis cases stand out in this regard because the juries that decided their fate were majority-black, a fact that made and continues to make a major difference in court cases that revolve around African Americans' right to bear arms and their right to use them in self-defense.

Conclusion

The history of black self-defense against white attacks in the United States can be roughly divided into three major periods. During the pre-civil rights era, African American armed resistance against racist violence was occasionally successful, but it also tended to trigger brutal white retaliation, especially in those cases where armed blacks joined together to defend their communities. By contrast, the civil rights and Black Power era was characterized by the emergence of more sophisticated efforts among citizens of color to form self-defense groups. Especially in the southern civil rights struggle of the 1950s and the first half of the 1960s, such protective organizations succeeded in repelling white supremacist attacks from the Ku Klux Klan and other racist terrorists. Black Power activists believed self-defense to play a key role in the African American struggle for liberation, because armed force was

52 See, for example, Mark Halper, "Police Scour Streets for Murder Suspect", *Bryan Times*, November 21, 1986, 2; "Suspect in Shooting Still at Large" *Herald Journal*, November 23, 1986, 2; "Police Look for Gunman", *Lodi News Sentinel*, December 15, 1986, 2; "Man Acquitted in Shootout with the Police", *Toledo Blade*, November 21, 1988, 7.

53 Robert Louden, "Davis, Larry (1966–2008)", in *African Americans and Criminal Justice: An Encyclopedia*, ed. Delores D. Jones-Brown, Beverly D. Frazier, and Marvie Brooks (Santa Barbara, CA: Greenwood, 2014), 142–145; Robert D. McFadden, "Slain in Prison, But Once Celebrated as a Fugitive", *New York Times*, February 22, 2008, B1.

54 McFadden, "Slain in Prison, but Once Celebrated as a Fugitive", Jinnette Caceres, "Larry Davis, presente!" *Liberation*, March 8, 2008 at www.liberationnews.org/08-03-08-larry-davis-presente-html/; "Man Slain in N.Y. Prison Once Hailed on the Streets as a Hero", *Sun Journal*, February 23, 2008, 4; Marilyn Corsianos, *The Complexities of Police Corruption: Gender, Identity, and Misconduct* (New York: Rowman & Littlefield, 2012), 151.

55 Michelle Alexander, *The New Jim Crow: Mass Incarceration in the Age of Colorblindness*, rev. ed. (New York: New Press, 2011), 107, 120–123, 193–194.

intended not only to stop police brutality, but also to function as a form of revolutionary violence that would affirm black manhood and help African Americans to overthrow the yoke of racist oppression. While southern defense organizations faced surprisingly little harassment and retaliation, Black Power groups such as the Black Panther Party were confronted with state-led campaigns to stop their activities and to destroy their organizations. This striking difference can be explained by the fact that civil rights defense groups such as the Deacons for the Defense and Justice sought to merely prevent attacks from white supremacist groups, who, while frequently being condoned by police, operated outside the law. Post-1966 black militants, by contrast, directly challenged the state by confronting law enforcement officers and by suggesting that gun violence might be used to radically transform America's social and political status quo.

The third period, which began in the early 1970s, saw a few black victories in non-activist settings for citizens of color who claimed the right to self-defense after armed confrontations with white police officers. Ultimately, however, this period was dominated by narratives about white policemen who justified the killings of black citizens with self-defense arguments.[56] In fact, judging from the vantage point of the years since 1990, the cases of Hayward Brown and Larry Davis were exceptional victories for African Americans' right to self-defense during an era that was characterized by efforts to undo or at least to erode the civil rights movement's achievements. Between the late 1980s and the present, it was primarily the police who claimed the right to self-defense after using armed force in confrontations with suspected black criminals. Rising crime rates and gang warfare in poor inner-city neighborhoods in the late twentieth century, as well as the Los Angeles Riot of 1992, probably helped law enforcement officers to justify excessive violence against African Americans, as well as a wave of mass incarcerations.[57] Beginning in the second decade of the twenty-first century, more and more videos taken by bystanders with their cell phones helped black activists to put a new spotlight on unlawful police brutality against citizens of color, most famously the killing of Michael Brown in Ferguson, Missouri, in 2014. These widely shared videos and the public outrage they triggered not only led to new efforts to hold police officers accountable for the types of illegal actions that they had previously been able to cover up. They also energized a new generation of African American civil rights activists, whose Black Lives Matter movement calls for an end to racial profiling and police brutality. Yet, although cell phone videos and black protest have led to an unprecedented number of investigations and a few indictments, most police officers who shot and killed African Americans during traffic stops or other seemingly routine encounters were ultimately cleared of any wrongdoing or did not face serious repercussions.[58]

56 On such cases, see, for example, Sam Howe, "Man's Shooting By Texas Police Provokes Anger", *New York Times*, February 21, 1994 at www.nytimes.com/1994/02/21/us/man-s-shooting-by-texas-police-provokes-anger.html; Jon Nordheimer, "Racial Stress Divides Town After Death of Black Youth", *New York Times*, May 9, 1994 at www.nytimes.com/1994/05/09/nyregion/racial-stress-divides-town-after-death-of-black-youth.html; Robet Hanley, "Charges Sought for Troopers Involved in Turnpike Shooting", *New York Times*, December 14, 2000 at www.nytimes.com/2000/12/14/nyregion/charges-sought-for-troopers-involved-in-turnpike-shooting.html; David Kocieniewski, "Troopers Are Off the Hook, But the State Is Still Mired", *New York Times*, January 20, 2002 at www.nytimes.com/2002/01/20/nyregion/on-politics-troopers-are-off-the-hook-but-the-state-is-still-mired.html.

57 See Elizabeth Hinton, *From the War on Poverty to the War on Crime: The Making of Mass Incarceration in America* (Cambridge, MA: Harvard University Press, 2016); Alexander, *The New Jim Crow*.

58 For the first assessments of the Black Lives Matter movement, see Keeanga-Yamahtta Taylor, *From #Black Lives Matter to Black Liberation* (Chicago: Haymarket Books, 2016); Jordan T. Camp and Christina

The conspicuous continuities that can be observed during all three periods of the history of black self-defense – chief among the white Americans' tendency to perpetuate deep-seated stereotypes about black criminality and African Americans' belief that black lives matter little to white authorities – help in understanding black citizens' reasoning behind the founding of such organizations as Yafeuh Balogun's Huey P. Newton Gun Club or the People's New Black Panther Party (founded in 2014) during the second decade of the twenty-first century.[59] The history of African Americans' past and current efforts to protect themselves and their communities with armed force complicates the scholarly discussion of the Second Amendment in general and restrictive gun legislation in particular. Since the 1990s, the legal historians Robert Cottrol and Raymond Diamond have lamented the fact that scholars of the Second Amendment generally neglect its racial dimensions.[60] Especially the post-civil rights era is a scholarly blind spot that calls for a thorough analysis of this particular aspect of the right to bear arms and black efforts to use them in self-defense. So far, only very few historians and legal scholars have heeded Cottrol's and Diamond's pleas, which is unfortunate, since only a more inclusive research agenda will ultimately help us to fully understand the complexities of the Second Amendment, American "gun culture," and the idea of American freedom itself.

Heatherton, eds., *Policing the Planet: Why the Policing Crisis Led to Black Lives Matter* (Brooklyn, NY: Verso, 2016).

59 John Eligon and Frances Robles, "Amid Broad Movement Against Police Abuse, Some Act on the Fringe", *New York Times*, July 23, 2016, A13.

60 See Cottrol and Diamond, "'Never Intended to Be Applied to the White Population,'" 1307–1335; Cottrol and Diamond, "The Second Amendment: Toward an Afro-American Reconsideration", 309–361.

6 From virtuous armed citizen to "cramped little risk-fearing man"

The meaning of firearms in an insecure era

Kevin Yuill

It is worth considering, in view of the overwhelming liberal and left-wing support for gun controls today, the very different perspective of radicals at the turn of the last century. The ill-fated Karl Liebknecht, one of the founders of the German Communist Party who was shot dead after the abortive Spartacist Uprising in 1919, penned *Militarism and Anti-militarism* in 1907. Whereas today firearms are decried as corruptors of persons,[1] Liebknecht argued that the ideal situation would be one in which every man and woman should possess not just a gun, but the ability to destroy the entire world. Praising a nineteenth-century futurist work by Edward Bulwer-Lytton, *The Coming Race*, Liebknecht argued:

> And indeed we can suppose that the time will come – even if it is far in the future – when technique and the easy domination by men of the most powerful forces of nature will reach a stage which makes the application of the technique of murder quite impossible, since it would mean the self-destruction of the human race. . . . The exploitation of technical progress will then take on a new character; from a basically plutocratic activity it will to a certain extent become a democratic, general human possibility.[2]

When the Prussian people were armed, Liebknecht continued,

> [t]he value of man increased. His social quality as a creator of wealth and a prospective taxpayer, together with his natural-physical quality as a bearer of physical power, as a bearer of intelligence and enthusiasm, took on decisive significance and raised his rate of exchange.[3]

1 See, for instance, Craig A. Anderson, Arlin J. Benjamin J. and Bruce D. Barlow, "Does the Gun Pull the Trigger? Automatic Priming Effects of Weapon Pictures and Weapon Names", 9 *American Psychological Science* 308–314 (July 1998). Jennifer Klinesmith, Tim Kasser and Francis T. McAndrew, "Guns, Testosterone, and Aggression: An Experimental Test of a Mediational Hypothesis", 17(7) *Psychological Science* 568–571 (2006).

2 Karl Liebknecht, *Militarism and Anti-Militarism: With Special Regard to the International Young Socialist Movement* (Cambridge: Rivers Press, 1973), 12. Such praise of the instruments of powers echoed Friedrich Engels, who also noted that force, or violence, 'is the midwife of every old society pregnant with a new one' 'Anti-Duhring', Bruce B. Lawrence and Aisha Karim, *Violence: A Reader* (Greensboro, NC: Duke University Press, 2007), 39–61, 61.

3 Ibid., 15.

Self-sovereignty but also equality, freedom and social solidarity – the bond of trust and common interest that unites a people – grew with the arming of the citizen. With a weapon, the citizen had an elementary means of ensuring that her will could not be ignored and that her rights were not easily trampled upon. The armed individual grew in stature, virtue and importance; only good things accrued from as wide as possible possession of the most destructive weapons, noted Liebknecht.

The specific characteristics of the United States – its revolutionary heritage, plentiful wilderness, historic battles on the frontier and, most importantly, its declared dedication to equality – ensured a relationship between gun ownership and citizenship, despite the country's lack of enthusiasm for the socialist revolutionism expressed by Liebknecht. With no established social scale, the gun became a tool to enforce order amongst equals. The arming of citizens ensured that there were limits to how far the audacious could, through force, impose their wills on others.

Yet today, the freedom of the average man to be armed is defended only by conservatives. Such a turn of events is very recent; as Adam Winkler has shown, in the 1960s, radicals like the Black Panthers reacted to attempts by conservative icon Ronald Reagan, then governor of California, to disallow loaded guns to be carried. The National Rifle Association – the *bête noire* of gun control groups – approved of the 1968 Gun Control Act.[4] Liberals express the fears that conservative elites expressed in earlier eras, and conservatives support Liebknecht's armed citizen.

Both sides of the debate today wish to disarm the private individual – one through passing laws and the other by pointing even more deadly weapons back at that individual. Part of this assault is waged as a cultural assault. In the eyes of many liberals, this powerful, independent, self-sovereign individual, the backbone of the United States up until 50 years ago, should be banished to a shabby and disreputable past, under attack for his (the male pronoun is appropriate because gun culture is almost always used to describe the attachment men have to their firearms as well as to the image of the armed citizen) poisonous 'gun culture' – for the very power celebrated by Liebknecht. He has moved from the hero to villain of history, from the ever-vigilant protector of towns and farms who patrolled the edges of civilization to a murderer of Native and African Americans. To many liberals today, he is a relic of a violent and unenlightened era. Any power allowed him today seems only to result in destruction and increasingly wanton violence. As Obama said, these people are angry, bitter and confused, and they 'cling to their guns or religion or antipathy towards those that are not like them'.[5] To Obama and others, the armed citizen lost his or her virtue, if it existed in the first place. The peacekeeping guns now seem to threaten our peaceful coexistence.

Yet the response from those resisting gun control legislation seems also to emanate from sense of deep distrust for one's fellow citizens. Rather than pointing to the rarity of mass shootings, the infinitesimally small chances of children being killed by guns at schools, or the rarity of terrorist incidents, the National Rifle Association (NRA) and others advocate armed guards being posted at schools or more 'certified' citizens carrying weapons. It may be true that the only way to stop a bad guy with a gun is with a good guy with a gun, as

4 Adam Winkler, "The Secret History of Guns", *The Atlantic*, September 2011 at www.theatlantic.com/magazine/archive/2011/09/the-secret-history-of-guns/308608/. See also Adam Winkler, *Gunfight: The Battle Over the Right to Bear Arms* (New York: W. W. Norton and Co., 2011), X, 68–70.

5 Cited in Janell Ross, "Obama Revives His 'Cling to Guns or Religion' Analysis – for Donald Trump Supporters", *Washington Post*, December 21, 2015.

NRA Executive Vice President Wayne LaPierre noted, but to imagine the world is populated by bad guys with guns is no less irrational than imagining that a machine made of metal, plastic and wood is capable of morally corrupting its possessor. Both sides of the debate argue as violent crime and homicide rates have dropped to a historically low point in the United States.[6]

This chapter gives a historical background to the recent campaign for gun controls, distinguishing attempts to control arms today from those of the past. It suggests that a paradigm shift occurred in the American, from virtuous armed citizen to what the critic Allan Bloom once called the 'cramped little risk-fearing man'.[7] Whereas the citizen of old gained strength and relied upon the knowledge that his or her fellows possessed potentially destructive arms, today's cramped little risk-fearing people (hereafter CLRFP) distrust their fellows and wish either to disarm them or to arm themselves to deal with the purported threat from their fellows.

In relation to policy, the target of gun control campaigns remains, as previous gun control attempts during the nineteenth and early twentieth centuries did, specific groups of people. In the past, gun controls were aimed at African Americans, socialists or immigrants. Today's campaign targets white, predominantly rural or suburban working-class Americans – those who, in the past, were regarded as the backbone of the country. Those campaigning for gun control do not attack being armed per se – it is private citizens being armed that they object to. Most have no problem with the authorities being armed, at least until their fellow citizens are disarmed. Nor do they campaign against destructive military power or the armaments industry, as their antecedents who campaigned against guns in the 1930s did.

But those who wield guns to protect themselves hardly resemble their historical precedents, either. Rather than using them as a tool in specific situations, many today use them to ward off almost-entirely imaginary threats. In 2014, the homicide rate was lower than at any time since 1957. Crime of almost every description is trending downwards.[8] Yet Americans are nearly twice as likely to carry a gun for protection in 2013 than they were in 1999.[9] Gun sales increase after mass shootings and terrorist attacks, although the chances of Americans being killed in a mass shooting or terrorist attack are infinitesimal. As Angela Stroud has written, holders of concealed carry licenses 'become increasingly dependent on their guns to feel secure'. Stroud also shows that those with concealed licenses see their licenses as important for making them feel they are 'good guys'.[10] The 'gun-carry revolution',

6 Wayne LaPierre made the statement after the Sandy Hook massacre. See http://washington.cbslocal.com/2012/12/21/nra-only-way-to-stop-a-bad-guy-with-a-gun-is-with-a-good-guy-with-a-gun/ For crime and homicide statistics, see endnote 8.

7 Allan Bloom, "John Rawls Vs. The Tradition of Political Philosophy", 69(2) *The American Political Science Review* 648–662, 659 (June, 1975).

8 See Federal Bureau of Investigation, "Crime in the United States", 2015 at https://ucr.fbi.gov/crime-in-the-u.s/2015/crime-in-the-u.s.-2015/tables/table-4 (accessed January 10, 2017). It should be noted that homicides and violent crime crept up in 2015 from 2014, from 4.5 to 4.9 per 100,000 but were still at less than 2011 levels and still far below the historic high of 1980 – 10.2 per 100,000. Historic crime rates available in James Alan Fox and Marianne W. Zawitz, *Homicide Trends in the United States Bureau of Justice Statistics* (2006) at www.bjs.gov/content/pub/pdf/htius.pdf (accessed January 10, 2017).

9 According to a Pew research poll, 49 per cent of Americans who owned guns said they did so for protection in 2013, contrasted to 1999, where the figure was 26 per cent. Cited in Bruce Drake, "5 Facts About the NRA and Guns in America", *Pew Research Center*, April 24, 2014 at www.pewresearch.org/fact-tank/2014/04/24/5-facts-about-the-nra-and-guns-in-america/ (accessed January 10, 2017).

10 Not one of Stroud's correspondents reported being in a position where they might have used a gun to prevent a crime. Angela Stroud, *Good Guys With Guns: The Appeal and Consequences of Concealed Carry* (Chapel Hill, NC: University of North Carolina Press, 2015), 2, 147.

as Jennifer Carlson called it, began in 1976, just after the organizations attempting to disarm the American population got off the ground (The Brady Campaign began as the National Council to Control Handguns in 1974).[11] Fellow citizens are in CLRFP's crosshairs, whether they favour more gun controls or not.

Is the gun fetishized in recent discussion? Several texts – most recently Pamela Haag's contribution to the history of the gun industry – discuss the fetishization of the gun. Undoubtedly, the gun has been associated with human characteristics in the past. God made men; Sam Colt made them equal, goes the old Western adage. Manhood, self-reliance, and even equality, have been symbolized by the gun. As Simon Wendt has shown, African Americans associated imbued ownership of firearms with all of these qualities.[12]

The relationship today is reversed. Rather than people holding guns, guns seem to have a hold over people. Humanity is under the gun. Phrases like 'epidemic of gun violence' belie a propensity to lend these simple machines, which throw lead very quickly and accurately, differing only in degree over hundreds of years, magical qualities whereby human beings are manipulated or 'infected'. The hugely different stories behind deaths caused by firearms are lumped simplistically together as if all are simply the consequence of allowing private citizens to be armed.

Moreover, different varieties of gun have different purposes. For civilian use – the focus of this study – rifles are used primarily for hunting (although so-called assault weapons are not particularly useful for hunting), but may also be used for protection of one's home. Rifles are not easily concealable or portable and thus are not as useful for self-protection outside of the home. Shotguns, also too large to carry for self-protection, are generally used for hunting birds. Rarely are either used in crimes. In 2014, according to the Federal Bureau of Investigation (FBI), out of a total of 8,124 murders using firearms, 262 murders were committed using rifles (including assault weapons) and 248 by shotgun. Handguns are primarily used for protection but may also be used in the commission of a crime. But, even though handguns were used in most of the remainder of the 8,124 homicides, less than 0.5 of 1 per cent of handguns possessed by Americans have *ever* have been used in homicides. So, their primary use is not killing but as protection or security.[13]

Treating guns as tools – and focusing on the uses specific to the form of each type of gun – might at least begin a conversation about them. But the trigger for the discussion about guns is less about guns per se and more about the perceived characteristics of those who might wield them.

The first section of this chapter briefly traces the evolution of the relationship between citizens and firearms, showing how the ideal of the private citizen armed for defence of home, family and property, and as a last line of civil defence, survived up until the 1960s (although such conceptions still exist, they have less influence than in the past). Then, a new discussion of violence, separated from the human purposes behind violence, began to associate its increase with an armed population. Since the 1970s, the assumed virtue

11 Jennifer Carlson, *Citizen-Protectors: The Everyday Politics of Guns in an Age of Decline* (New York: Oxford University Press, 2015), 5.

12 Simon Wendt, *The Spirit and the Shotgun: Armed Resistance and the Struggle for Civil Rights* (Gainesville, FL: University Press of Florida, 2010).

13 In 2009, Americans owned 114 million handguns, 110 million rifles and 86 million shotguns. William J. Krouse, *Gun Control Legislation* (Congressional Research Service, 2012), 8 at https://fas.org/sgp/crs/misc/RL32842.pdf. If a different handgun were used for every handgun murder over the past 50 years, and we overestimated them at 10,000 per year, it would be less than half of 1 per cent that was used to murder.

of the virtuous, armed citizen was no longer assumed. Instead, the dangerous armed citizen became the focus for CLRFP. As Christopher Lasch observed: "Self-preservation has replaced self-improvement as the goal of earthly existence."[14] The goal of self-preservation dictated that it is best to disarm all others, whilst keeping an armoury of weapons for self-defence against any threats.

The virtuous armed citizenry

Liebknecht's futuristic conception of citizenry was, in some ways, a logical extension of the concept of the armed citizen being necessary for the maintenance of the Republic put forward by Machiavelli and being transferred within the United States by James Harrington, James Burgh and others.[15] Even in England, the armed citizen was considered the paragon of virtue, except by some members of the elite during times of insecurity. Not only was possession of weapons a right, but a duty. In August 1819, a nervous establishment caused the Peterloo Massacre in Manchester, England, whereby a crowd of 60,000 assembled in front of banners proclaiming REFORM, UNIVERSAL SUFFRAGE, EQUAL REPRESENTATION and, touchingly, LOVE, was charged by troops on horseback, killing 18 and seriously wounding over 700. In the aftermath, a Seizure of Arms bill was proposed in Parliament. During the discussion in late 1819, Lord Rancliffe noted that if he was attacked in his house, it was 'his duty and his right, feeling as an Englishman, to resist the assailants.' Mr Protheroe, while clearly concerned about possible revolution, believed seizure of arms was 'utterly inconsistent with freedom and with the existence of a civilized society.'[16] The virtue of the armed citizen was, as Mr Brougham reminded the House,

> not merely . . . that he might use them against the lawless measures of bad rulers, but to remind those rulers that the weapon of defence might be turned against them if they broke the laws, or violated the constitution.

The virtuous citizen was regarded as both a keeper of the peace and as a guard against bad government.[17]

Americans greeted technological developments in weaponry as a great boon to mankind. In 1852, the *Hartford Daily Times* described the revolver patented by Samuel Colt as 'not without its moral importance'. Citing the argument that the invention of gunpowder diminishing 'the frequency, duration, and destructiveness of wars', it argued, foreshadowing Liebknecht's later arguments, that with the arrival of 'a process by which a whole army could be killed . . . the Millennium will arrive, and the lion and the lamb will lie down

14 Christopher Lasch, *The Culture of Narcissism: American Life in an Age of Diminishing Expectations* (New York: W. W. Norton and Company, 1979), 53.
15 See Robert E. Shalhope, "The Armed Citizen in the Early Republic", 49(1) *Law and Contemporary Problems* 125–141 (1986); Stephen P. Halbrook, *That Every Man Be Armed: The Evolution of a Constitutional Right* (Albuquerque: University of New Mexico Press, 2013), and J.G.A. Pocock, *The Machiavellian Moment: Florentine Political Thought and the Atlantic Republican Tradition* (Princeton, NJ: Princeton University Press, 1975).
16 *Hansard*, HC Deb vol 41 cc1124–65, "Seizure of Arms Bill", December 14, 1819, 1125, 1127.
17 Ibid., 1141.

together'. If a machine were invented that could destroy a thousand lives, 'wars among civilized nations would cease forever'.[18]

The importance of firearms to freedom made itself heard many times in relation to African Americans. In 1854, Frederick Douglass told African Americans to keep a

> good revolver, a steady hand and a determination to shoot down any man attempting to kidnap. . . . Every slave hunter who meets a bloody death in his infernal business is an argument in favor of the manhood of our race.

In 1857, Justice Taney, ruling on the infamous Dred Scott case, reaffirmed the relationship between firearms and citizenship, albeit negatively.[19] Just after the Civil War ended, a publication of the African Methodist Episcopal Church explained to newly freed blacks in South Carolina: 'We have several times alluded to the fact that the Constitution of the United States guarantees to every citizen the right to keep and bear arms.' If African Americans were more often denied citizenship to which they aspired in the ensuing years, their attachment to guns, as Nicholas Johnson has demonstrated, indicates the relationship between a free people and the proliferation of firearms.[20]

The existence of the virtuous, armed citizenry was assumed during the nineteenth century, although many wished to prevent African Americans from entering their ranks. In the United States, the connection between virtue and an armed citizenship survived right through into the 1960s. Gun controls, in any real sense, arrived in 1911, were consolidated in the 1930s, with the National Firearms Acts of 1934 and 1938, but most meaningfully restricted by the 1968 Gun Control Act. Gun controls, when they were enacted, were directed against those who, it was imagined, might threaten the peace. In Great Britain, the first real gun controls took place in the aftermath of the Bolshevik revolution, when soldiers returned from the First World War.[21]

In the United States, the concept of the virtuous armed citizen survived pressure for gun controls in the first part of the twentieth century, but only in a narrow definition that excluded immigrants and non-white citizens. One of the most vociferous campaigns for gun controls followed the 1906 Atlanta Riot. There was little reticence, in the *Atlanta Journal*, about who should be disarmed: 'With the negroes without firearms there is little to be feared, for the white people are calm and quiet and there will be no more violence unless the rioting is started by the blacks.'[22] At this time, the assumption was that a body of 'law-abiding citizens' should be, or, at least, should be allowed to be armed. When the Sullivan Law, the first real gun control act in the United States, was enacted in 1911, it

18 Cited in William Hosley, "Guns, Gun Cultures, and the Peddling of Dreams", in Jan E. Dizard, Robert Muth, Stephen P. Andrews (eds.), *Guns in America: A Reader* (New York: New York University Press, 1999), 47–85, 52.

19 If African Americans were citizens, observed Chief Justice Taney in *Dred Scott v. Sandford*, 'it would give to persons of the negro race . . . the full liberty of speech . . . ; to hold public meetings upon political affairs, *and to keep and carry arms wherever they went.*' Cited in Stephen P. Halbrook, "The 14th Amendment and the Right to Keep and Bear Arms: The Intent of the Framers", *Report of the Subcommittee on the Constitution of the Committee on the Judiciary, United States Senate, 97th Cong., 2d Sess., The Right to Keep and Bear Arms, 68–82 (1982)* Reproduced in the 1982 Senate Report, 68–82.

20 Cited in Nicholas Johnson, *Negroes and the Gun: The Black Tradition of Arms* (Amherst and New York: Prometheus Books, 2014), 80.

21 Joyce Malcolm, *Guns and Violence: The English Experience* (Cambridge, MA: Harvard University Press, 2002), 142–145.

22 "Disarm the Negroes", *The Atlanta Journal*, September 25, 1906, 6.

was designed to 'strike hardest at the foreign-born element', particularly Italians.[23] Fear of insurrection, the specific fear of the elite, but also of non-elite Southern whites, prompted generalized gun controls, but there was no doubt that their enforcement was selective. As the Baltimore *Afro-American* sardonically noted in 1930 about impending gun legislation in Louisiana:

> Hereafter if you are a coloured man you will be jailed if you carry a gun here. A white man is not molested. A relentless drive to arrest and disarm all Negroes found in possession of firearms has been ordered by Superintendent of Police Theodore A. Ray.[24]

But, in the United States, the target of gun controls in earlier periods differs from that of campaigns since 1970. Surveying reports in the press of the early twentieth century, it is the 'gun toter' or 'pistol toter' – not the gun itself – who was the target of the Sullivan Law and the various other legislation leading up to the 1934 National Firearms Act. As Barrett Sharpnack notes,

> not everyone who carried a weapon was automatically condemned as a menace. Indeed, the term gun toter could be contrasted directly with the ideal "armed citizen" that had been part of American military and political thought since the foundation of the United States.[25]

The armed citizen carried a gun only when he or she had to; a pistol toter carried a gun as a matter of course. The various municipal laws were used by the courts to prosecute those who were 'looking for trouble' and seldom used against armed citizens.[26]

There was some agitation, it is true, for universal gun controls in the interwar years, particularly in the 1930s. But for most the distinction was made between the gangster – a large concern at the time – and the ordinary citizen. The push for regulation reflected such a distinction. The NRA and manufacturers of firearms cooperated on the legislation. A model law, suggested by Karl T. Frederick, president of the NRA in the 1920s and 1930s, required

23 See Lee Kennett and James LaVerne Anderson, *The Gun in America: The Origins of a National Dilemma* (Greenwood Press: Westport, CT, 1975), 165–186. T. Markus Funk, "Gun Control in America: A History of Discrimination Against the Poor and Minorities", in Jan E. Dizard, Robert Merrill Muth, and Stephen P. Andrews, Jr. (eds.), *Guns in America: A Reader* (New York: New York University Press, 1999), 390–402, 393.

24 "Disarm Negroes, But Leave Whites Alone", *Afro-American (1893–1988)* January 11, 1930, 13. On the racially selective disarmament at between the Civil War and Second World War, see Kevin Yuill, "'Better Die Fighting Against Injustice than to Die Like a Dog': African-Americans and Guns, 1866–1941", in Karen R. Jones, Giacomo Macola and David Welch (eds.), *A Cultural History of Firearms in an Age of Empire* (London: Ashgate Press, July 2013), 211–232. See also Robert J. Cottrol and Raymond T. Diamond, "Never Intended to Be Applied to the White Population: Firearms Regulation and Racial Disparity – The Redeemed South's Legacy to a National Jurisprudence", 70 *Chicago-Kent Law Review* 1307–1335 (1994–1995); James L. Anderson and Lee Kennett, *The Gun in America: The Origins of a National Dilemma* (New York: Praeger, 1975); Clayton E. Cramer, "The Racist Roots of Gun Control", 17 *Kansas Journal of Law and Public Policy* 17–33 (1994–1995); Stefan Tahmassebbi, "Gun Control and Racism", 2(1) *George Mason University Civil Rights Law Journal* 67–100, 72 (Summer 1991).

25 Barrett Sharpnack, "Firepower by Mail: 'Gun-Toting', State Regulation, and the Origins of Federal Firearms Legislation, 1911–1927", MA thesis, Case Western Reserve University, May 2015 at https://etd.ohiolink.edu/!etd.send_file?accession=case1433579362&disposition=inline, 16.

26 See for example, "Pistol Toter Fined" *Oregonian*, Portland, Oregon, October 18, 1955; John Lowery, "Pistol-Carrying License Makes Some Think Using a Weapon is Legal", *Marietta Journal*, Marietta, Georgia, March 30, 1958. "Jails Pistol Toter" *Idaho Statesman*, Boise, Idaho, March 30, 1956.

that no one except 'suitable' people carry concealed handgun in public. Gun dealers would maintain a system of registration. 'I have never believed in the general practice of carrying weapons. . . . I do not believe in the general promiscuous toting of guns. I think it should be sharply restricted.'[27]

An illustration of the difference between the movement for gun controls in the 1930s and in the 1960s and 1970s can be found in the story of the attempted assassination of Franklin Roosevelt in 1933 by Guiseppe Zangara. Although the eight-dollar pawnshop pistol used in the attempt on Roosevelt's life generated some calls for tighter handgun controls, such comments were few and far between. As Carole Leff and Mark Leff commented: 'More concern centered on the fact that the President elect's assailant was a naturalized citizen, prompting anti-anarchist and anti-alien sentiment.'[28]

1960s and 1970s: the present controversy takes shape

In the period after the Second World War, with its Cold War emphasis on military preparedness and the freedom Americans had in relation to Soviet Bloc countries, the few calls for gun control that were heard were drowned out. Whereas some had consistently urged generalized gun controls from the 1930s onwards,[29] the purported need for a citizenry used to weapons and drilled in marksmanship kept gun control off the table in the war years and at the height of the Cold War. The virtuous armed citizen, at this time, was needed to defend the country.[30]

The next successful attack on guns was part of concern about violence that occurred as Americans reeled in the wake of consecutive summers of rioting and anti-Vietnam War demonstrations. In 1968, a bemused President Johnson set up The National Commission on the Causes and Prevention of Violence, following the assassinations of Martin Luther King and Robert F. Kennedy. The emphasis on violence – as opposed to the motives behind it – was new. Moreover, it was a sign of a sea-change in liberal criticism. Prior to the late 1960s, most liberals saw violence as the result of inequalities in society. As the editors of one of the commissioned studies that looked at the history of violence noted: 'Until fairly recently, American historians have been inclined to regard economic motives as paramount, and to explain violence either sympathetically as the protest of the have-nots or unsympathetically as a by-product of the defense of privilege.'[31]

An attack on violence, as the Commission hinted, was an indictment of a society that wielded sophisticated technology but lacked the ethical ability to use it responsibly. The fact that it concentrated on violence per se effectively delegitimized the reasons justifying violence in the past. As Hannah Arendt noted in a response to the Commission on Violence, it is only a means for some specific end. 'Violence is by nature instrumental; like all means, it always stands in need of guidance and justification through the end it pursues. And what

27 Cited in Winkler, *Gunfight*, 210.
28 Carol Skalnik Leff and Mark H. Leff, "The Politics of Ineffectiveness: Federal Firearms Legislation, 1919–38", 455 *Annals of the American Association of Political and Social Science* 48–62, 55 (May 1981).
29 See Leff and Leff, "The Politics of Ineffectiveness".
30 Before that, George Gallup had conducted a campaign to register all guns, but it had got nowhere. See George Gallup, "Stricter Firearm Law Favored by Americans", *Dallas Morning News*, Dallas, Texas, August 30, 1959. Carl Bakal, *The Right to Bear Arms* (New York: McGraw-Hill Book Co., 1966), 177.
31 Ted Robert Gurr and Hugh Davis Graham, eds., *The History of Violence in America: Historical and Comparative Perspectives* (New York: Frederick A. Praeger, 1969), xxviii.

needs justification through something else cannot be the essence of anything.' It was far easier to attack violence than it was the complex and often contradictory reasons why it occurs. And, as Arendt noted, blaming 'violence' for the riots was at once blaming everyone and no one, as no one was assigned responsibility for it.[32]

Given the separation of violence from the human purposes behind it, it is hardly surprising that the instruments of violence – firearms – were no longer treated as tools, but ascribed the power to corrupt. In 1967, psychologists Leonard Berkowitz and Anthony LePage published a summary of the results of an experiment they conducted, 'Weapons as Aggression-Eliciting Stimuli'. Berkowitz and LePage concluded that guns not only permit violence, but they can stimulate it as well. As Berkowitz stated in 1968, 'The finger pulls the trigger, but the trigger may also be pulling the finger.'[33] Berkowitz and LePage were early expositors of a new approach that de-emphasized moral responsibility for the actions of those who used weapons, focussing instead upon corrupting qualities of the weapon itself. As Berkowitz admitted, '[g]un control may not be too effective in protecting ordinary citizens against criminals or Presidents against assassins, but it may, nevertheless, save some ordinary citizens from other ordinary citizens like themselves.'[34] It is instructive that, to Berkowitz, the 'bad guys' were one's fellow citizens.

The conversion of Dr Benjamin Spock from a pro-gun to a pro-control perspective is indicative of the changes occurring. Spock, whose book *Baby and Child Care* advised American parents on child-raising, told parents not to worry about their children playing with guns. Noting that by age 6, a boy will stop pretend-shooting at his parents because 'his own conscience has . . . turned stricter,' Spock argued that 'playing at war is a natural step in the disciplining of the aggression of young boys.' But in 1968, he revised his book after concluding that casual TV violence begets increased cruelty in both children and adults. 'Parents should firmly stop children's war play or any other kind of play that degenerates into deliberate cruelty or meanness,' he wrote.[35] As Glen Utter and James True noted, the term to describe a collector of weapons changed from the post-war 'gun bug' to the less positive 'gun nut'.[36]

As a corollary to the emphasis on violence and gun-related homicide as triggers for psychological problems, firearms, by the end of the 1970s, were re-imagined as a medical problem. By 1979, American public health officials adopted the 'objective to reduce the number of handguns in private ownership'. Firearm violence was now an 'epidemic' and 'a public health emergency'. In the 1990s, health advocates claimed that 'guns are not . . . inanimate object[s], but in fact are a social ill.'[37] In the 1990s, health advocates claimed that

32 Hannah Arendt, "Reflections on Violence", *New York Review of Books*, 27 February, 1969 at www.nybooks.com/articles/1969/02/27/a-special-supplement-reflections-on-violence/.

33 Leonard Berkowitz and Anthony LePage, "Weapons as Aggression-Eliciting Stimuli", 7 *Journal of Personality and Social Psychology* 202–207 (1967).

34 Leonard Berkowitz, "How Guns Control Us", 15(6) *Psychology Today* (June 1981).

35 Marc Fisher, "Bang: The Troubled Legacy of Toy Guns", *Washington Post*, December 22, 2014.

36 Utter and True, "The Evolving Gun Culture in America".

37 Karl Adler, Jeremiah Barondess, Jordan Cohen, Saul Farber, Spencer Foreman, Gary Gambuti, Margaret Hamburg, Nathan Kase, Jacqueline Messite, Robert Michels, Robert Newman, Herbert Pardes, Dominick Purpura, Allan Rosenfield, John Rowe, Richard Schwarz, David Skinner, William Speck, and Rock Tonkel, "Firearm Violence and Public Health: Limiting the Availability of Guns", 271(16) *Journal of the American Medical Association* (JAMA) 1281–1283, 1283 (April, 1994). Cited in Don B. Kates et al., "Guns and Public Health: Epidemic of Violence or Pandemic of Propaganda?", 61 *Tennessee Law Review* 513–596, 514 (1994).

'guns are not . . . inanimate object[s], but in fact are a social ill.' Many august bodies, from the *American College of Physicians*, the *American Academy of Pediatrics* to the *American Medical Association*, treat gun violence as a medical, rather than moral, issue.[38]

The cultural attack on the virtuous, armed citizen

Also beginning at this time was the attack on 'gun culture'. Whereas the motivation behind the 1968 Gun Control Acts was a barely veiled attempt to remove cheap weapons from ghetto residents after the consecutive summers of rioting across American cities in the mid-1960s, an attack on gun culture allowed some liberals to avoid the difficult racial issues that had been connected to gun controls in the past.

One of the surprising aspects that seems to elude the recent scholarship on the history of guns is that the term 'gun culture' did not exist before 1970. In fact, it is difficult to find associations between American culture and gun violence. Then, it featured in a bad-tempered essay by Richard Hofstadter. Hofstadter noted 'the presence and easy availability of guns magnify the violent strain in the American character, multiplying its deadly consequences.'[39] Other books have questioned why America has a gun culture without questioning whether the condemnation of a gun culture might be historically specific rather than the much more amorphous 'gun culture' itself.[40]

This cultural swipe, like the Commission on Violence, avoided difficult questions about who wielded the gun and why, focussing instead on violence as an inheritance of the past, essentially stripping the virtuous armed citizen of his virtue. The 'good guys' of the Western went bad, and the role they symbolically played in ranging the frontier, repelling attacks from Native Americans, and enforcing law and order – hitherto seen as heroic – was part of this 'violent strain'. If guns were themselves corrupt their user, it makes sense to attack those who proudly possess them, both in history and today, instead of those who use them for criminal purposes.

38 Adler et al., 'Firearm Violence and Public Health', See also Institute of Medicine, "Priorities for Research to Reduce the Threat of Firearm-Related Violence", June 5, 2013 at www.iom.edu/Reports/2013/Priorities-for-Research-to-Reduce-the-Threat-of-Firearm-Related-Violence.aspx. R. Butkus, R. Doherty and H. Daniel, "Reducing Firearm-related Injuries and Deaths in the United States: Executive Summary of a Policy Position Paper From the American College of Physicians", 160 *Annals of Internal Medicine* 858–860 (2014); American Academy of Pediatrics, "Federal Policies to Keep Children Safe" at www.aap.org/en-us/advocacy-and-policy/federal-advocacy/Pages/AAPFederalGunViolencePreventionRecommendationstoWhiteHouse.aspx. American Medical Association, "H-145.997: Firearms as a Public Health Problem in the United States – Injuries and Death" at https://ssl3.ama-assn.org/apps/ecomm/PolicyFinderForm.pl?site=www.ama-assn.org&uri=%2fresources%2fhtml%2fPolicyFinder%2fpolicyfiles%2fHnE%2fH-145.997.HTM (accessed November 1, 2016).

39 Richard Hofstadter, "America as a Gun Culture", 21(6) *Heritage Magazine* (1970). For defences of 'gun culture', see Glen H. Utter and James L. True, "The Evolving Gun Culture in America", 23(2) *Journal of American & Comparative Cultures* 67–79 (2000) and William R. Tonso's, ed., *The Gun Culture and Its Enemies* (Columbus, OH: Merrill,1990).

40 Besides Joan Burbick, *Gun Show Nation: Gun Culture and American Democracy* (New York and London: The New Press, 2006) and Michael Bellesiles, *Arming America* (New York: Borzoi Books, 2000), see Peter Squires, *Gun Culture or Gun Control?: Firearms and Violence: Safety and Society* (New York: Routledge, 2000), Robert J. Spitzer, *The Politics of Gun Control* (Washington, DC: Congressional Quarterly Press, 2004), especially 8–13, William Hosley, "Guns, Gun Culture and the Peddling of Dreams", in Jan E. Dizard, Robert Merrill Muth, and Stephen P. Andrews, Jr. (eds.), *The Gun in America: A Reader* (New York: New York University Press, 1999), 47–85. More sympathetic to gun culture are Abbey Kohn, *Shooters: Myths and Realities of America's Gun Culture* (New York: Oxford University Press, 2004); William R. Tonso, *The Gun Culture and Its Enemies* (Bellevue, WA: The Second Amendment Foundation, 1990) argues that no real gun culture exists but an attachment to guns.

The indictment of the hitherto virtuous armed citizen began in earnest. As Wendy Brown has argued: 'The republican link between arms, freedom, and civic virtue (and virtue) depends upon the existence of responsible, active, public-minded citizens bound together in at least a modicum of civic solidarity.' Brown suggested, in 1989, that such citizens no longer existed.[41] But it was in the late 1960s that the virtuous armed citizen retreated under a withering attack and calls for gun controls grew louder.

Part of the attack on gun culture appears to be an attempt to morally isolate the problem of American racism. As Joan Burbick acerbically notes, the gun in America 'reeks of white power' and is historically tied to romantic tales of 'white frontier heroes and valiant Southern plantation owners rescuing their white daughters from the hands of black predators'. For Burbick, the gun is a 'political fetish' that operates as a cultural symbol of white male power.[42] Earlier, the now-disgraced historian Michael Bellesiles noted that 'this Hobbesian heritage of each against all emerged the modern American acceptance of widespread violence'. Bellesiles argued that 'gun culture' emerged with widespread advertising by gun manufacturers in the 1870s, rather than being a cultural continuation since the days of the American Revolution. Today, he adds, it is not just a minority 'who idolize and even fetishize firearms'.[43]

As Pamela Haag notes, '[t]he gun today is mired in political fetishization' but, as she also notes, such fetishization is recent.[44] However, it was not the embattled virtuous armed citizen that fetishized firearms, at least not first. There was, prior to 1970, an appreciation that they were a means to an end, that end being good or bad. Treating violence without reference to its motives surely fetishizes violence. Even more obviously, the idea that 'the trigger pulls the finger' or identifying weapons as an 'infection' lends will to an inanimate object. If anything, 'gun culture', so much that it can be said to exist, no more fetishizes guns than those who enjoy cars or airplanes do those machines. Bellesiles and others who lend pieces of wood, steel and plastic a moral quality, as killers themselves, surely hit the definition of 'fetishize' more directly.

However, the cultural assault on weapons is actually an attack on the 'type' of people who own and keep weapons. The Federal Assault Weapon Ban (AWB) of 1994 indicates, in as clear a way as the ban on the Saturday Night Special in 1968 targeted African Americans,[45] the segment of the population targeted by the ban. The 'assault weapon', a new and, as it turned out, meaningless term, focused on 18 specific firearms, as well as certain military-type features on guns. As many observers at the time noted, there was little difference between assault weapons and ordinary semi-automatic guns (fully automatic guns were prohibited in 1986). The various military-style additions to assault weapons, such as pistol-grips, collapsible stocks and flash preventers, made no difference to the lethality of the weapon. But they convey a militaristic image and are favoured by collectors and by those who wish to see guns as symbols of power. Weapons manufacturers, some complained, marketed assault weapons directly to [s]urvivalists – who envisioned themselves fending off

41 Wendy Brown, "Guns, Cowboys, Philadelphia Mayors, and Civic Republicanism: On Sanford Levinson's The Embarrassing Second Amendment", 99(3) *The Yale Law Journal* 661–667 (1989).
42 Burbick: *Gun Show Nation*, 27, 131.
43 Bellesiles, *Arming America*, 8.
44 Pamela Haag, *The Gunning of America: Business and the Making of American Gun Culture* (New York: Basic Books, 2016), 176.
45 Robert Sherrill, *The Saturday Night Special* (New York: Penguin, 1975).

a horde of desperate neighbors from within their bomb shelters – loved the combat features of high ammunition capacity and anti-personnel striking power of assault weapons.[46]

Such an image belies the less sinister uses that the huge majority of those who own assault weapons have for them. Despite warnings by gun control advocates that assault weapons are the weapon of choice for criminals, they have never figured very highly in crime statistics. According to the AWB's author, Senator Diane Feinstein, introducing similar legislation in 2012, since the 1994 ban lapsed in 2004, assault weapons were responsible for around 48 homicides per year, a remarkably low number given the estimated 20–30m of these weapons in the United States. These weapons were used on average for less than half of 1 per cent of all gun homicides, and knife homicides were three times the number of assault weapon homicides between 2004 and 2012. Assault weapons are attacked for their symbolism and because certain types of persons wish to own them. In short, they are offensive to those who believe that weapons themselves bring death and destruction.[47]

The changing context

Why did the target of gun controls switch from the illegitimate use of firearms by specific groups to the armed citizen in general? Why, at this stage, were violence and weapons detached from their purposes to be condemned as too dangerous for the virtuous armed citizen to handle? These are very large questions and almost impossible to answer within the limits of this chapter. What follows is more a suggestion for the direction of future research than a comprehensive answer.

The many confusing elements of recent discussion about firearms – in particular its seemingly intractable nature – click into focus seeing through the lens of the very different context within which the debate since 1970s has occurred. It is the context of what sociologist Ulrich Beck termed 'risk society'. Morality, in the 'risk society', is seen in terms of *unintended consequences* rather than purposeful evil. Beck understood the characteristics of our most recent era as a decline in class societies, motivated by equality, and their replacement by risk societies, motivated by anxiety. In the latter

> one is no longer concerned with attaining something "good", but rather with preventing the worst; self-limitation is the goal which emerges. The dream of class society is that everyone wants and ought to have a share of the pie. The utopia of the risk society is that everyone should be spared from poisoning.[48]

As Mary Douglas and Aaron Wildavsky noted in their 1983 publication, *The Culture of Risk*, a fundamental shift occurred in the 1960s: 'In the amazingly short space of fifteen to twenty years, confidence . . . has turned into doubt.'[49]

Today, irrational fears frame the debate on guns. It is not that the virtuous armed citizen became evil; it is that firearms might 'infect' him, overcoming his virtue. 'Our ethical tools – the code of moral behaviour, the assembly of the rules of thumb we follow – have not been,

46 www.vpc.org/studies/militarization.pdf.
47 www.feinstein.senate.gov/public/index.cfm/press-releases?ID=28d0c499-28ec-42a7-902d-ebf318d46d02 (accessed October 31, 2016).
48 Ulrich Beck, *Risk Society: Towards a New Modernity* (London: Sage, 1998), 49.
49 Mary Douglas and Aaron Wildavsky, *Risk and Culture: An Essay on the Selection of Technological and Environmental Dangers* (London: University of California Press, 1983).

simply, made to the measure of our present powers.'[50] Americans no longer trusted themselves with the power they wield. The 'pivot', as Nicholas Johnson called the 180-degree change of perspective of African Americans in the 1970s in relation to firearms – from an insistence on the right to bear arms to campaigning to have them taken away – was the result of this new context within which the debate takes place.[51]

In a 'risk society', the assignment of moral responsibility is beside the point when prevention of a catastrophe is the highest aspiration. When unintended consequences, rather than purpose, are perceived to be the problem, objects that may be used for destructive purposes must be removed or neutralized.

Understanding the paradoxes

A series of paradoxes clouds the gun debate. Most Americans support gun controls but 56 per cent feel that America would be safer if more Americans carried concealed weapons.[52] The 'gun control paradox' – after high profile shootings, firearm sales surge to record levels – surely reflects broad insecurities rather than fears that restrictions will prevent them from buying a gun. Though numbers of gun purchases after 9–11 have been exaggerated, they did surge in the short-term.[53] It does not make much sense to buy a gun for self-defence, let alone to ward off terrorist attacks. In 2014, 277 justifiable homicides by civilians took place, according to the FBI. According to the Gun Violence Archive, a non-partisan compilation of gun data, there were fewer than 1,600 verified defensive guns uses, meaning a police report was filed. But in 2013, there were 505 unintentional firearm deaths.[54] What that means is that, with owning a gun, the chances of killing oneself or a family member accidentally are nearly twice as high as killing someone in self-defence. But the chances of neither happening are many, many times better.

Americans increasingly respond emotionally rather than rationally, in policy terms, to events like Sandy Hook. American schools, with a population similar to that of the United Kingdom, are statistically safer than American homes, and that, if American schools were in fact a country, they would have fewer homicides than any other country where murders have occurred in a given year.[55] But in the wake of Sandy Hook, not only was there a surge in support for banning assault weapons, the NRA suggested that armed guards be posted within schools.[56]

50 Zygmunt Bauman, *Postmodern Ethics* (Oxford: Blackwell, 1993), 18.

51 See Chapter 8 "The Pivot" in Johnson, *Negroes and the Gun*, 285–296.

52 Data from 2016, 2015. www.pollingreport.com/guns.htm (accessed January 13, 2017).

53 Tom W. Smith, "Surge in Gun Sales? The Press Misfires" at https://ropercenter.cornell.edu/public-perspective/ppscan/134/134005.pdf (accessed January 14, 2017).

54 www.cdc.gov/nchs/data/nvsr/nvsr64/nvsr64_02.pdf (accessed January 14, 2017).

55 According to the National Center for Educational Statistics, there were 75,900,000 people enrolled in educational institutions in the United States in 2010, of which 55,350,000 were enrolled in K–12 schools (for ages 5–18). The rate of homicide at school is approximately one homicide or suicide per 2.7 million school-age students in 2009–2010, according to the Center for Disease Control. To put that in perspective, that rate is lower than that of any country in the world that records homicides (Lichtenstein and Iceland often have no homicides over a year). The United Kingdom's overall rate of homicide with its similar population (64m) to the US schools and educational facilities combined population is 32 times higher, and the United States' overall homicide rate is 127 times higher. American schools and higher education facilities are incredibly safe places.

56 Cheryl Gay Stolberg, "Report Sees Guns as Path to Safety in Schools", *New York Times*, April 2, 2013 at www.nytimes.com/2013/04/03/us/nra-details-plan-for-armed-school-guards.html.

The less commented-upon paradox, however, is that those who call for gun controls never extend these policies to the police or other authorities. It is random violence by private citizens they fear. As spokesman Peter Hamm from the Brady Center to Prevent Gun Violence, one of the most prominent gun control advocate organizations, noted, 'police officers need to be able to defend themselves and the rest of us, and they need the weapons to do so.' As James F. Pastor observed: 'Since the Brady Center is devoted to gun control laws, it is rather surprising to note that they are advocating heavier weaponry for the police.'[57] The Coalition to Stop Gun Violence, even as it condemns the intimidation of carrying guns in public, says nothing about the police carrying arms.[58]

The overarching paradox is that Americans are more fearful of crime almost in proportion to the huge fall in crime in the past 25 years. The violent crime rate and the homicide rate have been coming down steadily in the United States. From 1993 to 2014, the rate of violent crime declined from a rate of 79.8 per 1000 persons over the age of 12 to 20.1 per 1,000.[59] Homicides in 2013 and 2014 were at their lowest rate per 100,000 since 1957.[60] Moreover, gun homicides declined from 1993 to 2013 by 49 per cent,[61] whereas gun sales climb ever higher, making record sales in 2016, totalling some 23.1m.[62]

Most firearms, in other words, will not be discharged for the purpose their owners bought them for. Many people own many items for security to offset even the most incredibly low risks. We could hardly justify preventing them from having an item simply because it is useless. But restrictions on guns involve policing the behaviour of others. All will admit that restricting a freedom of another must be at least justified. But, amidst the falling crime rates and the lack of any relation between numbers of guns and homicides or the bizarre idea that gun ownership might exacerbate or prevent terrorist attacks, new measures to bureaucratize and regulate gun ownership are being put forward. If my neighbour purchases weapons in the name of security, one might smile tolerantly at his folly and use extreme caution if knocking unannounced. If he, for his own security, orders all others on the street to remove all firearms from their houses house, that is quite another thing.

A risk-averse mentality can only accept the (impossible) goal of reducing risks to zero. Security – a risk-free world – can never be achieved and is, in the end, self-defeating. As Isaiah Berlin noted, insecurity creates neither a free nor, ironically, a secure environment. 'The logical culmination of this process of destroying everything through which I can possibly be wounded is suicide. . . . Total liberation in this sense (as Schopenhauer correctly perceived) is conferred only by death.'[63]

Conclusion

The relationship of Americans to firearms switched paradigmatically over the past 50 years. Firearms empowered individuals, promoted equality and freedom, and were endowed with moral qualities in the nineteenth and twentieth centuries. They expressed America's unique

57 James F. Pastor, *Terrorism and Public Safety Policing: Implications for the Obama Presidency* (Boca Raton, FL: CRC Press, 2010), 132.
58 http://csgv.org/issues/concealed-carry/ (accessed January 15, 2017).
59 www.bjs.gov/content/pub/pdf/cv14.pdf (accessed January 15, 2017).
60 https://ucr.fbi.gov/crime-in-the-u.s/2014/crime-in-the-u.s.-2014/tables/table-1 (accessed January 15, 2017).
61 www.pewsocialtrends.org/2013/05/07/gun-homicide-rate-down-49-since-1993-peak-public-unaware/ (accessed January 15, 2017).
62 www.washingtonpost.com/news/wonk/wp/2016/01/05/gun-sales-hit-new-record-ahead-of-new-obama-gun-restrictions/?utm_term=.1ca4b05ea5a0 (accessed January 15, 2017).
63 Isiah Berlin, *Four Essays on Liberty* (Oxford University Press: Oxford, 1979), 139–140.

experiment with equality and freedom, where ordinary citizens enjoyed more power than their European brethren. The proliferation of privately held arms set the United States apart as a bastion of equality, at least for the majority of society.

If we accept the United States as a 'risk society', the ensuing paradigm shift, from virtuous armed citizen to CLRFP, clicks into focus. In the past, firearms were endowed with the positive qualities of the ordinary citizen; they embodied empowerment and symbolized equality. They were a machine that exuded the equalitarian pretensions of their possessor. Today, the relationship is reversed; the negative connotations of the gun infect ordinary people with their destructive capabilities. The specific uses of various guns – shotguns, rifles and pistols – are forgotten because all destructive power can infect the ordinary citizen.

The division between those who favour restrictive firearms policies versus those who oppose them reflects a cultural divide between Americans who believe that the state should have the monopoly on force in order to allay their insecurities and Americans who seek a more individual solution, who refuse to trust the state with their security. The former's 'nightmare' is summed up by Pamela Haag:

> A "good guy", noted by his neighbors as a quiet, upstanding citizen, can snap, becoming a monstrous villain with no apparent warning. We watch horrified as the armed, acting out of mental illness rage, impulse, sadness, or other unknown and perhaps unknowable causes or motivations harm others or themselves.[64]

Yet, in order to gain security, those who would more tightly control firearms have assented to a ridiculous concentration of arms within the police and other parts of the state. Arguably, the militarization of the police only became apparent to most Americans with the riots in Ferguson in 2014. Why not protest about police – who sometimes snap – arming themselves with ever more destructive weapons against their own citizens?

But the nightmare scenario of those who need a gun because they fear personal violence is well captured in Jennifer Carlson's correspondent: 'When I'm with my family, I can defend them. I'm not a karate expert, so I never had a feeling of safety until I had a firearm.'[65] This is despite consistently falling crime rates and despite the fact that only one of Angela Stroud's correspondents – who all carried guns for self-protection – could recount any situation where they might have actually used a gun.[66]

The problem is not with America's 'gun culture', or with the number of guns, or with a villainous percentage of the population that is out to kill honest upstanding citizens. It is distrust of one's fellow citizens, it is that the virtue of one's fellow human beings is no longer assumed, it is fear of other people, of crime statistics and newspaper headlines. It is, as Franklin D. Roosevelt, 'fear itself – nameless, unreasoning, unjustified terror which paralyzes needed efforts to convert retreat into advance'.[67]

64 Haag, *The Gunning of America*, 367.
65 Carlson, *Citizen-Protectors*, 99.
66 Stroud, *Good Guys With Guns.*
67 www.presidency.ucsb.edu/ws/?pid=14473 (accessed January 15, 2017).

7 Gun rights and the rule of law

Firmin DeBrabander

Ours is "a government of laws, not men." With these words, inscribed in the Massachusetts state constitution of 1780, John Adams declared that rule of law is a defining feature of democracy. Law enforces equality and protects our freedom; law keeps the peace and ensures the smooth functioning of society. Not men.

This is a key distinction. When individual men are called upon to enforce justice, we are at the mercy of their individual judgments and limited perspectives, their abilities and emotions. For John Locke, civil society aims as far as possible to remove us from this tenuous situation; it aims to deliver us to something more stable, more consistent, more predictable – something that may deliver enduring peace.

I will argue that the contemporary gun rights movement in the United States poses a threat to rule of law. I have argued elsewhere that expansive gun rights, as currently championed by the gun lobby in America – the National Rifle Association (NRA) – undermine basic rights we enjoy in this democracy, and which are essential to democracy: freedom of speech and freedom of assembly. Simply put, the pervasive, and sometimes glaring, presence of guns in the public sphere has a dampening effect on speech – because guns are instruments of violence, and they issue a threat in themselves – a threat that gun owners themselves proudly admit. But I have concluded that the gravest danger posed by expansive gun rights is the threat to rule of law. For, this is the bedrock of a functioning, flourishing society as such; without rule of law, nothing can get done – there can be no daily life, never mind sophisticated commerce, cultural exchange, or democratic debate. Without rule of law, life is reduced to a day-to-day struggle for existence.

Countless nations around the world desperately toil to establish rule of law. Development experts agree, nations cannot attract investment, and sow the seeds of prosperity, without rule of law. But this institution is very fragile, and elusive, and is exceedingly difficult to attain, taking decades, if not centuries to germinate. Rule of law must worm its way into a nation's traditions; it takes time for a people to realize, and trust, that corruption and violence are no longer the law of the land. And yet, remarkably, we here in America take this precious commodity for granted. We tempt fate, and invite violence and vigilantism, returning the ultimate judgment of law – death – back to the arbitrary wills of individual men.

Locke is an important resource here. Many gun rights advocates consider him an ally, and invoke Social Contract theory more broadly. This would be a fortuitous connection, since Locke's political philosophy also provided considerable inspiration for our founding fathers, thereby embedding the gun rights movement deep in the heart of the nation's origins. In its current, extreme incarnation, however, the gun rights movement can make no such claim. This is because numerous items on its agenda threaten rule of law, about which our founding fathers, and John Locke, cared deeply. This threat to rule of law is exemplified by stand-your-ground legislation, as I will discuss shortly.

Gun rights advocates consider Locke a natural ally, for one thing, because he acknowledges a natural and God-given right of self-defense. This is also cited as the main justification behind stand-your-ground legislation.

In the fashion of natural law theory, which Locke aims to build on, the right to self-defense follows from our inherent drive for self-preservation. And from our right to self-defense follow the rights to punish transgressors and demand reparations of them. These are justified, Locke explains in his *Second Treatise on Government*, because they deter would-be offenders. Such are the rights we have and recognize in a state of nature, for Locke, prior to or outside civil society. By nature, we recognize a wrong when it is committed, we recognize a right to punish – whether or not I am the victim – *and* we understand what constitutes fair and adequate punishment. This is all quite remarkable, and Locke knows it. He admits it is a "strange doctrine" that "in the State of Nature every one has Executive Power of the Law of Nature" and is empowered and driven to adjudicate fair punishment and reparations.[1]

We are inherently animated by a robust sense of justice, according to Locke, but as individuals in nature, tragically, we are not equipped to carry it out. Locke explains: "it's unreasonable for Men to be judges in their own cases, that self-love will make men partial to themselves and their friends – and that ill nature, passion, revenge will carry them too far in punishing others."[2] And when they do so, they effectively turn themselves into offenders and aggressors, violators of the law of nature, justifiably subject to the wrath of others who would prosecute the law of nature – also excessively, perhaps. Our sense of justice, in concert with our native limitations, is likely to land us in a state of war. Such are the "inconveniences of the State of Nature," Locke explains, for which "Civil Government is the proper remedy."[3]

In particular, civil society, and the social contract that grounds it, recognizes a common judge – an independent, indifferent, and objective agent – that carries out our instinct for justice, and can do so better than ourselves, limited as we are. In civil society, people seek as far as possible to rely on the rulings of this common judge – and not their own judgment and executive power.

This is rule of law, as invoked by John Adams. In civil society, we refuse to be ruled by mere men. We refuse to be ruled by partial, and often arbitrary judgments of individuals, and instead defer to a common judge. We wish to be ruled by that impartial entity, which we all intuit – the law of nature – but of our own devices, we cannot achieve such an arrangement. To follow the law of nature as accurately and effectively as possible – to submit to the rule of law – and satisfy our instinct for justice, we must defer to a common judge, according to Locke. The superior resources and broader perspective of this common judge allow him to adjudicate with greater fairness and consistency

Locke sums up the terms of his social contract neatly here:

> [B]ecause no political society can be nor subsist without having in itself the power to preserve the property, and in order thereunto punish the offenses of all those in that society; there and there only is political society, where everyone of the members hath

1 John Locke, *Two Treatises on Government* (Cambridge: Cambridge University Press, 1988), 275.
2 Ibid., 275.
3 Ibid., 276.

> quitted this natural power, resigned it up into the hands of the community in all cases that exclude him not from appealing for protection to the law that established it.[4]

Civil society upholds and defends our natural rights better than we can of our own efforts. This is the main principle of Social Contract theory as such. For Locke, we are faulty instruments of justice. Of ourselves, we are also ill equipped to defend ourselves and our property. To emend this situation, we must transfer to government our "natural powers," Locke maintains. Civil society fulfills, completes, and perfects our nature.

There is a basic, foundational exchange here: I surrender my right to use violence to punish others and extract just reparations, as Locke puts it. What of self-defense? In a passage oft cited by gun rights advocates,[5] Locke says it is

> lawful for a man to kill a thief who has not in the least hurt him, nor declared any design upon his life . . . because using force where he has no right to get me into his power, let his pretense be what it will, I have no reason to suppose that he . . . would not . . . take everything else.[6]

Locke says this right to kill a thief, "though he be in society and a fellow subject," exists because I must presume the worst of him, and because he "allows not time to appeal to our Common Judge."[7]

Tellingly, this passage follows Locke's chapter on the state of nature and the inconveniences of that state, which compel us to leave it; it also comes well before Locke introduces the social contract itself. The right of self-defense emerges again at the end of the *Second Treatise* when Locke contemplates our return to a state of nature; it is the foundation of a right to rebel against government that defies the social contract, preys upon us, and has already returned us to a state of nature. Does Locke recognize an individual's right to self-defense in civil society? I think he does – but it is clear he would want to circumscribe this right. His example of killing a thief invokes the inconveniences of nature that lead to mayhem and cycles of violence. Because I must presume the worst of a thief, and may *kill* him even if he means me no harm (maybe I'm mistaken that he's a thief at all); this is all the more reason for civil society to limit such occasions, the violence I may inflict, the damage I may do, and the perceived injustices I may leave in my wake – all of which may lead to war, as Locke conceives it, between individuals, and between groups in society.

Locke offers a good framework for understanding what is wrong with stand your ground laws, championed by the radical gun rights movement, and now on the books in 25 states.[8] A lawyer's comments in one stand your ground case are illuminating. In early 2014, Curtis Reeves shot and killed Chad Oulson in a Tampa movie theater after the two men argued, and Oulson stood over Reeves and threw popcorn in his face. Reeves' lawyer immediately

4 Ibid., 324.

5 See for example David French, "The Biblical and Natural Right of Self-Defense", *The Corner* (blog), *National Review*, January 25, 2013 at www.nationalreview.com/corner/338845/biblical-and-natural-right-self-defense-david-french.

6 Locke, *Two Treatises*, 279–280.

7 Ibid., 280.

8 Cora Currier, "The Twenty Four States that have Sweeping Self-Defense Laws Just Like Florida's", *ProPublica*, March 22, 2012 at www.propublica.org/article/the-23-states-that-have-sweeping-self-defense-laws-just-like-floridas.

announced he would seek stand-your-ground protections for his client, telling reporters that Reeves felt threatened with "great bodily harm," as the Florida law stipulates – and that was enough. At that moment, the lawyer reasoned, in the darkened theater, Reeves did not know what Oulson intended to do to him; he did not know that Oulson had no weapon, only popcorn. According to the letter of Florida's stand-your-ground law, the lawyer maintained, Reeves was permitted to presume the worst. The law is not concerned with how petty the argument was between the two men, or that a tragic mistake was involved. No, the lawyer explained, the law is only concerned with whether "Reeves *thought* Chad Oulson would hurt him."[9]

Florida's stand your ground statute, widely copied by other states, says a person may "use deadly force if he or she reasonably believes . . . [it] is necessary to prevent imminent death or great bodily harm." Such a person "does not have a duty to retreat and has the right to stand his or her ground if [he or she] is not engaged in criminal activity and is in a place where he or she has a right to be."[10]

That the law may protect citizens who mistakenly shoot and kill perceived threats, simply because they *believe* they are in danger, is quite disastrous for Locke. It reintroduces the inconveniences of a state of nature, from which civil society would remove us. It reintroduces that state where justice is tenuous, or endangered, and the sense of injustice may linger, fester, and grow. The father of an unarmed man shot by a neighbor, who was subsequently given stand-your-ground immunity, complained that "somehow we've reached the point where the shooter's word is the law. The victim doesn't even get his day in court."[11] One prosecutor worried that

> you lose faith in the legitimacy of the justice process if you feel cases are unresolved or resolved in a way that suggests a sort of unfair or biased result. At a very basic level [stand-your-ground laws] change how we view the sanctity of human life. If we're allowed to shoot somebody for reaching into your car to grab your purse, does it mean that we don't value human life the way we thought we did?[12]

With this last statement, the prosecutor invokes the expansion of Castle doctrine, from which stand your ground emerged. According to English common law, which undergirds and informs our own legal system, persons faced with a threat – in public – have the duty to withdraw or avoid confrontation if possible, and use force only as a last resort. Historically, castle doctrine is a common law doctrine that absolves an individual of the obligation to retreat if he feels threatened in his home – his "castle." At home, faced with a threat, a person may use force as a first resort. Castle doctrine has been incorporated into law in some form in 46 states, and in many cases, expanded beyond the home to include, among other

9 Melanie Michael, "Popcorn Defense: Can Accused Florida Movie Shooter Use 'Stand Your Ground'?" *KSDK.com*, January 15, 2014 at www.ksdk.com/story/news/nation/2014/01/15/popcorn-defense-can-accused-florida-movie-shooter-use-stand-your-ground/4488939/.

10 "Title XLVI Chapter 776: Justifiable Use of Force", *The 2013 Florida Statutes* at www.leg.state.fl.us/statutes/index.cfm?App_mode=Display_Statute&URL=0700-0799/0776/Sections/0776.013.html.

11 Patrik Jonsson, "Trayvon Martin Case Reveals Confusion Over How Stand Your Ground Works", *Christian Science Monitor*, April 11, 2012 at www.csmonitor.com/USA/Justice/2012/0411/Trayvon-Martin-case-reveals-confusion-over-how-Stand-Your-Ground-works.

12 Jonsson, "Trayvon Martin Case Reveals Confusion."

things, one's car, and one's workplace.[13] Stand-your-ground laws absolve an individual *anywhere* of the duty to retreat, if a person perceives a threat.

Stand your ground laws have given rise to numerous controversies, and tragedies. Perhaps the most notable of them is the 2012 shooting of Trayvon Martin. The teenager's killer, George Zimmerman, was acquitted of murder, which elicited widespread protest and outrage. Defenders of stand your ground point out that Zimmerman's lawyers waived his pretrial stand-your-ground hearing, which would have granted him immunity from criminal prosecution, and instead sought to defend him before a jury. Thus, they have argued, this was no stand your ground controversy at all; that law is blameless. And yet, it turns out, "the issue of stand your ground was in the jury instructions under the self-defense rubric in which justifiable use of force was to be considered."[14] Thus, as many commentators observed at the time, the verdict was wholly unsurprising: stand your ground produced this horrific decision – the jury felt compelled by that law to rule as it did. How could you deny that Zimmerman *felt* threatened by the boy? And the boy was no longer alive to give his side of the story.

In his capacity as neighborhood watchman, Zimmerman followed Martin, who was not engaged in any criminal activity. Zimmerman merely thought the hooded boy looked suspicious. Zimmerman ignored a police dispatcher's advice to leave Martin alone and wait for assistance. He exited his car to confront Martin face to face, armed, and after a scuffle ensued, shot the teenager dead. Stand your ground is founded on self-defense, supporters say. And yet, based on the facts, the claim that Zimmerman killed the unarmed teenager as an act of self-defense seemed unconvincing. There was a distinct air of vigilantism surrounding his actions.

Journalist Amel Ahmad argues that stand-your-ground laws "influence society long before they reach the courtroom."[15] Their mere existence potentially emboldens armed citizens, either to be over-zealous in exercising self-defense, and needlessly killing someone, or even lapsing into vigilantism. Regarding the latter, the Florida statute says stand your ground protections may also extend to those who use their firearms "to prevent the imminent commission of a forcible felony."[16] Private citizens lack the training of law enforcement. Will they have the insight to detect with any accuracy the "imminent commission of a forcible felony"? Chances are good they will make mistakes – like Zimmerman – and at a higher proportion than police officers, who are also liable to error on occasion. Why encourage this? To the extent that stand your ground blatantly invokes vigilantism, this is perfectly disastrous for rule of law, according to Locke. It leads back to the state of nature where people act as executives of the law of nature – partially, and imperfectly – sowing injustice, inciting revenge, and no one is secure.

The very existence of stand-your-ground laws suggest to everyone that it is a good idea to be armed and ready to draw their weapon quickly and instinctively in public. The *Tampa*

13 State of Connecticut General Assembly: Office of Legislative Research Report, *The Castle Doctrine and Stand-Your-Ground Law*, by Hendrik DeBoer and Mark Randall, April 24, 2012 at www.cga.ct.gov/2012/rpt/pdf/2012-R-0172.pdf.

14 Matt Pearce, "NRA Isn't Budging in Post-Verdict 'Stand your Ground' Standoff", *Nation Now* (blog), *Los Angeles Times*, July 12, 2013 at www.latimes.com/nation/nationnow/la-na-nn-nra-stand-your-ground-20130717-story.html.

15 Amel Ahmad, "Mixed Verdict in Dunn Trial Result of 'Stand Your Ground,' Experts Say", *AlJazeera.com*, February 18, 2014 at http://america.aljazeera.com/articles/2014/2/17/dunn-trial-blamethelawnotthejuryexpertssay.html.

16 "Title XLVI Chapter 776: Justifiable Use of Force", *The 2013 Florida Statutes.*

Bay Times reports that "as stand your ground claims have increased, so too has the number of Floridians with guns. Concealed weapons permits now stand at 1.1 million [as of 2014], three times as many as in 2005 when the law was passed."[17] This development is understandable in one respect: What if you are faced with a Curtis Reeves who will pull his gun on you at the slightest threat, though he is mistaken? Who knows what he, or anyone for that matter, finds threatening? What if you are shadowed by a would-be George Zimerm-man, who feels emboldened by stand your ground to keep an eye out for the "imminent commission of a forcible felony" – and he deems you suspicious? It makes good sense to be armed and ready, against anyone over-exuberant in identifying and confronting a threat. Here is the central problem: the very notion of threat is highly subjective, and variable – and often wrong. It also incites irrational behavior. As John Timoney, the former Miami police chief explained,

> citizens feel threatened all the time, whether it's from the approach of an aggressive panhandler or squeegee pest or even just walking down a poorly lighted street at night. . . . In tightly congested urban areas, public encounters can be threatening. . . . This is part of urban life. You learn to navigate threatening settings *without* resorting to force.[18]

This captures the spirit of Locke's project, his aim for civil society. We cannot rule out the use of force; there may be a place for it, in cases of self-defense for example, when law enforcement is not present, and there are no other options. And yet, what distinguishes and defines civil society *as such* is that it strives to limit individuals' reliance on force, reliance on their own judgment and perspective in the heat of the moment, when results could be deadly. Stand your ground leads in the other direction: it says one may resort to force – first – and force may be an acceptable or understandable response to everyday conflicts and common misjudgments. Indeed, as more people are armed in Florida, and emboldened by the law, or put on edge by it, they may well be more inclined to shoot over minor disputes, for fear their disputant will draw first.

Perusing the stand-your-ground cases documented in the *Tampa Bay Times*, it is alarming to see how many conflicts were needlessly escalated by individuals merely flashing their guns and issuing a threat, elevating petty disagreements into deadly fights. One Florida lawyer said, "I see cases where I'll think, 'this person didn't really need to kill that person but the law, as it is written, justifies their action.'"[19] Or as an editorial in the *Tampa Tribune* put it,

> People who fear for their lives through no fault of their own shouldn't be prosecuted. But that was already the rule of law, and the "stand your ground" law eliminates any duty to retreat, which is enabling people to participate in violent disputes to end them by using lethal force.[20]

17 Connie Humburg, Kris Hundley and Susan Taylor Martin, "Florida 'Stand Your Ground' Law Yields Some Shocking Outcomes Depending on How the Law Is Applied", *Tampa Bay Times*, June 1, 2012 at www.tampabay.com/news/publicsafety/crime/florida-stand-your-ground-law-yields-some-shocking-outcomes-depending-on/1233133.

18 John Timoney, "Florida's Disastrous Self-Defense Law", *New York Times*, March 24, 2012 at www.nytimes.com/2012/03/24/opinion/floridas-disastrous-self-defense-law.html?_r=0.

19 "Florida's Stand Your Ground Law Yields Some Shocking Outcomes", *Tampa Bay Times*.

20 "Editorial: Stand Your Ground Continues to Rear Its Ugly Head", *The Tampa Tribune*, July 18, 2014 at www.tbo.com/list/news-opinion-editorials/editorial-stand-your-ground-continues-to-rear-its-ugly-head-20140718/.

In a civil society, where our preference should be to resolve threatening situations without resorting to force that may lead to greater tragedy, enduring conflict, and mounting injustices, the duty to retreat (which does not rule out force, if you are unable to retreat) satisfies the demands of self-defense eminently for Locke.

As for rule of law, stand your ground is quite destructive. Rule of law is an act of faith: people presume and trust that everyone around them understands or knows the law, at least its main tenets, and will act predictably. I must presume this in order to get on with my business on a daily basis; I have to trust that others know and obey the law – and are not prepared to kill. If there is a greater likelihood that minor disputes may end in death, that changes everything; it makes me less willing to get on with my business. It undermines my faith in the public sphere – and what is a vibrant democracy without a public sphere? It makes me inclined to enter the public sphere armed and on edge, on the lookout for threats – and when we are on the lookout for said threats, will we be more likely to find them? I think so. This is the nature of fear: we lash out at things that do not deserve our fear, because we imagine otherwise. A stand-your-ground society offers ample opportunities to imagine the worst, from people you argue with, or cut off in traffic, or who think they are upholding the law.

Stand your ground urges us to feel, or fear, that at any given moment, rule of law no longer pertains – that Law no longer rules over us – and governs our daily interactions. It recommends that we should be armed and prepared to rely on our fears and judgment if we feel threatened. Stand your ground surrenders us progressively to the arbitrary judgment of individual men; and as such, it risks making interpersonal behavior intolerably unpredictable and deadly. Security is endangered in this environment – my personal security may be at the mercy of someone's irrational fears, or my own. If people feel more and more that they must rely on themselves and their weapons for their daily, basic protection, and feel emboldened, or obliged, to resolve disagreements violently – because others increasingly do so – then we are very far from Locke's civil society. Rule of law is the key to security in a democratic society, not personal firearms and their emboldened owners.

Adding to the perversity of stand-your-ground laws, and further eroding rule of law, Craig Whitney points out that "criminals can take advantage of these same laws and make it more difficult for police to prosecute them."[21] A robber, for example, only has to say – if there are no other witnesses – that the unarmed citizen he shot on the street had attacked *him*. His victim, if dead, cannot give testimony to the contrary. Stand-your-ground privileges the shooter. And it puts police at a disadvantage in bringing killers with criminal intent to justice, which is why law enforcement is generally against stand-your-ground laws. Affirming the advantage these laws offer criminals, one Florida prosecutor explains, "people who've been through the legal system are going to be more seasoned to using the law. And it doesn't take a master of fiction to turn a homicide into stand your ground."[22]

In its survey of Florida cases where stand your ground immunity was sought, the *Tampa Bay Times* noted that the law was invoked "with unexpected frequency, in ways no one imagined, to free killers and violent attackers whose self-defense claims seem questionable at best."[23] For one thing, the study revealed that the stand-your-ground defense was very successful, with nearly 70 per cent of the people requesting immunity receiving it.[24] Such

21 Craig Whitney, *Living With Guns: A Liberal's Case For the Second Amendment* (New York: Public Affairs, 2012), 26.
22 Paul Solotaroff, "A Most American Way to Die", *Rolling Stone*, April 25, 2013 at www.rollingstone.com/culture/news/jordan-davis-stand-your-grounds-latest-victim-20130425.
23 "Florida's Stand Your Ground Law Yields Some Shocking Outcomes", *Tampa Bay Times*.
24 Ibid.

success, naturally, will inspire more lawyers to invoke the defense – and in more creative ways. This has produced a disturbing state of affairs, the study notes:

> People often go free under "Stand your Ground" in cases that seem to make a mockery of what lawmakers intended. One man killed two unarmed people and walked out of jail. Another shot a man as he lay on the ground. Others went free after shooting their victims in the back. In nearly a third of the cases the *Times* analyzed, defendants initiated the fight, shot an unarmed person or pursued their victim – and still went free.[25]

There is also a troubling racial aspect to the law. The *Times* study revealed that whites who kill blacks are more likely to be granted stand-your-ground immunities than if the situation were the reverse. In its study of the impact of stand your ground laws nationwide, the *Urban Institute* noted a huge racial disparity: "a white shooter who kills a black victim is 350 percent more likely to be found to be justified than if the same shooter killed a white victim."[26] This, too, should be unsurprising since a subjective feeling of threat is at the heart of the law: building off of existing and lingering racial prejudices, some whites will be more likely to consider a person of color inherently threatening – like Trayvon Martin in his hoodie. And it is very difficult to question or doubt a person's feeling – again, an actual threat is not the core of the law, but merely the *feeling* of threat.

In a way, stand your ground is the logical culmination of expansive gun rights. Why have a gun, why carry it in public, as open carry and concealed carry allow, if you are not also protected in using it? The gun lobby has worked hard to expand the number of public places people may bring their guns. The next step is protecting gun owners when they use their weapons in public. After all, how else are we to fully realize the deterrent power of guns? If criminals know that the law has released gun owners to use their firearms with full force, this will make them think twice before attacking. Thus, stand your ground enhances the deterrent power of guns, making society safer for us all, warning off "bad guys."

Of course, it hasn't exactly worked out this way. Criminals invoke stand your ground protections. And a prominent study found that the law bore no deterrent effect when it comes to a variety of crimes – but it noticed an uptick in homicides.[27] It was predictable that stand your ground would fail to deter criminals. Indeed, knowing that citizens are emboldened to use their weapons against perceived threats, criminals will simply arm themselves better, which the NRA has made all too easy, since it has fought the assault weapons ban and universal background checks on gun purchases. What's more, stand your ground will simply prompt criminals to shoot first – which, of all people in society, they were most inclined to do anyway.

There is a deep irony in the fact that the radical gun rights agenda, exemplified by stand your ground, threatens rule of law. For, rule of law is cherished by prominent conservative thinkers – and gun rights advocates fancy themselves staunch conservatives.

There are few figures more revered on the right than Milton Friedman, the University of Chicago economist and laissez faire capitalist, who inspired monetary policy from the Reagan

25 Ibid.

26 "National Task Force on Stand Your Ground Laws: Final Report and Recommendations", *American Bar Association*, September 2015 at www.americanbar.org/content/dam/aba/images/diversity/SYG_Report_Book.pdf.

27 David K. Humphreys, Antonio Gasparrini and Douglas Wiebe, "Evaluating the Impact of Florida's 'Stand your Ground' Self-defense Law on Homicide and Suicide by Firearm", *Journal of the American Medical Association*, January 2017 at http://jamanetwork.com/journals/jamainternalmedicine/article-abstract/2582988.

Administration onwards. Friedman was also a proponent of strong rule of law, and he argued that, in the interest of protecting a free market economy, where the market is properly dynamic, we must step back – "let it be" – and not tolerate bureaucratic meddling. The market must be allowed to function against the backdrop, or within the superstructure, of law – nothing else. Friedman claimed that the duties and reach of government extend no further than articulating the law, making sure it is heeded, adjudicating differences between citizens and corporations, and prosecuting offenses against them. Beyond that, Friedman affirms, government should let the law and market do its work, with the compliance of free and rational citizens. As he put it, the government ought merely play the role of architect and umpire of the law; when it sticks its finger into the market actively or intermittently, it mucks things up.[28]

Another respected conservative thinker, twentieth-century British philosopher Michael Oakeshott, calls rule of law "the greatest single condition of our freedom, removing from us that great fear which has overshadowed so many communities, the fear of the power of our own government."[29] Indeed, the latter was a major concern of our founding fathers, who aimed to construct a government where lawmakers' arbitrary power was constrained as far as possible. Gun rights advocates cite this same fear of government power as a principal justification for expansive gun rights. As commentator Andrew Napolitano put it, "The historical reality of the Second Amendment's protection of the right to keep and bear arms is not that it protects the right to shoot deer. It protects the right to shoot tyrants, and it protects the right to shoot at them effectively."[30] In other words, gun control would only limit our ability to depose government when it slides into tyranny. This is the main intention behind the Second Amendment. By the grace of all our guns, we keep government honest and upright.

For Oakeshott, however, rule of law performs this task eminently. As he explains:

> [Government] by rule of law . . . is itself the emblem of that diffusion of power which it exists to promote, and is therefore peculiarly appropriate to a free society. It is the method of government most economical in the use of power; it . . . leaves no room for arbitrariness; it encourages a tradition of resistance to the growth of dangerous concentrations of power which is far more effective than any promiscuous onslaught however crushing; it controls effectively without breaking the grand affirmative flow of things; and it gives a practical definition of the kind of limited by necessary service a society may expect from its government, restraining us from vain and dangerous expectations.[31]

Rule of law is simply the most elegant, effective – economical – way for government to exercise power, and preserve our freedom. It imposes an agenda that is limited, impersonal, and credible. It creates the least intrusion and constitutes the most secure foundation for authority. What does Oakeshott mean when he says that rule of law is the most *economical* means to keep government limited – superior to any "promiscuous onslaught"? Rule of law is better than violence at constraining government, because violence – even the threat of it, I will argue – serves as an invitation for government to abandon its adherence to rule of law, and react in kind. Violence is not economical; violence is messy, often ineffective and

28 Milton Friedman, *Capitalism and Freedom* (Chicago: University of Chicago Press, 2002), 25–27.
29 Michael Oakeshott, "The Political Economy of Freedom", in *Rationalism in Politics and Other Essays* (Indianapolis, IN: Liberty Fund, 1991), 391.
30 Andrew Napolitano, "The Right to Shoot Tyrants, Not Deer", *Washington Times*, January 10, 2013 at www.washingtontimes.com/news/2013/jan/10/the-right-to-shoot-tyrants-not-deer/.
31 Oakeshott, "The Political Economy of Freedom", 390.

counter-productive. It urges those who govern us to lapse into arbitrary rule, as is their perennial temptation. A free state is one where power is strictly impersonal. Liberty requires diffusion of power; on this, Oakeshott and our founders agree. There is no greater force for said diffusion of power, Oakeshott explains, than when rule of law is strong.

The conservative Oakeshott offers sobering words for the prospect of violent rebellion or upheaval. So does Locke, it turns out. This, too, is perhaps surprising for gun rights advocates. Locke seems most firmly in their corner because he also sanctions the citizens' right to dissolve government – and use their guns to do it. Locke expresses concern at one point that disarming subjects may enable the ruler to "make prey on them when he pleases."[32] Just the kind of thing contemporary gun rights advocates like to say. Locke says civilian rebellion is justified when the lawmaker alters the laws without consent of the people, and "sets up his own arbitrary will in place of laws"; or when the ruler aims to destroy or lay claim to the people's property.[33] Of course, people may say that a lot of complaints against the government meet Locke's conditions. They might – and often do – call any number of government actions clear evidence of tyranny. Locke understood this; he anticipated that critics would say his "hypothesis lays the ferment for frequent rebellion."[34] But he was not worried. He explained that people will not be quick to rebel over every little complaint, but only for a "long train of abuses."[35] Why? Because rebellion is no trivial matter – and it should not be cited for trivial complaints. Rebellion carries tremendous risks, including the demise of the state and civil society, Locke understands – and a possible return to a state of nature. Accordingly, Locke insisted, the right to rebellion is itself "the best fence against rebellion."[36] Simply knowing that the people retain this right, our leaders should resist bad behavior.

More importantly, Locke maintained, the people must be careful in how they wield the right to rebel, and issue threats. It is treacherous and foolish for citizens to invoke the threat of rebellion often, or casually, or for minor and isolated complaints. For, Locke warned, those in power have the "temptation of force . . . and the flattery of those around them."[37] In short, the threat of rebellion may cause rulers to worry about their self-preservation, and urge them into abandoning the law, or any pretense thereof, and turning to naked violence. This threat tells the government that a portion of the electorate seriously contemplates violence, and is prepared for it – assault weapons in tow – and the government must respond in turn. One ardent gun rights supporter wont to issue such threats acted on them, with murderous effect: Timothy McVeigh, who bombed the Alfred P. Murrah federal building in Oklahoma City in 1995 and killed 168 people. As a result, our government will not take the threats of insurrection lightly. Some gun rights extremists will respond approvingly – the government had better take them seriously. But this is naïve. For, this effectively urges the government to be oppressive, and abandon adherence to rule of law, in favor of violence. It prods government to disregard civil rights in pursuit of such threats.

Oakeshott and Locke agree that the threat of violent rebellion is not the best means of ensuring that government remains limited. In fact, it is quite dangerous, and it endangers our freedom. How shall we ensure that government remains limited and hews to rule of law – the condition of diffused, impersonal power, as Oakeshott puts it? How to ensure,

32 Locke, *Two Treatises*, 359.
33 Ibid., 408–409.
34 Ibid., 414.
35 Ibid., 415.
36 Ibid., 415.
37 Ibid., 416.

short of armed insurrection, that government does not lurch into arbitrariness, but remains respectful of the will of the masses? Civil disobedience, and nonviolent protest, offer a compelling answer. As Thoreau conceived it, according to legal scholar Bernard Harcourt, "civil disobedience accepts the legitimacy of the political structure and of our political institutions, but resists the moral authority of the resulting laws."[38] In this vein, nonviolent protest aims *not* to throw into question or undermine the larger political structure. If this structure is a democracy, nominally devoted to the equal rights of all citizens, the nonviolent protester wishes to encourage the democratic state to live up to its name and promise. The nonviolent protester who follows Thoreau's advice aims to achieve something constructive, not destructive. Thoreau realized that justice, freedom, and equality can be achieved only within the confines of the state. If democratic protest undermines the state, it undermines its own cause.

Such is the virtue of nonviolence: it works to change the state without destroying it. It works to change the political order without abandoning order as such – and without abandoning the hope for justice in that political order. There can be no hope for justice outside the political order. In his famous "Letter from a Birmingham Jail," Martin Luther King writes that

> One who breaks an unjust law must do so openly, lovingly, and with a willingness to accept the penalty. I submit that an individual who breaks a law that conscience tells him is unjust, and who willingly accepts the penalty of imprisonment in order to arouse the conscience of the community over its injustice, is in reality expressing the highest regard for law."[39]

Nonviolent disobedience, King claims, sends the message that one believes in the state, and the law; it says that one is not lawless, angling for anarchy, or pursuing selfish goals. Nonviolent disobedience embodies a hope for justice. The genius of this approach is that it is protest in the spirit of rule of law. It affirms law, and the rule of law; it aims to leave rule of law intact, and perhaps stronger, because its legitimacy is more broadly believed.

There is of course ample evidence of the power of nonviolence. But consider one case in particular, the pro-democracy protests in Tiananmen Square in China, in 1989, and the subsequent NRA response. These protests were ultimately squashed, and violently, by the Chinese government, and any talk of them has been subsequently censored at home. At the time, the NRA issued an ad bearing the image of a battered student surrounded by troops; it read

> The students of Beijing did not have the 2nd Amendment right to defend themselves when the soldiers came. America's founding fathers understood that an armed people are a free people . . . free to rise up against tyranny. That's why the individual armed citizen remains one of democracy's strongest symbols.[40]

In fact, the enduring image of Tiananmen Square suggests exactly the opposite: the single protester, unarmed, holding a line of tanks in check, stepping side to side to halt their advance. How would a gun have enhanced his effort? He is facing a line of tanks – would a gun let him do so more effectively? To the contrary, the Chinese government would have welcomed a gun. This

38 Bernard Harcourt, "Political Disobedience", in W. J. T. Mitchell, Bernard E. Harcourt, and Michael Taussig (eds.), *Occupy: Three Inquiries in Disobedience* (Chicago: University of Chicago Press, 2013), 46.
39 Martin Luther King Jr., "Letter from a Birmingham Jail", in James M. Washington (ed.), *A Testament of Hope* (New York: Harper Collins, 1986), 294.
40 Osha Gray Davidson, *Under Fire: The NRA and the Battle for Gun Control* (Iowa City: University of Iowa Press, 1998), 156.

would have given them an immediate excuse to blow him away. It was precisely because he was unarmed that the tank drivers were stymied and unsure how to act. And it is precisely because of the power of this image that it is so assiduously censored in Chinese media to this day: it indicates the astounding power of individuals – unarmed – to frustrate one of the most fearsome regimes on the planet. If the protester had been armed and shooting at tanks, the regime would have been less reluctant to transmit the image. A gun would have made it easier for the government to control and distort the narrative by depicting him as a terrorist or criminal.

Tyrannical governments hardly fear rifles, handguns, even assault weapons in the hands of citizens. Such weapons are an invitation for tyrannical government to act thuggishly. Tyrannical governments fear citizens insisting upon rule of law – lawfully – and en masse. As King put it,

> there is more power in socially organized masses on the march than there is in guns in the hands of a few desperate men. Our enemies would prefer to deal with a small armed group rather than with a huge, unarmed but resolute mass of people.[41]

With its expansive agenda, exemplified by stand-your-ground legislation, the contemporary gun rights movement claims to help us protect ourselves against our fellow citizens, when they are dangerous, or mean to do us harm. Stand your ground is upheld on the premise of self-defense. However, I have argued, the law puts too much power – deadly power – in the hands of individual persons, with their imperfect judgment, partial knowledge, and irrational fear. As Locke saw it, a civil society is one that strives to remove power from individuals in precisely such circumstances, and under such conditions, and hand it over to impersonal law. In a stand your ground society, people have reason to fear the dangerous and the law abiding alike – because the latter, imperfect humans as they are, are empowered by this law to shoot mere threats, which is entirely too subjective and variable a notion. When or if society becomes pervasively fearsome as a result of this law, everyday life becomes nearly untenable.

Even if stand your ground has not yet lead to open chaos, the law has not enabled people to defend themselves better; indeed, it has increased the number of threats in society, from the dangerous and the upstanding alike – especially the upstanding who misperceive threats. Stand your ground poses an intolerable, unnecessary threat to rule of law.

The gun rights movement also claims to protect us against the government. Those who govern us will want to accumulate and consolidate power, over and against the democratic populace. This was the view of the founders who crafted our Constitution; and the gun rights movement argues that the Second Amendment was written to allay concerns about government expansion. However, government is best constrained by rule of law. It is a conservative principle that we have strong rule of law in society; it is the superstructure in which humans are to act freely and responsibly. When people threaten the government with force, and sometimes act on it, this effectively urges those who govern us to abandon rule of law, trample our civil rights, and perhaps resort to violence. In short, such threats, Locke and Oakeshott perceive, prod the government to become big and nasty – just what our founders feared. In issuing threats to government, the gun rights movement again undermines the rule of law that would constrain government most effectively, and preserve our liberty.

41 Martin Luther King Jr., "The Social Organization of Non-violence", in James M. Washington (ed.), *A Testament of Hope* (New York: Harper Collins, 1986), 33.

8 To endure for all time or to change with the times? The Supreme Court and the Second Amendment

Emma Long

Introduction

In June 2008, the US Supreme Court handed down its decision in *District of Columbia v. Heller*, ruling for the first time that the Second Amendment to the US Constitution guaranteed an individual right to bear arms for the purposes of self-defence. Gun rights activists responded with joy that a majority of the Justices had endorsed a reading of the Amendment that they had advocated for nearly three decades. Gun control supporters expressed disappointment at the Court's ruling, which struck down what were the strictest gun laws in the nation, but also argued that *Heller* offered support for their position too. In fact, both leading presidential candidates, John McCain and Barack Obama, publicly offered their support for *Heller*.[1] How could both sides in the seemingly Manichaean debate between greater gun rights and greater gun control claim support from the same ruling? Because, in reality, *Heller offered* something to both sides. While finding the Amendment protected an individual right to own firearms separate from militia participation, the Court also clearly stated that right was not unlimited, and it offered what one commentator called a "laundry list" of regulations on gun ownership and use that remained acceptable under the Second Amendment.[2] Thus in answering one question (the scope of the right protected by the Amendment), the Court's ruling in *Heller* offered up an array of others (exactly what regulations were permitted), guaranteeing continued debate about guns in American society that ensured the Second Amendment would remain relevant well into the twenty-first century.

Heller also presented, in stark terms, a clash between two competing theories of constitutional interpretation: originalism versus living constitutionalism. Justice Antonin Scalia, who wrote for the five-Justice majority in *Heller*, described the ruling as the greatest "vindication of originalism."[3] Emerging initially as a means by which conservatives could criticise the liberal, individual rights rulings of the Warren Court, originalists argued that the meaning of the Constitution should be found by seeking the "intent" of those who created it. Objecting to what they saw as activist judges ignoring the words and meaning of the Constitution in favour of writing their own personal policy preferences into law, advocates offered originalism as a method of restraining the judiciary

1 See Dan Balz and Keith Richburg, "Historic Decision Renews Old Debate," *Washington Post*, June 27, 2008.
2 Adam Winkler, "*Heller's* Catch-22," 56 *UCLA Law Review* 1551–1577 (June 2009), at 1564.
3 Quoted in Marcia Coyle, *The Roberts Court: The Struggle for the Constitution* (New York: Simon & Schuster, 2013), 163.

and "returning" the Constitution to the meaning intended by the Founding Fathers. Scholarly criticism of the methods of original intent led to the development of what has come to be known as "original public meaning," the version of originalism found in *Heller*. The approach places less emphasis on the intentions of those who created the Constitution and more on the way in which the provisions would have been understood by ordinary eighteenth-century Americans. Judges remain constrained by the historical meaning of the constitutional provision, but without the methodological difficulties that inhered in original intent.

Originalism is offered as an alternative to what is commonly referred to as "living constitutionalism." A broad umbrella term which encompasses many differing methodologies, advocates generally adhere to Chief Justice John Marshall's 1819 statement in *McCulloch v. Maryland* that the Constitution was "intended to endure for ages to come and, consequently, to be adapted to the various crises of human affairs."[4] To remain relevant, advocates assert, the words and phrases of the Constitution must be understood in their contemporary, not their historical, context. Guided by history, precedent, legislative action, scholarly works, and public opinion, living constitutionalism, advocates assert, is a framework for ensuring a document created more than two centuries ago does not become obsolete through irrelevance: a strong Constitution must change with the times. In *Heller*, the two jurisprudential theories competed for acceptance among the Justices.

Despite the complexity of the ruling, *Heller* has been hailed, particularly by conservatives, as a triumph of originalism.[5] Such claims appear based in large part on the fact that both Justice Antonin Scalia for the majority and Justice John Paul Stevens for the dissenters made extensive use of history and historical sources to build a case for their respective readings of the Second Amendment. That oral argument was dominated by discussions of the late eighteenth century, that Scalia, the long-time advocate of originalism on the Court, wrote the majority opinion, and that Stevens, not usually considered an originalist, responded on originalist grounds all supported the claim of originalism's success. But, in fact, *Heller* was not a triumph of Second Amendment originalism, nor even close to a triumph. It cannot be for three reasons that this chapter will explore. First, the history and historical methods of both the majority and the dissent have been subject to extensive criticism from historians and legal scholars alike. Second, the majority was inconsistent in its application of history to gun control laws, suggesting at the very least that original public meaning cannot answer every question raised by a Second Amendment challenge. And third, the largely overlooked dissent filed by Justice Stephen Breyer indicated that at least one alternative jurisprudential philosophy can effectively stand against the originalist approach.

4 *McCulloch v. Maryland* 17 US 216, 407 (1819).

5 See, for example, Justice Scalia quoted at n.3; Randy Barnett, "News Flash: The Constitution Means What It Says," *Wall Street Journal*, June 27, 2008; National Rifle Association, "*Heller*: The Supreme Decision," June 27, 2008 (https://www.nraila.org/articles/20080627/heller, accessed June 1, 2015); Alan Gura, "*Heller* and the Triumph of Originalist Judicial Engagement: A Response to Judge Harvey Wilkinson," 56 *UCLA Law Review* 1127–1169 (June 2009), at 1129. For those noting the importance of originalism without hailing the decision, see Debra Cassens Weiss, "Second Amendment Ruling is Justice Scalia's Originalism 'Legacy,'" *ABA Journal*, June 27, 2008 (http://www.abajournal.com/mobile/article/second_amendment_ruling_is_justice_scalias_originalism_legacy, accessed 1 June 2015); J. Harvie Wilkinson, "Of Guns, Abortions, and the Unravelling of Law," 95 *Virginia Law Review* 253–323 (April 2009), at 256; Jeffrey Toobin, *The Oath: The Obama White House and the Supreme Court* (New York: Doubleday, 2012), 111–112; Mark Tushnet, *In The Balance: Law and Politics on the Roberts Court* (New York: W.W. Norton & Co., 2013), 149, 185.

Heller and history

Original public meaning relies heavily on history and historical discussion dominated Scalia and Stevens' opinions in *Heller*. But historians and legal scholars have not been reticent in criticising the history employed by both the majority and the dissent. Stevens' historical readings have been variously described as "historically false or patently nonsensical," "non-sense on stilts," "pseudointellectual gibberish," "idiosyncratic," "stingy [and] irrelevant," and "fantastical academic constructs."[6] Alternatively, Scalia's history has been categorised as a "magician's parlor trick," "historical ventriloquism," "methodologically irregular," full of "logical flaws and inconsistencies," as presenting a "Salvador Dali-like historical landscape," and like "Bach played on a kazoo."[7] Away from the colourful criticisms, however, a veritable cottage industry of Second Amendment scholarship with a historical focus has developed, sometimes to further illuminate our understanding of the issue of gun ownership and regulation in the early Republic, sometimes to praise or criticise a particular historical interpretation. Scholars themselves cannot seem to agree on whose interpretation has the most support.[8] Don Kates, one of the lawyers involved in the *Heller* litigation, argued in 2009 that "the overwhelming conclusion of legal and historical writers is that the Second Amendment preserves the right of all responsible, law-abiding adults to be armed for the defense of themselves, their homes and their families." Legal scholar Cass Sunstein noted, however, that "many historians have concluded and even insisted that the Second Amendment did not create an individual right to use guns for non-military purposes."[9]

Little of the relevant history remains without discussion in some form, but for those not steeped in the history of the early American nation, the literature is both overwhelming and seemingly inconclusive. Scholarly studies have followed the template established by Scalia and Stevens in *Heller* and sought the "proper" meaning of key Second Amendment phrases "the people," "arms," and "keep and bear arms," providing contradictory readings, while criticising the historical understanding of those with whom they disagree. Others have fundamentally disagreed, as did Scalia and Stevens, about the proper role and understanding of preambles generally and the Second Amendment's prefatory clause ("A well regulated militia, being necessary to the security of a free State . . .") in particular in the context of eighteenth-century legal interpretation. In addition, a variety of different readings have been offered of the meaning and relevance of state constitutional requirements

6 Don Kates, "A Modern Historiography of the Second Amendment," 56 *UCLA Law Review* 1211–1232 (June 2009), at 1226, 1227; Joyce Lee Malcolm, "The Supreme Court and the Uses of History: *District of Columbia v. Heller*," 56 *UCLA Law Review* 1377–1398 (June 2009), at 1383, 1385; Nicholas Johnson, "Rights Versus Duties, History Department Lawyering, and the Incoherence of Justice Stevens's *Heller* Dissent," 39 *Fordham Urban Law Journal* 1503–1526 (October 2012), at 1519; Gura, "Originalist Judicial Engagement," 1129.

7 Saul Cornell, "Originalism on Trial: The Use and Abuse of History in *District of Columbia v. Heller*," 69 *Ohio State Law Journal* 625–640 (2008), at 626, 632; Saul Cornell, "The People's Constitution vs. The Lawyer's Constitution: Popular Constitutionalism and the Original Debate Over Originalism," 23 *Yale Journal of Law and the Humanities* 295–337 (Summer 2011), at 301; Saul Cornell, "Meaning and Understanding in the History of Constitutional Ideas: The Intellectual History Alternative to Originalism," 82 *Fordham Law Review* 721–755 (November 2013), at 740; Reva Siegel "*Heller* and Originalism's Dead Hand – In Theory and Practice," 56 *UCLA Law Review* 1399–1424 (June 2009), at 1416; Winkler, "*Heller's* Catch-22," 1551; Dennis Henigan, "The *Heller* Paradox," 59 *UCLA Law Review* 1171–1210 (June 2009).

8 Kates, "A Modern Historiography," 1231.

9 Cass Sunstein, "Second Amendment Minimalism: *Heller* as *Griswold*," 122 *Harvard Law Review* 246–274 (November 2008), at 255. Sunstein also noted that many historians support Stevens' narrower, militia-connected reading of the Second Amendment (at 256).

both contemporaneous with and subsequent to ratification of the Second Amendment; the drafting history of the Second Amendment and the relative importance of language ultimately discarded by the First Congress; the exemption of Quakers and the debate over conscientious objection; the Pennsylvania Constitution; English common law; and nineteenth-century sources in understanding the meaning of the Second Amendment.[10] And yet, there are no clear or obvious conclusions to be drawn from this voluminous history, except perhaps for Richard Schragger's 2008 observation that "the meaning of the Second Amendment is complicated,"[11] which, while accurate, provides little guidance in navigating through the proffered alternative readings. What this complexity does offer, however, is a major challenge to those who claim *Heller* was a triumph of originalism. If history is to play a major role in interpreting constitutional provisions, the debate among the Justices and within subsequent scholarship suggests the question of *which* history has yet to be discovered or decided.

A second major challenge to originalism, offered primarily by historians, is that the history employed by originalists does not meet the rigorous methodological requirements of professional history, but is instead "law office history."[12] Such history has been defined as "a results oriented methodology in which evidence is selectively gathered and interpreted to produce a preordained conclusion."[13] "There is a marked difference," Sunstein wrote, "between the care, sensitivity to context, and relative neutrality generally shown by historians and the advocacy-oriented, conclusion-driven, and often tendentious treatments characteristic of academic lawyers."[14] Criticisms of history used by lawyers and legal scholars as ideologically motivated or selectively chosen are not new, nor are they limited to any particular constitutional provision. They have, however, been prevalent in Second Amendment scholarship.[15] In 2008, Professor Joyce Lee Malcolm praised Scalia's "carefully reasoned and scholarly opinion," which "painstakingly assessed both favorable and unfavorable

10 Most studies address more than one of these subjects. See, for example, Robert Churchill, "Gun Regulation, the Police Power and the Right to Keep Arms in Early America: The Legal Context of the Second Amendment," 25 *Law and History Review* 139–185 (Spring 2007), at 161; Saul Cornell, "*Heller*, New Originalism, and Law Office History: 'Meet the New Boss, Same as the Old Boss,'" 56 *UCLA Law Review* 1095–1125 (June 2009), at 1106–1110; Cornell, "Originalism on Trial," 632–635; Henigan, "The *Heller* Paradox," 1176–1182; David Konig, "Arms and the Man: What Did the Right to 'Keep' Arms Mean in the Early Republic?" *Law and History Review*.

11 Richard Schragger, "The Last Progressive: Justice Breyer, *Heller*, and 'Judicial Judgment,'" 59 *Syracuse Law Review* 283–297 (2009), at 283.

12 Or, as Mark Tushnet has termed it, "history-in-law." Mark Tushnet, "*Heller* and the New Originalism," 69 *Ohio State Law Journal* 609–624 (2008), at 610.

13 Cornell, "New Originalism," 1098.

14 Sunstein, "Second Amendment Minimalism," 256

15 The role of history in law has been extensively debated. For an introduction, see Martin Flaherty, "History 'Lite' in Modern American Constitutionalism," 95 *Columbia Law Review* 523–590 (April 1995); Larry Kramer, "When Lawyers Do History," 72 *George Washington Law Review* 387–423 (December 2003); John Reid, "Law and History," 27 *Loyola of Los Angeles Law Review* 193–223 (November 1993); Mark Tushnet, "Interdisciplinary Legal Scholarship: The Case of History in Law," 71 *Chicago-Kent Law Review* 909–935 (1996). For criticisms of law office history in Second Amendment scholarship, see Carl T. Bogus, "The History and Politics of Second Amendment Scholarship: A Primer," 76*Chicago-Kent Law Review* 3–25 (2000); Cornell, "New Originalism," 1098; Henigan, "The *Heller* Paradox,"; Gura, "Originalist Judicial Engagement," 1129; Kates, "A Modern Historiography," 1226–1227; Sandford Levinson, "Some Preliminary Reflections on *Heller*," *Balkanization*, June 26, 2008 (http://balkin.blogspot.co.uk/2008/06/some-preliminary-reflections-on-heller.html, accessed 30 June 2008); Jack Rakove, "Thoughts on *Heller* From a 'Real Historian,'" *Balkanization*, June 27, 2008 (http://balkin.blogspot.co.uk/search?q=rakove+heller, accessed June 30, 2008); Mark Tushnet, "More on *Heller*," *Balkanization*, June 27, 2008 (http://balkin.blogspot.co.uk/2008/06/more-on-heller.html, accessed 30 June 2008); Tushnet, "New Originalism," 610.

historical evidence," while criticising Stevens for "disregard[ing] inconvenient facts and employ[ing] linguistic devices that distort the plain meaning of the original text."[16] Saul Cornell has been arguably the most prolific and frequent critic of the *Heller* majority, and originalists generally, for their reading of early American history.[17] Criticising one group or another for participating in law office history has similarities to claiming that those same individuals are misreading history: it seeks to delegitimize the conclusions reached. In the latter, it does so by claiming those conclusions are wrong, in the former by holding that the methods employed are not sound. That the criticisms are aimed at all sides in the debates fundamentally weakens any claim for the "triumph" of originalism in *Heller*. If the history offered by lawyers and employed by the Justices in their opinions is all equally tainted by claims of results-orientation, then the biggest loser of all is the methodology that encourages and draws on that history.

One need not be an expert in early American history, however, to see the problems inherent in originalism: the opinions in *Heller* exposed them clearly. Absent the restraint of significant precedent, the Justices were able to write on "as near a clean slate as modern constitutional law presents"[18] which only made more stark the limitations of originalism, at least on its own terms. The biggest problem, so clear to historians, is that *the* original meaning sought by originalists does not and cannot exist. While it is possible to criticise the methodology and readings of the history employed by Scalia and Stevens in their respective opinions, their clash of views revealed the fundamental problem of originalism, one which most historians would recognise: even using similar sources and methodologies, individuals can quite reasonably come to different conclusions about the events portrayed in those sources. When those individuals start using different sources and employing methodologies which weight those sources differently, then the possibility of different outcomes increases exponentially. Thus, Scalia and Stevens might both be equally correct in their readings, just as they might be equally wrong, but both are *reasonable* understandings of the history revealed in their sources.

This is because history at its best is a work of interpretation. Historians, unlike law office historians, generally do not pick and choose their sources according to their preferred outcomes nor do they deliberately seek to reinforce a political agenda with the history they write. But historians do bring their own beliefs, experiences, opinions, and personalities to what they do, and with those things come choices, about which sources to trust, which are more or less reliable, which are more historically significant, which were more influential or representative. And such choices entail judgment, the very thing originalism claims to expunge from the process of judging. Scalia and Stevens' differing histories can be accounted for by differences in judgment just as much as strengths and weaknesses in their history. As Mark Tushnet observed:

16 Malcolm, "Uses of History," 1378

17 See, in particular, references at n.7. Lawyers and legal scholars have also criticised their opponents for misusing history, but since they are generally also the targets of such criticism it is entirely possible to see these criticisms as part of the political or ideological agenda for which they are arguing. See for example, Alan Gura's praise for the *Heller* majority's refusal to be distracted by arguments "driven by modern ideological dogmas and backed by historical revisionism or selective citation," implying this was exactly what the dissenters had done (Gura was the lead attorney for Dick Heller). Gura "Originalist Judicial Engagement," 1129. Or, Dennis Henigan's critique of Scalia's majority opinion as "an unprincipled abuse of judicial power in pursuit of an ideological objective" (Henigan is former Vice President of the Brady Center to Prevent Gun Violence). Henigan, "The *Heller* Paradox," 1171.

18 Linda Greenhouse, "'Weighing Needs and Burdens:' Justice Breyer's *Heller* Dissent," 59 *Syracuse Law Review* 299–308 (2008), at 307.

> *Heller* was a test for conservative originalists' claim that modern originalism's exclusive focus on historical materials would keep judges from advancing their policy views while pretending to interpret the Constitution. Originalism didn't quite fail the test, but it got a grade of C+ or so – pretty much the grade you'd give every other method of constitutional interpretation.[19]

The fact that Scalia and Stevens, ostensibly both taking an originalist approach, could ultimately come to different conclusions about the meaning of the Second Amendment was the simplest, clearest sign of the most significant weakness in originalism's methodology: historical scholarship requires judgment and, because of that, there is no "correct" or "true" history to be found. To the extent that originalists seek *the* historical meaning of constitutional provisions in a way that prevents or limits judicial judgment, therefore, they seek something nonexistent. The danger then becomes that originalism presents itself as a neutral method of judicial interpretation while it is, in reality, a "theory no less subject to judicial subjectivity and endless argumentation than any other."[20]

Inconsistency and the majority

Originalists and non-originalists alike have offered a further critique of the originalism employed by Scalia for the majority: that it was inconsistent in addressing questions of possible limits to the Second Amendment right. "Like most rights," Scalia stated in *Heller*, "the right secured by the Second Amendment is not unlimited." Throughout the nineteenth century, Scalia noted, courts and commentators recognised that "the right was not a right to keep and carry any weapon whatsoever in any manner whatsoever and for whatever purpose."[21] Yet, as noted by Justice Breyer in dissent and by many commentators since, the majority offered no historical support for these exemptions.[22] After more than fifty pages of historical discussion of the meaning of the Second Amendment, the lack of any such discussion on this point was notable and Scalia's defence, that in the first case considering such a major issue not all possible areas of controversy could be discussed in detail, failed to address the inconsistency. The founding era offered many examples of gun regulations that the majority could have referenced. Scalia's opinion dismissed those offered by Breyer as of minimal relevance but, those aside, the scholarly literature offered additional examples that the majority might have used as colonial era analogues of the modern gun control laws they found acceptable.[23] At the very least, the principle of regulations on gun ownership had been established. From an originalist perspective, however, such examples were problematic in that none offered direct equivalents to those listed in the majority opinion; making

19 Tushnet, *In The Balance*, 168.
20 Wilkinson, "Of Guns," 256
21 *District of Columbia v. Heller* 554 US 570, 626 (2008).
22 *District of Columbia v. Heller* 554 US 570, 720 (2008) (Justice Breyer, dissenting); See, for example, Winkler "*Heller's* Catch-22," 1561–1563; and Enrique Schaerer, "What the Heller? An Originalist Critique of Justice Scalia's Second Amendment Jurisprudence," 82 University of Cincinnati Law Review 795–830 (Spring 2014), at 811–813). *District of Columbia v. Heller* 554 US 570, 720 (2008) (Justice Breyer, dissenting).
23 For example, military musters where weapons could be inspected, registration of firearms, and regulations for the safe storage of gunpowder. See Saul Cornell, *A Well-Regulated Militia: The Founding Fathers and the Origins of Gun Control in America* (New York: Oxford University Press, 2006), 26–30; Churchill, "Gun Regulation," 161–165; Brief of amici curiae Jack Rakove et al. in support of the petitioners, *District of Columbia v. Heller* (available from the American Bar Association website, http://www.americanbar.org/content/dam/aba/publishing/preview/publiced_preview_briefs_pdfs_07_08_07_290_PetitionerAmCuRakove.authcheckdam.pdf, accessed June 1, 2015).

connections and finding equivalencies would require a degree of interpretation and judgment that originalists decry. But providing no historical evidence for those limits accepted by the majority also contradicted an originalist approach and created an anomaly within the *Heller* majority opinion.

A second area of controversy has been the inconsistent treatment of handguns in the majority opinion. Reading the Court's own 1939 precedent, *US v. Miller*, as permitting restrictions on certain *types* of weapons, the *Heller* majority accepted that such a limitation "is fairly supported by the historical tradition of prohibiting the carrying of dangerous and unusual weapons." Thus, the weapons protected by the Second Amendment were those "in common use at the time."[24] Yet in discussing the specifics of the District's law later in the opinion, the majority noted, "handguns are the most popular weapons chosen by Americans for self-defense in the home."[25] The majority's language, the context of the discussion, and the lack of any historical references in this section combined to give the impression that this was a judgment based not on colonial era self-defence, but on twenty-first-century choices. As Adam Winkler commented, "Scalia looks to the fickle dynamics of contemporary consumer choices. Handguns are protected because people today choose handguns for protection."[26] In an opinion so self-consciously originalist, which criticised both dissents for poor history and a lack of proper historical grounding, the majority's apparent reliance upon current public opinion rather than historical understanding was jarring. The decision to follow, if not to actually make, a policy choice about the types of weapons protected under the Second Amendment potentially implied that the entire historical reading offered earlier in the opinion was equally influenced by policy choices. The lack of historical evidence and the apparent influence of contemporary decisions by ordinary Americans combined to offer a challenge to the majority's claimed originalism from within the opinion itself.

The majority's defence of gun regulations can be explained by a number of factors, all of which speak to the general working of the Court. First, remembering Justice William Brennan's "rule of five," it is possible that the language was inserted to gain or keep the five-Justice majority.[27] While Justices Scalia and Clarence Thomas had been consistent advocates for an originalist perspective, Chief Justice John Roberts and Justices Samuel Alito and Anthony Kennedy often looked to other sources and may not have been entirely convinced by an entirely originalist argument.[28] Second, the comments can be read as a response to the dissenters' concerns about the potential dangers of an unlimited right to gun.[29] Challenged by claims that the Court's ruling would lead to inconsistent decisions, policy-making by judges, and increased danger to law-abiding Americans, the majority sought to defend their approach and dispel such claims by indicating the limits to the scope of their holding. Third, the majority's discussion of handguns in particular spoke to the importance of *stare decisis* in light of the reference to *Miller*. Scalia had previously stated that he believed precedent

24 *District of Columbia v. Heller* 554 US 570, 627 (2008) (internal quotations omitted).
25 *District of Columbia v. Heller* 554 US 570, 629 (2008).
26 Winkler, "*Heller*'s Catch-22," 1560.
27 On Brennan's views about the working of the Court, including his "rule of five," see Dawn Johnsen, "Justice Brennan: Legacy of a Champion," 111 *Michigan Law Review* 1151–1181 (April 2013), at 1159.
28 In 2013, Mark Tushnet confidently claimed that the list of exceptions was included to secure the vote of Justice Anthony Kennedy. Although plausible, Tushnet provides no definitive evidence for this. Tushnet, *In The Balance*, 182.
29 Henigan, "The *Heller* Paradox," 1196; Wilkinson, "Of Guns," 273, 281

might offer an acceptable exception to an originalist reading of a constitutional provision.[30] Recognising that certain types of weapons may be eligible for regulation (and by implication, others may not) fitted with Scalia's own judicial philosophy. Fourth is the question of public legitimacy. The exact relationship between public opinion and the Supreme Court is unclear but most scholars agree that the Court is rarely out of line with public opinion for long and the Justices are aware that the Court's institutional legitimacy is threatened when making decisions which challenge public opinion.[31] Studies suggest that most Americans support both an individual right to own guns for self-defence and reasonable gun regulations; thus a ruling challenging either of these might lead to a public backlash against the Court. A rational actor, seeking to preserve their influence in the most effective way, might judge that conceding on the issue of reasonable, already-existing regulations, while pressing a preferred reading of the broad right in general, might offer the best way to ensure continued legitimacy and the opportunity to revisit the issue at a later date.[32] Or, in the words of one commentator, "the originalists on the Court had to sell their originalist souls to survive."[33]

To Court scholars all of these explanations for the apparent contradiction between the self-confessed originalism of the majority's approach and the acceptance of certain kinds of limits on gun ownership are reasonable; each speaks to an accepted understanding of the way in which the Court operates. In the context of *Heller*, however, the fact is that all of them undermine any claim to a "triumph of originalism." Concessions to keep a majority, to maintain public support, to address or limit criticisms from dissenters, or to recognise the importance of *stare decisis* or other jurisprudential considerations, ensured the majority won the battle to define the overarching right embodied in the Second Amendment, but none of them rested on an historical interpretation of the original public meaning of the scope of the Second Amendment. Thus, while *Heller* offered a showcase of what originalism could achieve, it also revealed clearly its limitations.

Justice Breyer and the living Constitution

Nothing shows how dominant has been the view that the importance of *Heller* lay in its originalism than the almost complete absence of any significant discussion of Justice Breyer's dissent. Linda Greenhouse, former Supreme Court correspondent for the *New York*

30 Antonin Scalia, "Originalism: The Lesser Evil," 57 *University of Cincinnati Law Review* 849–865 (1989).

31 The literature on the Court and public opinion is voluminous. As a starting point see Christopher Casillas, Peter Enns, and Patrick Wohlfarth, "How Public Opinion Constrains the US Supreme Court," 55 *American Journal of Political Science* 74–88 (January 2011); Lee Epstein and Andrew Martin, "Does Public Opinion Influence the Supreme Court? Possibly Yes (But We're Not Sure Why)," 13 *University of Pennsylvania Journal of Constitutional Law* 263–281 (December 2010); Kevin McGuire and James Stimson, "The Least Dangerous Branch Revisited: New Evidence on Supreme Court Responsiveness to Public Preferences," 66 *The Journal of Politics* 1018–1035 (November 2004); William Rehnquist, "Constitutional Law and Public Opinion," 20 *Suffolk University Law Review* 751–769 (Winter 1986).

32 Jeffrey Jones, "Americans in Agreement With Supreme Court on Gun Rights," *Gallup*, June 26, 2008 (http://www.gallup.com/poll/108394/Americans-Agreement-Supreme-Court-Gun-Rights.aspx, accessed June 3, 2015); "Washington Post Poll: Most Americans Say Amendment Covers Individuals and Militias," *Washington Post*, March 16, 2008 (http://www.washingtonpost.com/wp-dyn/content/graphic/2008/03/16/GR2008031600072.html, accessed June 3, 2015); Pew Research Center, "Public Continues to Oppose Banning Handgun Sales," May 14, 2008 (http://www.people-press.org/files/legacy-pdf/419.pdf, accessed June 3, 2015).

33 Winkler, "*Heller*'s Catch-22," 1565. See generally Siegel, "*Heller* and Originalism's Dead Hand."

Times, noted this absence in 2009, offering her own interpretation of Breyer's opinion as a *mea culpa* for giving "short shrift" to the opinion in her initial coverage for the *Times*.[34] Yet discussion of Breyer's dissent remains curiously absent from the debate about *Heller*, drowned out by "the titanic clash of the competing historical visions" offered by Scalia and Stevens.[35] The reasons for this are unclear. Breyer's opinion, at forty-four pages, was only marginally shorter than Stevens' dissent (forty-six pages) and was certainly no less detailed or effectively argued. It directly addressed and criticised the majority's approach and offered alternative readings of key state provisions in terms of early American gun control legislation, criticisms to which Scalia responded. In addition, Breyer was seen as Scalia's most frequent sparring partner on and off the Court in regards to methods of constitutional interpretation. The battle between the two was noted and commentated upon, making it all the stranger that its continuation in the pages of *Heller* has been so under-explored.[36]

One hint comes in Jeffrey Toobin's 2012 study of the Roberts Court. Writing about *Heller*, he commented, "It was left to Breyer to write the kind of dissent that the justices used to produce."[37] From this perspective, the dominance of originalism in the majority opinion in particular was unusual and noteworthy, the first time the Court had so clearly and heavily made use of history to interpret a major provision of the Constitution; by contrast, Breyer's approach represented something older, something more familiar, and therefore less striking. It is certainly true that Breyer's jurisprudence was a version of living constitutionalism. The general failure to address Breyer's *Heller* dissent may, therefore, be a simple case that familiarity breeds contempt. But this significantly underestimates the importance of Breyer's particular approach to living constitutionalism and its role in *Heller*. In his dissent, Breyer offered a clear, compelling alternative way of understanding the Court's role in interpreting the Second Amendment and a critique of some of originalism's weaknesses, while also showing that living constitutionalism had not disappeared from the Court's jurisprudential toolbox, no matter how much commentators would like to concentrate on originalism.

Like Scalia, Breyer began his opinion with history. His understanding, however, differed from that of the majority. Colonial history, he wrote, "offers important examples of the kinds of gun regulation that citizens would then have thought compatible with the 'right to keep and bear arms.'"[38] Boston, Philadelphia, and New York, Breyer noted, all had laws restricting the discharge of firearms within the city limits; in effect, laws governing the use of guns in urban areas. This would become crucial later in his opinion. In addition, several towns and cities regulated the storage of gunpowder for fire safety reasons. This had relevance for the District's law in two particular ways according to Breyer. First, it prevented individuals from keeping loaded weapons in the house to use immediately against an intruder. Second, it prevented individuals carrying their guns in the city, unless they had

34 Greenhouse, "Weighing Needs and Burdens," 300.
35 Greenhouse, "Weighing Needs and Burdens," 299.
36 See, for example, Dahlia Lithwick, "Justice Grover Versus Justice Oscar," *Slate*, December 6, 2006 (http://www.slate.com/articles/news_and_politics/jurisprudence/2006/12/justice_grover_versus_justice_oscar.html, accessed May 12, 2015); Adam Young, "Supreme Court Justices Spar on Lubbock Stage," *Lubbock Avalanche-Journal Online*, November 13, 2010 (http://lubbockonline.com/local-news/2010-11-13/supreme-court-justices-spar-lubbock-stage, accessed June 1, 2015); Andrea Seabrook, "Justices Get Candid About the Constitution," *NPR Online*, October 9, 2011 (http://www.npr.org/2011/10/09/141188564/a-matter-of-interpretation-justices-open-up, accessed May 12, 2015).
37 Toobin, *The Oath*, 112.
38 *District of Columbia v. Heller* 554 US 570, 683 (2008) (Justice Breyer, dissenting).

no intention of entering a building or were willing to unload their weapon before going inside.[39] Dismissed by the majority as of minor relevance, Breyer's argument was not that these laws were exact analogues of the District's law, but that they established, in principle, the fact that Americans of the colonial era were familiar with laws that burdened in several ways their ability to use and carry firearms, at home or in public.[40] Such laws might, as in the case of gunpowder storage, be motivated by concerns for public safety, indicating that any right to gun ownership was tempered by concerns for public welfare. Thus Breyer, as well as Stevens, offered a reading of history which challenged that offered by the majority. But for Breyer, history was not dispositive; it was only the beginning, not the end of the discussion. Having established that some restrictions on Second Amendment rights might be permissible, the question was at what point the acceptable became unconstitutional.

Assessing constitutionality according to Breyer required a balancing of interests, "with the interests protected by the Second Amendment on one side and the governmental public safety concerns on the other, the only question being whether the regulation at issue impermissibly burdens the former in the course of advancing the latter" (689). Far from being a novel approach to constitutional interpretation, the balancing of interests has traditionally been the way the Court has resolved such disputes.[41] Breyer, then, followed more closely than the majority the Court's traditional path for adjudicating constitutional disputes. "[I]mportant interests lie on both sides of the constitutional equation,"[42] Breyer argued, offering in advance a challenge to critics who might be tempted to claim his approach failed to take seriously Second Amendment rights. Crucially, however, Breyer argued that more than simply Second Amendment rights were at stake and worthy of consideration.

In his 2005 book, *Active Liberty*, Breyer emphasised the importance of "the freedom of the individual citizen to participate in the government and thereby to share with others the right to make or control the nation's public acts."[43] The views of the people, as expressed through their legislatures, are entitled to respect in a democratic system. While that does not mean the Court should always defer to legislative judgments, it does mean their views are entitled to a degree of consideration when their actions are challenged. "The majority's view cannot be correct unless it can show that the District's regulation is unreasonable or inappropriate in Second Amendment terms. This the majority cannot do," Breyer asserted in *Heller*.[44] Presenting in some detail statistical evidence on gun deaths and gun crime, Breyer showed the extent of the problem identified by the District. Discussing statistics on gun deaths generally, and accidental death and deaths of children in particular,

39 *District of Columbia v. Heller* 554 US 570, 683-6 (2008) (Justice Breyer, dissenting). The first challenged the majority's view that self-defence requires operable weapons.The second challenged those who argued the self-defence rationale permits unrestricted carrying of weapons in public. *District of Columbia v. Heller* 554 US 570, 683–686 (2008) (Justice Breyer, dissenting).

40 "And, in any event, as I have shown, the gunpowder-storage laws would have ***burdened*** armed self-defense, even if they did not completely ***prohibit*** it." *District of Columbia v. Heller* 554 US 570, 687 (2008) (Justice Breyer, dissenting – emphasis in original).

41 Traditionally the Court considers laws subject to constitutional challenge under one of three levels of scrutiny: strict scrutiny, intermediate scrutiny, or rational basis. While each begins with a different level of scepticism about the constitutionality of the challenged law, each category, in effect, weighs the balance between government needs and individual rights. Breyer's approach in *Heller* simply continued this approach.

42 *District of Columbia v. Heller*, 554 US 570, 689 (2008) (Justice Breyer, dissenting).

43 Stephen Breyer, *Active Liberty: Interpreting Our Democratic Constitution* (New York: Alfred A. Knopf, 2005), 3.

44 *District of Columbia v. Heller* 554 US 570, 681 (2008) (Justice Breyer, dissenting).

as well as figures about gun crime in urban areas, Breyer presented the District's law as a reasonable, common sense response to a growing problem. Recognising that debate existed about whether gun regulation actually reduced gun crime and gun death, Breyer nevertheless noted, "a legislature might respond, we want to make an effort to try to dry up that urban sea [of guns], drop by drop. And none of the studies can show that effort is not worthwhile." Indeed, not only did the studies fail to show the worth of the attempt, "they do not by themselves show that those judgments are incorrect."[45] While the statistics quoted by Breyer presented a picture of needless, tragic loss, his primary aim was to support his understanding of proper constitutional interpretation: "legislators, not judges, have primary responsibility for drawing policy conclusions from empirical fact. And, given that *constitutional allocation of decision-making* responsibility, the empirical evidence presented here is sufficient to allow a judge to reach a firm *legal* conclusion."[46] Because the legislative judgment was based on a reasonable (even if not necessarily correct) interpretation of the information available to it, that judgment was entitled to considerable weight when judging the law's constitutionality.

With his emphasis on public safety concerns, Breyer also drew on a constitutional understanding at least as old as the Second Amendment. Under the federal system, states maintained responsibility for protecting the health, safety, and welfare of their citizens: the so-called police powers of the states.[47] Long-recognised by the Court, police powers justifications offered a legitimate state interest, worthy of consideration. The role of police powers was evident in Breyer's discussion of the statistics considered by the District in passing the challenged law but was even clearer in his analysis of whether the burdens placed on individuals' self-defence rights by that law were the least-restrictive and proportionate to the aims sought. "[T]he very attributes that make handguns particularly useful for self-defense are also what make them particularly dangerous," Breyer observed. As a result, "although there may be less restrictive, *less effective* substitutes for an outright ban, there is no less restrictive *equivalent* of an outright ban."[48] The District had reasonably judged that the lives and safety of its citizens were in danger from uncontrolled access to and use of handguns and thus had sought to regulate that access and use; the District's interest in protecting the lives and safety of its citizens was legitimate; an alternative law could not achieve the same level of protection as the one passed by the District; thus, by implication, an alternative law would not permit the District to meet its police powers obligation. If taking police powers seriously, the law should stand since it represented both a reasonable judgment and the only way in which the District's aims could be fully met and its duties fully discharged.

Breyer's opinion thus offered a significant challenge to both the outcome and the methodology of the majority. That he was only able to convince three colleagues to join him in *Heller* should not detract from the importance of his approach. Recognising the importance of the history of the founding era, Breyer nevertheless rejected undue deference to that history. The history he did provide supported the fact revealed by a comparison of the opinions of the majority and Stevens: that history may be read in many different ways and

45 *District of Columbia v. Heller* 554 US 570, 703 (2008) (Justice Breyer, dissenting).

46 *District of Columbia v. Heller* 554 US 570, 704 (2008) (Justice Breyer, dissenting – first emphasis added, second in original).

47 Although the police powers doctrine is traditionally applied to states, in principle it can apply to any body with responsibility for governing: the council of the District of Columbia can thus have been considered as imbued with many of the same rights and responsibilities as other governments.

48 *District of Columbia v. Heller* 554 US 570, 711–712 (2008) (Justice Breyer, dissenting).

thus originalism's claim as a neutral method of constitutional interpretation could not be supported. Breyer made clear, however, that history should only be part of the enquiry, and not necessarily the definitive part. Instead, Breyer argued, the role of the Court was to balance the competing interests before it: the rights of citizens protected by the Second Amendment against the right and duty of states to protect their citizens under their police powers. In judging the correct balance, deference was due to the historical scope of the right, but also to the policy decisions of democratically elected legislatures in light of the evidence available to them. Acknowledging such an approach required an element of judicial judgment, Breyer nevertheless rejected the majority's characterisation of his approach as "judge-empowering" by asserting the limits placed on such judgment. In fact, he argued, his approach was far more transparent than that of the majority who made judgments about the value of particular historical sources and debates without clearly showing either that they were doing so or why and who failed to provide any reasoning justified by their own methods for the gun regulations they accepted. Breyer thus offered both a critique of originalist methodology and a workable alternative approach that the Court could follow in future cases. Whether or not Breyer is able to convince his colleagues to adopt his approach at some future point, his contribution to the debate demands more attention than it has to date received.

Conclusion

Frustrating gun rights supporters who saw in *Heller* an understanding of the Second Amendment that would free gun owners from most, if not all restrictions, lower courts have largely borne out Scalia's observation that Second Amendment rights are not unlimited. By March 2015, more than 900 gun-related cases had been heard at state and federal level, and while not all gun control laws survived the challenge, the vast majority were upheld by the courts.[49] (Significantly for originalism, most regulations were upheld under the "common use" doctrine or the list of possible exceptions offered by the *Heller* majority. Courts have shown little interest in following the historical approach to the Second Amendment laid out in *Heller* or the Supreme Court's 2010 ruling in *McDonald v. Chicago*, which applied the earlier ruling to the states.[50] The combination of heavy reliance on the non-originalist part of *Heller* and the relative absence of historical enquiry by lower courts challenges a reading of *Heller* as a triumph of originalism, suggesting instead that history remains only one of a number of factors taken into consideration by courts when assessing Second Amendment claims.[51] The Supreme Court's subsequent absence from the debate, rejecting review, as of the time of writing, in all Second Amendment cases since

49 Law Center to Prevent Gun Violence, "Post-*Heller* Litigation Summary: 31 March 2015," p. 1 (http://smartgunlaws.org/wp-content/uploads/2014/11/Post-Heller-Litigation-Summary-March-2015-Final-Version.pdf, accessed June 3, 2015).

50 See in particular, Allen Rostron, "Justice Breyer's Triumph in the Third Battle Over the Second Amendment," 80 *George Washington Law Review* 703–763 (April 2012), at 709. *McDonald v. Chicago* 561 US 742 (2010).

51 *Heller* continues to inspire political action, however, and gun rights advocates have had significant success, particularly in relation to rights outside the home. See recent legislative trends at Law Center to Prevent Gun Violence at http://smartgunlaws.org/category/gun-laws-policies/new-gun-legislation/ (accessed June 03, 2015) and the National Rifle Association's Institute for Legislative Action website at www.nraila.org.

McDonald, in effect, permitted the continuation of such approaches and their gradual embedding into state and federal law.[52]

Heller was thus not the triumph of originalism that many claimed it to be. The conflicting histories offered by Scalia and Stevens revealed that originalism could not do what its advocates claimed and offer a way of understanding the Second Amendment free from judicial judgment. The fundamental nature of historical scholarship made this impossible. Thus the originalists in the majority failed to be clear about the judgments they were making and offered, at best, only partial explanations for their reasoning. The failure of lower courts to make extensive use of *Heller*'s originalist reading suggests the competing interpretations of Second Amendment history offered by Scalia and Stevens served only to confuse rather than clarify. Scalia's majority opinion, with its inconsistent use of history and failure to provide historical support for either its favouring of handguns or for regulations on gun ownership, indicated that originalism alone could not address all contemporary Second Amendment concerns. In addition, the focus on originalism overlooks Breyer's contribution to the debate, which shows that there *is* a debate to be had, legally and politically. Legally, Breyer offered an alternative way to approach constitutional interpretation generally and Second Amendment jurisprudence specifically. And, as ongoing debates in the nation's legislatures show, the exact meaning of the Second Amendment remains an open question to be further explored: *Heller* did not and cannot end the debate. Gun rights and gun control supporters both point to the Constitution and to *Heller* in support of their position. Given this, the Second Amendment's relevance for twenty-first-century debates about guns and American society is ensured.

52 In the summer of 2015, Justices Thomas and Scalia dissented twice from the Court's rejection of gun law cases. See *Jackson v. San Francisco* 576 US _ (2015), docket no. 14–704 (Justice Thomas dissenting from denial of *certiorari*) and *Friedman v. City of Highland Park, Illinois* 577 US _ (2015), docket no. 15–133 (Justice Thomas dissenting from denial of certiorari). Two cases heard by the Court after *McDonald* addressed gun rights: *Abramski v. US* 573 US _ (2014), raised the question of whether one person may be prevented from buying a gun on behalf of someone else, so-called straw buyers, but did not involve a Second Amendment challenge; *Caetano v. Massachusetts* 577 US _ (2016) addressed the Second Amendment, but in the context of stun guns rather than firearms.

9 Mr Gingrich's bequest

Globalising the Second Amendment?

Peter Squires

'*The Second Amendment is an amendment for all mankind.*'[1]

Former Speaker of the US House of Representatives and one-time Republican presidential candidate, Newt Gingrich, made an unusual claim in 2012. Speaking at the National Rifle Association (NRA) Annual Convention in St. Louis, he argued that '*the Second Amendment* is an amendment *for all mankind.*' Hitherto, the debate about the Second Amendment had largely been concerned with the interpretation of this supposedly 'embarrassing' clause *within* the United States,[2] adding a global dimension to the debate might be seen as an entirely new departure in the gun debate. In fact, however, Gingrich's remarks represented a relatively late tactical foray into a debate that the NRA had been contesting for around a decade. Trying to raise the stakes with a bullish and opportunist gesture, Gingrich claimed that the NRA leadership had been 'too timid' – few people had ever suggested that before – and he went on to conclude his speech by noting that, should he ever successfully bid to enter the White House, he would work towards pushing the United Nations to extend the right to bear arms to the rest of the world, so that 'violent crimes like rape and child murder' might be prevented by armed citizens.[3]

The nature of Gingrich's remark plays into a number of the NRA's core concerns: in the first place, taking the fight to the United Nations which, since 2001, had been working towards a global policy to restrict the availability of small arms and light weapons (SALW); in the second place, to encourage more women to take up firearms for personal and family protection; and, in the third place, to reinforce the citizen protector model of gun ownership[4] that, later in the year, following the Sandy Hook school shooting, was succinctly

1 Cited in Jill Lepore, "The Lost Amendment", *New Yorker*, April 19, 2012 at www.newyorker.com/news/news-desk/the-lost-amendment (accessed March 15, 2017).

2 See Stanley Levinson, "The Embarrassing Second Amendment", 99 *The Yale Law Journal*, 637–659 (1989).

3 One of my fellow contributors to this volume, David Kopel, suggests that I have written 'too narrowly' as if 'self-defence rights were invented in America.' Readers may judge for themselves that this is clearly not the case; I even cite prominent NRA advocates who argue that 'self-defence rights are as old as civilisation.' I have no difficulty with that. On the contrary, my argument is simply that Newt Gingrich and others of his political and ideological persuasion are aiming at the globalisation of a largely mythical, contrived and seemingly absolute Second Amendment right to carry firearms for personal protection in the face of compelling global evidence of the damaging public policy consequences and inevitable harms.

4 Jennifer Carlson, "'I Don't Dial 911': American Gun Politics and the Problem of Policing", 52(6) *British Journal of Criminology*, 1113–1132 (2012).

voiced by Wayne LaPierre, Executive VP of the NRA: 'the only way to stop a bad guy with a gun . . . is a good guy with a gun.'[5]

The movement for gun rights had been successful on a number of domestic fronts, culminating in the Heller and MacDonald Supreme Court judgements which, in 2008 and 2010 respectively, struck down wide-ranging firearms prohibitions in Washington, DC, and Chicago. A growing majority of states had passed mandatory, shall-issue, concealed firearm carry permit laws to citizens wanting a firearm for personal protection. Many had also passed versions of the 'no duty to retreat' or 'Castle Doctrine' law, which had lately become notorious following the fatal shooting of young African American, Trayvon Martin, by neighborhood watch co-ordinator George Zimmerman in 2011. In other states, legislation was under consideration to disallow 'gun-free zones' on, for instance, university college campuses and, in other places, Michigan and Texas included, groups of citizens were actively taking their open carry firearm protests to the streets, demanding the right to openly carry their firearms while out shopping, eating in restaurants, collecting children from school or visiting national parks.

In the international political arena, however, it was a rather different story. Following mass shooting incidents in a number of countries,[6] where tighter firearms controls were becoming associated with reducing rates of gun violence, perhaps most obviously the United Kingdom, Australia, Canada, South Africa and Brazil, a global gun control movement had begun to take shape connecting with the pioneering work of peacemaking non-governmental organisations (NGOs) in war-torn parts of the 'global south' – especially in Africa and Latin America. Gun control, human rights and economic development organisations in societies suffering the consequences of small arms proliferation came increasingly to recognise that national solutions for gun crime would need to be matched by concerted international action.[7] Likewise, disarmament and development workers in some of the dangerous locations where most of the killing occurs, appreciated the need for more effective regulation of the supply side to stem the flows of firearms, which undermined their efforts and threatened their lives. Disarmament, demobilisation and reintegration (DDR) could no longer be simply about fire-fighting and peace-keeping. Important as these issues were, DDR needed to look forwards to more globally relevant security and development strategies.[8] In similar fashion, the arms control and international relations research communities increasingly came to acknowledge the rather porous character of much existing arms control and enforcement practice, including fraudulent end-user certification practices.[9] As Greene and Marsh have noted of the research base, policy-making and enforcement in the fields of small arms and light weapon governance (including DDR, post-conflict management, security sector and arms trade reform, the removal of weapon surpluses and regulation of stockpiles, criminal trafficking and domestic law enforcement) needed to be substantially more 'joined-up'.[10]

5 Cited in Peter Overbury, "NRA: 'Only Thing that Stops a Bad Guy With a Gun Is a Good Guy With a Gun'", *NPR*, December 21 2012 at www.npr.org/2012/12/21/167824766/nra-only-thing-that-stops-a-bad-guy-with-a-gun-is-a-good-guy-with-a-gun.

6 A. Lankford, "Public Mass Shooters and Firearms: A Cross-National Study of 171 Countries", 31(2) *Violence and Victims* 187–199 (2016).

7 See chapter 8 of Peter Squires, *Gun Crime in Global Contexts* (London: Routledge, 2014), 275–320.

8 Michael Bourne and Owen Greene, "Governance and Control of SALW After Armed Conflicts", in Owen Greene and Nic Marsh (eds.), *Small Arms, Crime and Conflict: Global Governance and the Threat of Armed Violence* (London: Routledge, 2012), 183–206.

9 Mark Bromley and Hugh Griffiths, "End-User Certificates: Improving Standards to Prevent Diversion. *SIPRI Insights on Peace and Security* 2010/3, March 2010 at http://books.sipri.org/files/insight/SIPRIInsight1003.pdf (accessed March 15, 2017).

10 Greene and Marsh, "Introduction", in Greene and Marsh, *Small Arms, Crime and Conflict*, 1–20.

United Nations: action on small arms

Accordingly, from the late 1990s, the international arms control community – national gun control groups, NGOs working in the field of peace, security and development, weapons trade researchers (such as IANSA, the Small Arms Survey, Amnesty International, Oxfam and War on Want) had been working through the United Nations to build an international framework for global arms control. In 2001, this was accepted as a 'Programme of Action' for the UN in much the same way as the UN had earlier sought to restrict the distribution of nuclear and biological weapons, cluster munitions and landmines. The critical issue in respect of 'small arms and light weapons' is that these munitions were actually responsible for far greater rates of death and injury than the others put together. After much debate, periodic review conferences and diplomatic wrangling, the UN finally agreed, by an overwhelming majority vote, an Arms Trade Treaty in 2013 which was designed to bring visibility and accountability to the international trade in SALW, while preventing the distribution of weapons to 'non-state actors'.[11] By late 2013, the Treaty had been signed by 114 UN member states, although incorporated into the national legislation of only a few of these. Throughout the early UN deliberations on the planned UN Programme of Action on SALW, and until 2008 and the election of Barack Obama as US President, US negotiators at the UN conferences had vehemently sought to block the arms control proposals, which they had wilfully misconceived as a threat to civilian ownership of firearms in the United States. A delegation of US negotiators, led by US Under-Secretary of State John Bolton and supported by a number of prominent members of the NRA were firmly opposed to any conception of 'small arms and light weapons' that went beyond a narrow band of military specification weapons.[12] They also opposed the proposed restrictions on the transfer of arms to so-called non-state groups, arguing that this amounted to a challenge to the idea of civilian gun ownership cherished by the Second Amendment. In fact, nothing could have been further from the truth. The aim of the Arms Trade Treaty was to render visible, accountable and subject to law, *large scale* arms transfers rather than individual weapon sales; the treaty aimed to prevent the clandestine and criminal distribution of firearms to terrorists, insurgents and organised criminal groups. The NRA's position on the arms trade treaty was one of the clearest indicators that the organisation looked primarily to the fortunes of the gun industry rather than US gun owners. It was chiefly concerned with proposals to restrict the free market in guns, nothing in the UN Programme of Action sought to restrict private citizens owning, buying or selling individual firearms.

Ironically, the NRA's stance appeared to tolerate the distribution of firearms to terrorist and insurgent groups, thereby linking it ideologically with the far-right libertarian and insurrectionist militias which had periodically sought to disaffect, by force of arms, from the US federal government such as at Waco, Texas, in 1993.[13] Furthermore, the disingenuous suggestion that only 'military specification' weapons – fully automatic machine guns – were appropriate to be covered by the trade ban ignored the fact that for years US gun manufacturers had been responsible for the substantial 'militarization' of the stock of weapons

11 Sarah Parker, "Breaking New Ground: The Arms Trade Treaty, in the Graduate Institute, Geneva", *Small Arms Survey 2014* (Cambridge: Cambridge University Press, 2014).

12 David Atwood and Owen Greene, "Reaching Consensus in New York: the 2001 UN Small Arms Conference", *Small Arms Survey 2002: Counting the Human Cost* (Oxford: Oxford University Press, 2002), 219.

13 Joshua Horwitz and Casey Anderson, *Guns, Democracy and the Insurrectionist Idea* (Ann Arbor: University of Michigan Press, 2009).

owned by US citizens. As Diaz has explained, this is precisely the way that gun industry marketing works. Firearms manufacturers produce weapons attempting to win government, military and law enforcement contracts. They often sell these weapons at reduced, almost 'loss-leader', prices, confident that, in the much bigger civilian market, the advertising tag 'as used by the FBI' will garner many more sales.[14] The more that 'elite' military units procure specialist weapons, the more that the general public appears to want them. From the manufacturer's point of view, in an already highly saturated weapons market, with every potential gun owner accounted for and each of them averaging up to eight guns,[15] the only way to expand the market, aside from niche marketing firearms to women (which began in earnest after the 1980s[16]) and special interest groups (for example, collectors, 'cowboy-action' shooters and hunters), has been to promise more and greater firepower, presumably to face a more substantially imagined criminal or terrorist threat.

At the first UN conference on the Programme of Action on Small Arms in 2001, Bolton, accompanied by a number of senior members of the NRA laid out the US/NRA position. In a tough-talking, no-nonsense, speech in which he specifically referred to the US Second Amendment; he argued that the proposed programme was flawed, in that it confused issues which should properly be dealt with by sovereign governments with those more appropriate to the UN. The United States, he argued, defined SALW, strictly, as *military grade* weapons and would never support: proposals to restrict the legal manufacture of SALW or their legal trade; proposals restricting civilian firearm ownership; or any measures to prevent the trade in SALW to non-state actors.[17] He opposed the idea of a mandatory Review Conference and urged the UN to restrict the arms control advocacy role of NGOs.[18] As we have noted, however, when Bolton spoke, the entry of military grade assault rifles into the US civilian market had already begun, and by 2001, the United States was over halfway through a ten-year federal ban on the civilian sale of new assault rifles (only new sales were banned, ownership of *existing* assault rifles was permitted and there was no buy-back, such as in Australia). The assault weapon ban, which was initially passed by the Clinton Administration, lapsed in 2004 under George W. Bush.[19] Since 2004, assault weapons have featured in some of the US most murderous recurring mass shootings – in Aurora, Colorado (2011); Newtown, Connecticut (2012); San Bernadino, California (2015) and, most recently, Orlando, Florida, (2016).

14 See Tom Diaz, *Making a Killing: The Business of Guns in America* (New York: The New Press, 2009) and *The Last Gun: How Changes in the Gun Industry Are Killing Americans and What It Will Take to Stop It* (New York: The New Press, 2013).

15 US General Social Survey data reveal that whilst, in the mid-1990s, the typical US gun owner owned between four to five firearms, by 2015 this figure had risen to an average of eight per gun-owning household. This conforms to a national trend in which the overall number of gun owners is falling, but those owning guns have more of them. See C. Ingraham, "The Average Gun Owner Now Owns 8 Guns – Double What It Used to Be", *The Washington Post*, 21 October 2015. See also L. Hepburn, M. Miller, D. Azrael, and D. Hemenway, "The US Gun Stock: Results From the 2004 National Firearms Survey", 31(1) *Injury Prevention* 15–19 (2007).

16 Paxton Quigley, *Armed and Female: Twelve Million American Women Own Guns, Should You?* (New York: St. Martins Paperbacks, 1989).

17 Atwood and Greene, "Reaching Consensus in New York", 219.

18 John R. Bolton, "Statement Made at the United Nations Conference on the Illicit Trade in Small Arms and Light Weapons in All Its Aspects", 9 July, US department of State Archive at http://2001-2009.state.gov/t/us/rm/janjuly/4038.htm (accessed March 15, 2017).

19 Christopher Koper, "America's Experience With the Federal Assault Weapons Ban, 1994–2004: Key Findings and Implications", in D.W. Webster and J.S.Vernick (ed.), *Reducing Gun Violence in America: Informing Policy With Evidence and Analysis* (Baltimore: Johns Hopkins University Press, 2013), 157–172.

The arguments put forwards by Bolton were no surprise to seasoned firearms control advocates; he drew upon the positions previously adopted by the World Forum on Shooting Activities (WFSA) established as a gun industry lobby organisation which had obtained NGO status for its UN negotiations. At a meeting in London, 2001, the WFSA had devoted itself to considering how to distinguish 'civilian appropriate' firearms from what they termed 'weapons of war'. Encouraged by the NRA members present, they eventually settled upon the idea of 'fully automatic firing' as the solitary relevant distinguishing feature of a weapon of war. Ignoring legal norms, practice and precedent and endorsing perhaps the most restrictive definition of military weapons possible, they advocated semi-automatic rifles for civilian ownership despite the fact that these were already prohibited in many jurisdictions – including the United States (at the time), the United Kingdom and Australia. Perhaps it goes without saying, but this definition of 'civilian appropriate' firearms was highly favourable to the US gun industry seeking new sales in a crowded domestic market, especially after 2004 when the federal assault weapon sales ban lapsed.

The guns rights movement: culture, identity and politics

Responding to what they represented as a global United Nations inspired global threat to civilian gun ownership and a challenge to the Second Amendment and Constitution, US firearms lobbyists began to mobilise with a global discourse of their own. This argument sought to transform a national – Common Law inspired – right to self-defence into a universal right to possess the weapons by which that right might most effectively be pursued. Implicitly, thereby, they centred the Second Amendment on self-defence gun ownership (rather than hunting and sports shooting). Over time, various NRA-aligned writers have attempted to develop this argument, and it is possible to detect, in many parts of the world, how this idea has achieved a degree of 'cultural purchase' where private citizens have responded to perceived vulnerabilities and insecurities by self-arming. At the same time, this globalised advocacy for the Second Amendment combines with more subtle cultural influences, such as forms of cultural imperialism disseminating sovereign individualist Second Amendment values facilitating the weaponisation of diverse communities around the globe by reference to a US-led universal neo-liberalism of the gun. As O'Neill has argued, although separated by culture, continents and oceans, 'white male identity politics' exercises a tenacious global grip. It is, he claims, a politics that the NRA itself has done a great deal to sustain.[20] Cukier and Sheptycki have similarly argued that what they term the 'global carriers of gun culture', by which they refer to 'technology, media and ideology' especially Hollywood movies, television cop shows, violent video games and popular music culture, have served to '(re)produce the links between masculinity, affluence and firearms' across many diverse cultures.[21] For a particular illustration of this, anthropologist Paul Richards discovered how repeated viewings of *Rambo* videos, seemed a particular, if perverse, source of inspiration to the young guerrilla fighters involved in the Sierra Leone civil war.[22]

20 Kevin O'Neill, "Armed Citizens and the Stories They Tell: The National Rifle Association's Achievement of Terror and Masculinity", 9 *Men and Masculinities* 457–475 (2007).

21 Rodrigo Bascuñán Christian Pearce, *Enter the Babylon System: Unpacking Gun Culture From Samuel Colt to 50 Cent* (Toronto: Random House, 2008). Wendy Cukier and James Sheptycki, "Globalization of Gun Culture: Transnational Reflections on Pistolization and Masculinity, Flows and Resistance", 40 *International Journal of Law, Crime and Justice* 3–19 (2012).

22 Paul Richards, *Fighting for the Rain Forest: War, Youth and Resources in Sierra Leone* (Oxford: The International Africa Institute, 1996).

At times, the cultural imperialism script has been specifically projected *outwards* to influence gun control debates in other societies. The NRA have been known to weigh in to support Canadian gun rights and help overturn gun regulations in Canada. In the wake of the Port Arthur Massacre in Australia, the organization donated money to support Australian firearms enthusiasts campaign against the proposed new Australian gun laws). Most significantly of all, the late shifts in voting intentions which changed the outcome of the 2005 Brazilian referendum on firearms controls have been attributed both to NRA money and campaign and advertising know-how. The fearful middle classes were apparently convinced by NRA propaganda that they had a lot to lose if they gave up their guns.[23]

The NRA's wider cultural and political script, as Melzer argues, has also exercised a powerful influence back in the United States too. Melzer approaches the NRA through a social movement perspective and, like Carlson, characterizes the organization by virtue of its membership demographics. In this sense, the NRA most completely represents a white, male, middle-aged, middle-class, suburban and, often, ex-military, population.[24] Carlson draws upon research which shows that white Detroit males, especially those who articulate racist views 'are more likely to own firearms for self-protection against crime'. She goes further, arguing that 'guns are socially deployed to express anxieties among white, male, conservative gun owners . . . [providing] a means for white, conservative heterosexual men to reclaim masculine privilege as part of a broader conservative "“backlash” against New Deal politics.'[25] Like Street's analysis of the 'Conservative backlash' which settled upon the movie cop figure of 'Dirty' Harry Callahan (played by Clint Eastwood) as the putative, maverick, big gun toting, 'solution' to both crime in the streets and the cultural crisis of contemporary American white masculinity.[26] Melzer makes the point that the NRA has successfully managed to represent the threat to gun ownership – via gun control – as a threat to American manhood and the freedom-loving US way of life.[27] In this sense, every United Nations' arms control initiative, rather like every gun control proposal, can be represented by the organisation as an attack on freedom and masculinity; as Melzer argues this assists the NRA leadership in both its recruitment campaigns and its fundraising. It helps enormously, as we shall see, if the UN can be represented as alien, socialist, bureaucratic and fundamentally un-American. Inadvertently, the UN has become an effective recruiting sergeant for the NRA. It also is this which has enabled the NRA, firearms industry-backed, four-million-members strong, powerful lobbyist and firmly positioned within the Conservative mainstream, to successfully represent itself as part of a beleaguered and misunderstood minority. This manner of representation, what might be referred to as the NRA's 'Alamo mindset', comprises a subtle brand of historical amnesia and creative myth-making. Taken together, each of these elements featured significantly when the NRA turned towards a global politics to contest the UN's emerging arms control agenda.

23 Simon Chapman, *Over Our Dead Bodies. Port Arthur and Australia's Fight for Gun Control* (Pluto Press/Sydney University Press, 2013). On the politics of gun control in Brazil, see Donna Goldstein, "Gun Politics: Reflections on Brazil's Failed Gun Ban Referendum in the Rio de Janeiro Context", in Charles F. Springwood (ed.), *Open Fire: Understanding Global Gun Cultures* (Oxford: Berg, 2007), 28–41 and Roxanna Cavalcanti, "Armed Violence and the Politics of Gun Control in Brazil: An Analysis of the 2005 Referendum", *Bulletin of Latin American Research* (No. 1, 2017).

24 Scott Melzer, *Gun Crusaders: The NRA's Culture War* (New York: New York University Press, 2009).

25 Carson, "I Don't Dial 911", 1115, 1117.

26 Joe Street, *Dirty Harry's America: Clint Eastwood, Harry Callahan, and the Conservative Backlash* (Gainesville: University Press of Florida, 2016)

27 Melzer, *Gun Crusaders.*

Aside from political forays into other country's firearms control debates, as referred to earlier, the NRA's global politics has taken broadly three principal forms. In the first place, there has been a concerted attempt to prove that gun control does not and cannot work – anywhere. This forms an important part of the academic war of position vis-à-vis international efforts at firearm violence reduction. If NRA scholars can show that firearms controls have been ineffective in other societies (typically societies where firearms are less prevalent and the laws already less permissive), often in the face of evidence pointing clearly in the opposing direction, it follows that the case for gun control in the United States itself might appear rather less compelling.

Academic self-defence wars

One of the first commentators deploying this line of argument was US historian Joyce Lee Malcolm, author of an erudite analysis of the way in which the 1688 English Bill of Rights served as a foundation for what became the US Second Amendment. However, fresh from advocating, on BBC Radio 4's Woman's Hour, that women should carry firearms in their own homes to protect themselves against the risk of domestic violence, in the weeks after the 2003 New Year's Eve 'drive-by' murders in Birmingham, she contributed an 'opinion' piece to a BBC news website. The article was provocatively titled 'Why Britain Needs More Guns'.[28]

The article began with the old NRA bumper sticker assertion 'if guns are outlawed only outlaws will have guns' and proceeded to relate 'leaping' rates of gun crime with the British government's seemingly perverse desire to seek to tighten already strict gun laws. Apparently, 'for 80 years the safety of the British People has been staked on the premise that fewer private guns means less crime, indeed that any weapons in the hands of men and women, however law abiding, pose a danger.'[29] In fact, she continued, the British had been deluding themselves, it was mere wishful thinking to assume that society could ensure the protection of private citizens, for general disarmament had not just failed to stem a rising tide of criminal violence, but far worse, it had rendered British citizens fatally vulnerable.

Malcolm's BBC opinion piece drew upon her book, published the year before: *Guns and Violence: The English Experience.*[30] At first, the historical discussion is wide-ranging and informative, exploring the gradual curtailment of private rights of redress and, from the early nineteenth century, the rise of a collective police power, accruing unto itself, in a typically British *collective paternalist* fashion, a monopoly of legitimate force in civil society: the Queen's Peace rather than the citizen's right. Unfortunately, Malcolm's analysis collapses headlong into a crude single-factor explanation of twentieth-century rates of violence. Apparently, Malcolm argues, beyond all else, interpersonal violence was kept in check by widespread civilian firearms ownership before the First World War. Thus, 'the nineteenth century ended with firearms plentifully available while rates of armed crime had been declining and were to reach a record low.'[31]

Malcolm presents widespread civilian firearms ownership as the crucial guarantee of responsible and democratic civilisation, a legacy that successive British Governments have

28 Joyce Malcolm, *To Keep and Bear Arms: The Evolution of an Anglo-American Right*, (Cambridge, MA: Harvard University Press, 1994). For Malcolm's interview on *BBC Radio 4* at www.bbc.co.uk/radio4/womanshour/2002_27_fri_01.shtml (accessed March 15, 2017). Joyce Malcolm, "Why Britain Needs More Guns" at http://news.bbc.co.uk/1/hi/uk_politics/2656875.stm (accessed March 15, 2017).

29 Malcolm, "Why Britain Needs More Guns".

30 Joyce Malcolm, *Guns and Violence : The English Experience* (Cambridge, MA: Harvard University Press, 2002).

31 Ibid., 130.

criminally squandered. The 1953 Prevention of Crime Act is singled out for particular attention as the key piece of twentieth-century legislation effectively ratifying the new paternalistic relationship which had gradually and almost imperceptibly replaced English common law rights of self-defence. Rather than a response to popular concerns about rising post-war violence and the use of weapons by criminal gangs, Malcolm presents the primary purpose of the legislation, which created a new offence of carrying offensive or 'potentially offensive' weapons, as establishing a new relationship between people, police and Government, criminalising the carriage of weapons and thereby transferring to the police 'sole responsibility for the protection of individuals'. And in so doing, she claims, it effectively outlawed an older common law right to self-defence.[32]

There are undoubtedly a number of important issues in critical historical criminology to be developed here. Unfortunately, Malcolm, being so keen to relate the whole of Britain's post-war, late modern, crime increases to successive governments' obsession with outlawing private firearms ownership, misses them. Rather tellingly, when discussing the rising crime rates and tightening gun controls of post-war Britain, she comments on Radzinowicz's important international analysis of the growth of crime, published in the late 1970s). 'Neither Radzinowicz nor other criminologists cited the availability of guns or other weapons as a factor in either the cause of crime or its deterrence.' No doubt, one may be inclined to think, this was for good reason. In fact, it is only Malcolm's desire to exonerate firearms as crime facilitators and herald them as guarantors of peace and freedom instead (an American ideology, after all) that leads her, quite wrongly, to install them at all as major factors in any account of twentieth-century British crime problems. Therefore, her claim that 'guns seldom contributed to violent crime [but] they may have helped keep it in check by deterring would-be burglars and muggers' is quite unrecognisable as a commentary on post-war Britain.[33]

This is not the place to refute all of Malcolm's claims; suffice it to say, her attempt to stretch a single-factor explanation for crime trend variations over several centuries gave a prominence to firearms as both facilitators of crime and as benefactors of peace and civilisation that they never have had in the British experience. Of central importance in her argument is a core ideological commitment to civilian ownership of firearms for self-defence. All would be well, according to Malcolm, if Britain took a lesson from the United States and reinstated a right to private firearms ownership for self-defence: 'in England, fewer guns have meant more crime. In America, more guns have meant less crime,'[34] and she draws approvingly on the work of John Lott, which is discredited in the eyes of many.[35] Malcolm, therefore goes further than many British firearms lobbyists ever dared during the post-Dunblane debates about handgun prohibition.[36] Then, most British shooters were very careful to

32 Ibid., 173.

33 Ibid., 168, 166. See Leon Radzinowicz and Joan King, *The Growth of Crime* (Harmondsworth: Penguin, 1977).

34 Malcolm, *Guns and Violence*, 252.

35 John Lott, *More Guns, Less Crime: Understanding Crime and Gun Control Laws* (Chicago: University of Chicago Press, 1998).

36 Lord Cullen, in his report on the Dunblane shooting incident (1996) briefly explored the 'net benefit' or utilitarian crime reduction argument in favour of civilian gun ownership, that widespread gun ownership prevented more crime and violence than it facilitated. This argument was summarily dismissed by Cullen. 'In this country the possession of firearms for self-defence has not been regarded for many years as a "good reason" for their possession and there never has been a policy of facilitating, let alone encouraging, the acquisition of firearms to discourage crime or limit its effects.' And, he concluded, accordingly. 'I do not see anything in the 'net benefit' argument that is relevant to this country.' See www.gov.scot/Resource/Doc/158868/0043149.pdf (accessed March 15, 2017), 112, para. 9.29).

develop a case almost entirely around the preservation of *sports* shooting.[37] Now, however, having decisively lost that argument, the stakes are being raised by American advocates engaging in a more global debate about arms control and the self-defence and self-determination arguments are surfacing too.

Malcolm's arguments are not about sports shooting at all, nor was she simply arguing a right to armed self-defence, her claim is that attempts to prohibit firearms ownership actually provoke greater violence and illegality and are, in effect, inevitably counter-productive. On this, she added her voice to a growing chorus of commentators arguing, in effect, for the 'human right' to bear arms. Unfortunately for Malcolm, timing also worked against her analysis. Although there was a short, sharp, upwards spike in gun-enabled crime in the four or five years following the British handgun bans, attributable, primarily, to an increase in street gang activity in the later 1990s and an unprecedented influx of 'junk guns' (imitations, conversions, recycled and modified air weapons and BB guns),[38] the publication of her book coincided with the beginning of a decade-long decline in the rates of gun crime in England and Wales, during which time firearm-enabled offences fell by close to 50 per cent. Furthermore, Malcolm's more general arguments about the crime suppressing character of civilian gun ownership failed to acknowledge that by 2002, overall crime in England and Wales had *already* been falling for some six years. There is certainly more than a little truth in the argument, most recently developed by Jock Young[39] that criminologists generally failed to anticipate and explain the post-war crime explosion until it was actually happening, and that they likewise failed to predict or, subsequently, satisfactorily account for, the more recent global crime drop.[40] However, not unlike Malcolm's rather misplaced critique of Radzinowicz and King, no credible social scientist, even in the United States where firearms clearly matter far more, has attempted to explain the evolution of complex crime trends entirely by the prevalence of firearms in a given population. On the contrary, beyond the need to demonstrate the failure of gun control in Britain, although rather in the face of the evidence to the contrary, Malcolm's book was little more than a further assertion of the NRA belief that the Britain, and beyond that the world at large, would be a safer place with more firearms.

Hard on the heels of Joyce Malcolm's foray into British gun control politics, in 2005 a group of US legal and criminological scholars, many of them broadly sympathetic to firearm rights, gathered at the George Mason University School of Law, in Arlington, Virginia, to debate self-defence, human rights and the right to bear arms.[41] The subject matter of

37 Peter Squires, *Gun Culture or Gun Control?* (London: Routledge, 2000).

38 For a fuller account of the growth and significance of this developing 'junk gun' market in the United Kingdom, refer to Squires, *Gun Crime in Global Contexts.*

39 Jock Young, *The Criminological Imagination* (Cambridge: Polity Press, 2011).

40 See Alfred Blumstein and Joel Wallman, *The Crime Drop in America* (Cambridge: Cambridge University Press, 2000); Andrew Karmen, *New York Murder Mystery: The True Story Behind the Crime Crash of the 1990s* (New York: New York University Press, 2000), and Jan Van Dijk et al., *The International Crime Drop: New Directions in Research* (Basingstoke: Palgrave MacMillan, 2012).

41 The symposium was named in honour of Mrs Bessie Jones, a 92-year-old wheelchair-bound black woman who, in 1993, shot and killed a youthful intruder who refused to leave her Chicago home. The youth was killed with an unregistered .38 calibre revolver she kept hidden behind a sofa cushion and which Mrs Jones had been given by her husband, shortly before he died in 1945. A number of participants at the conference unhelpfully compared the case with that of Norfolk, United Kingdom, farmer Tony Martin who, during 1999, had shot two burglars. In contrast to Mrs Jones, Martin was convicted of murder, later amended to manslaughter, and served a three-year prison sentence. There are significant factual differences between the cases, Martin effectively ambushed the burglars with an illegal pump action shotgun and shot them while they were attempting to escape. The case also raised issues about the police response

the symposium concerned the claimed human right to bear arms in pursuit of personal self-defence and collective self-determination. The issues entailed were often complex, multi-layered, intricate, and contested with scholars, often versed in different domestic, constitutional and international law traditions or academic specialties often arguing past one another. Nevertheless, the broad thrust of the developing arguments were broadly continuous with a growing current of American legal and firearm advocacy scholarship that, over the past three decades, had sought to effect a fundamental reinterpretation of the Second Amendment to the US Constitution. These issues involved core questions about how the Second Amendment might be interpreted; the proper scope for 'interpretative activism' in historical constitutional studies; what the original framers *might* have intended; and how, 200 years on, the Second Amendment might seem something of an anachronism.[42]

In any event, by the end of the twentieth century, a substantial body of legal and historical scholarship, including Malcolm's 1994 book, had conspired to develop an argument which had been successful to the extent that the so-called individual rights view of the Second Amendment had now become the 'standard' interpretation.[43] Prominent amongst many similar historical and legal revisionist writings were contributions by Don Kates, Stanley Levinson and Clayton Cramer, all of whom argued for an individualist interpretation of the right to bear arms.[44] As Winkler has argued, this growing body of legal scholarship reinforced and emboldened NRA gun rights advocacy, contributing to the 1986 Handgun Owners Protection Act and eventually paving the way towards the *Heller* and *McDonald* Supreme Court judgements that overturned generic handgun prohibitions first in Washington, DC (2008), and later in Chicago (2010).[45] For the benefit of the firearm advocacy scholars gathered in George Mason University law school in 2004, Nicholas Johnson reiterated the essential connectedness of this growing body of 'Second Amendment history and theory' with the fundamental human right of self-defence. 'The ancient right of self-defense' he argued, 'is in the first echelon of fundamental constitutional rights to "liberty" . . . [it lies] at the core of a proper understanding of the Second Amendment.'[46]

Johnson proceeds to develop a closely developed case, following Blackstone. While the US Constitution may not be the *original* source of the right to self-defence, taking together the Second, Ninth and Fourteenth Amendments, it is abundantly clear that the Constitution implicitly endorses this pre-existing and inalienable right, the most fundamental of all rights, argues Johnson. However, recognising that the Constitution does not dwell upon the kinds of low-level and 'private altercations' in which self-defence issues may sometimes arise, or, indeed, many other of the private tastes of individuals, he proceeds to distinguish

---

and their 'failure to protect', which have arisen subsequently in both the United Kingdom and United States.

42 Mark Tushnet, *Out of Range: Why the Constitution Can't End the Battle Over Guns* (Oxford: Oxford University Press, 2007).

43 Glenn Reynolds, "A Critical Guide to the Second Amendment", 62 *Tennessee Law Review* 461–475 (1995).

44 Drawing upon research by Carl Bogus, Jill Lepore has argued that 'at least sixteen of the twenty-seven law-review articles published between 1970 and 1989 that were favorable to the N.R.A.'s interpretation of the Second Amendment were "written by lawyers who had been directly employed by or represented the N.R.A. or other gun-rights organizations."' "The Lost Amendment", *New Yorker Magazine*, April 19th 2012. See also Adam Winkler, *Gunfight: The Battle Over the Right to Bear Arms in America* (New York, Norton & Co. 2011), 96–97.

45 Winkler, *Gunfight*. For a fuller contextual discussion of these themes and issues refer to Squires, *Gun Control in Global Context*, 146–156.

46 Nicholas Johnson, "Self-Defense?", 2(2) *Journal of Law, Economics and Policy* 187–212 (2006).

those areas that a state might legitimately interfere with and those it should not. Thus, the state might punish people for crimes committed, it might confiscate their (illegally obtained) property, or even attempt to make it more difficult or expensive for people to 'obtain or use particular defensive technologies'. But what it cannot do, according to Johnson, is prohibit a right to self-defence. 'Self-defense is like breathing', he continues, 'it is like the multitude of rights that . . . were part of the innumerable rights retained by the people'.[47] When we set aside questions of technology (in this case firearms), Johnson claims, few people – including even the United Nations – have difficulty with this idea of self-defence and where the United States permits citizens (those not disqualified) to own firearms, it must follow that those weapons be available to citizens to effectively exercise this right of self-defence. He concludes by setting this rights claim in a global context by quoting from the 1948 UN Charter itself. 'Nothing in the Charter shall impair the inherent right of individual or collective self-defense' (UN Charter, 1948, Article 51). In this fashion, a direct link was drawn between NRA advocacy for the Second Amendment and international human rights and, in turn, by appearing to restrict firearm ownership, sales and transfers, amongst citizens, the UN is construed to be impeding their right to self-defence.[48]

In light of this, it fell to Lance Stell to attempt to develop the self-defence rights argument specifically in respect of the ownership and possession of handguns, the self-defence 'weapon of choice'. Unfortunately, however, for the same reasons that it features as the self-defence weapon of choice (size, weight, ease of concealment and of use) the handgun is also the offender's weapon of choice, the weapon most likely to be employed in both violent and fatal assaults, statistically, it is America's most lethal weapon. Much is made in gun control debates of the gun rights advocacy claim, a so-called 'truth', that if firearms were prohibited, offenders – people who readily break laws – would be the last to give them up (*if guns were outlawed, only outlaws would have guns*). Leaving aside the reasonable objection that the groups 'criminal' and 'law abiding' are far from being watertight categories, similar weight is seldom given to another claim, no less verifiable, that if the population at large were readily armed, potential offenders would find it so much easier to acquire weapons.[49]

Notwithstanding such objections, Stell's central argument made the point that it would be an affront to justice for states to so tightly restrict the carrying of handguns that they were not effectively available for personal defence against attack. This, he argued, is especially the case where police protection entails no-one a 'right to protection' and correspondingly entails no particular duty to protect anyone at all (the police are not responsible for crime). In fact, recent developments in British law, heralded by the 2012 White Paper *Putting Victims First*, and carried into law by the *Anti-Social Behaviour, Crime and Policing Act* 2014, extend the police duty of care where victims are known to

47 And as guaranteed by the Ninth Amendment. Johnson, "Self-Defence?", 193, 194.

48 These arguments were taken up by other contributors to the symposium. Cerone, for example, disputed Johnson's claim and argued instead 'there is no norm of international law providing a human right to self-defense' adding that Article 51 refers only to self-defence actions by states (John Cerone, "Is there a Human Right of Self-Defense?", 2 *J.L. Econ. & Pol'y* 319, 311–344, 319–320 (2006). The only exception to this principle, he suggested, was the norm of international criminal law 'requiring state or international criminal courts to recognize self-defense as a basis for excluding criminal responsibility.' However, as he continued, 'such a norm could not reasonably be construed to imply a right of access to means of physically defending oneself' (329).

49 Lance Stell, "Self-Defense and Handgun Rights", 2(2) *Journal of Law, Economics and Policy* 265–308 (1996).

be particularly vulnerable or subject to hate-based victimisation. Such a principle stands in significant contrast to US law where, Stell argued, 'even when a court-ordered restraining order against a violent spouse declares that the police "shall" enforce its provisions by arresting and jailing him, the order's beneficiary has no reliance right to its enforcement' (*Ibid*, 266). The gap between the duties assumed by the police in the different jurisdictions is for Stell, 'compensated for' by permitting law-abiding private citizens in the United States access to self-defence handguns. A failure to allow citizens to own firearms, he suggested, is tantamount to the state engaging in a policy of de facto 'scarcity gun control' (making firearms excessively difficult to acquire), which, by disempowering potential victims, effectively allows criminal aggression to lie where it falls.

The final stages of Stell's arguments wove together a critique of Zimring and Hawkins' comparative and international analysis of firearms and violent crime: *Crime is not the problem*[50] an assessment of police protective capacity, and broad acceptance of Lott's *More Guns: Less Crime* thesis, referred to previously. And the conclusion he came to was that states must respect and protect equally 'the fundamental right to bodily integrity, which includes a fundamental, serious right to self-defense'.[51] And where they cannot afford such a guarantee, which is to say, in most jurisdictions around the world, they should, at the very least, not interfere with a citizen's capacity to protect himself or herself. In other words, 'prohibitory gun laws directly implicate the state's duty to respect equally each person's interest in bodily integrity. If the state bans civilian possession of 'equalizers', . . . it forbids those who are resultingly made vulnerable to offset the criminological effects of natural inequalities (of being frailer, smaller and weaker).[52] In international ideological perspective, Stell's analysis complements that of Malcolm's 2002 commentary, in the way that both construe gun regulation as a constraint on citizen freedom, especially so in an era (the second half of the twentieth century) of rising crime and seemingly diminishing police effectiveness.

These two issues, rising crime and perceptions of police effectiveness, have long been understood as two of the critical drivers of self-defence firearm purchase.[53] And, developing this series of themes, the symposium concluded with an international analysis purporting to demonstrate, around the world, vulnerable citizens, would-be beneficiaries of Mr Gingrich's bequest, crying out for the right to protect themselves with firearms against a rising tide of criminal perpetrators. Renee Lerner's paper went by the strange title, 'The worldwide popular revolt against proportionality in self-defense law'.[54] Her analysis, drawing chiefly upon examples from Florida, Britain and Belgium, is premised upon an

50 Franklin Zimring, and Gordon Hawkins, *Crime Is Not the Problem: Lethal Violence in America* (New York: Oxford University Press, 1997).

51 Stell, *Self-Defense and Handgun Rights*, 307.

52 Ibid., 307.

53 According to McDowall and Loftin, 'the demand for legal handguns is positively related to riots and crime rates and negatively related to a measure of resources devoted to collective security, the number of police per capita. We interpret this as evidence that legal handgun demand is responsive to evaluations of the strength of collective security.' David McDowall and Colin Loftin, "Collective Security and the Demand for Legal Handguns", 88(6) *American Journal of Sociology* 1146–1161, 1147 (1983); see also Gary Kleck, *Point Blank: Guns and Violence in America* (New York: Aldine De Gruyter, 1991), 27–33.

54 Renee Lerner, "The Worldwide Popular Revolt Against Proportionality in Self-defense Law", 2(2) *Journal of Law, Economics and Policy*, 331–364 (2006). The paper's peculiar title, 'against disproportionality in self -defense' begs a question about what 'disproportionate' self-defence might look like in practice. Perhaps 'gratuitous' or 'excessive' self-defence is aspired to. In this light, we have further evidence with which to equate the *demand* for firearms, and disproportionately violent retaliation with them, with the wider punitive turn of late-twentieth-century criminal justice, hyper-incarceration and the so-called rebalancing of criminal justice much discussed in the United Kingdom.

idea of paternalistic political elites failing Stell's test, failing to keep forces of crime and disorder in check and thereby rendering citizens vulnerable to violence and victimisation. Only in Florida, she argued, has the state, through its 'Castle Doctrine' law and 'stand-your ground' principle openly sanctioned the private use of lethal force in protection of life and property.[55] In European societies, she argued, even as citizens demanded more robust criminal sentencing and more permissive self-defence powers, professional political elites have blocked proposals to allow more violent leeway to those claiming self-defence. She cited the Martin case (referred to in footnote 41) in support of her argument, failing to recognise it was not a genuine case of self-defence. In fact, in England and Wales, there have been relatively few prosecutions for acts of genuine self-defence in face of imminent threat,[56] but this did not stop former Conservative Party Leader David Cameron muddying the water with an ill-advised remark while campaigning in 2010. 'The moment a burglar steps over your threshold . . . I think they leave their human rights outside,' he said.[57] Although when the Home Office and Crown Prosecution released a leaflet explaining the right to self-defence, it carefully elaborated the original common law principles, making no changes.

Under close scrutiny, Lerner's 'worldwide popular revolt' rather evaporates around a few misunderstood cases and some opportunist lobbying. Her supposed 'discovery' of a defence law revolt, reads more like an attempt to orchestrate one. The Florida story she was so keen to celebrate in 2006 led directly to a shabby, unprovoked 2011 shooting of a seventeen-year-old African American, Trayvon Martin, by volunteer neighbourhood watch co-ordinator, George Zimmerman. Zimmerman had allegedly racially profiled the black teenager as 'trouble' and contrary to police dispatcher guidance, confronted Martin and then shot him. The Martin/Zimmerman case made explicit what firearm rights advocates often overlook: firearm self-defence rights are often enacted in shooting: self-defence is activated by shooting to kill. A majority-white jury subsequently acquitted Zimmerman. For a fuller discussion, see Squires, Gun Crime in Global Contexts, 176, 180. The Martin case resonated with the politics of race and crime in the United States, with self-defence becoming a race issue and firearm self-defence liberalisation ultimately contributing little to overall public safety.[58]

Gun grabbers and global advocacy

The symposium contributors whose work has been critiqued in the foregoing pages share with Malcolm, discussed earlier, an a priori committed view that citizens are entitled to enact violent self-defence. They are also committed to the preservation of the individual

55 The self-defence law changes in Florida are acknowledged to be 'one of the latest in a series of state statutes around the USA, allowing defense of dwellings or vehicles' (Lerner, 2006: 336).

56 The same is manifestly not true of prosecutions of women, who having suffered years of domestic violence finally kill their abusers as an opportunity arises, even though a violent threat to them may not be imminent. The issue is discussed at length in Young, *Imagining Crime.*

57 David Cameron, "Burglars Leave Human Rights at the Door", *Daily Telegraph*, February 1, 2010 at www.telegraph.co.uk/news/politics/david-cameron/7104132/David-Cameron-burglars-leave-human-rights-at-the-door.html (accessed March 15, 2017).

58 Chandler McLellan and Erdal Tekin, "Stand Your Ground Laws and Homicides", *Bonn Institute for the Study of Labour: IZA Discussion Paper No. 6705*, July 2012 at http://ftp.iza.org/dp6705.pdf (accessed March 16, 2017), Cheng Cheng and Mark Hoekstra, "Does Strengthening Self-Defense Law Deter Crime or Escalate Violence? Evidence from expansions to Castle Doctrine", 48(3) *Journal of Human Resources* 821–854 (2013).

rights interpretation of the US Second Amendment, and it is all but self-evident to them, most clearly articulated in Stell's contribution, that the human right to self-defence also entails a right to the most efficacious means of ensuring one's self-defence – ownership of handguns. This is a view they have projected globally, even, in Lerner's case, perceiving the beginnings of a global movement demanding US self-defence rights. In this sense, they are all Newt Gingrich's academic advance guard, proclaiming the Second Amendment as a putative human right. No one, perhaps, has argued this case so long and so forcefully as Wayne LaPierre, executive vice president of the NRA, America's foremost firearm advocacy lobby.

As we have already seen, the NRA was never shy of foreign interventions, but it was the emerging UN Programme of Action on SALW which the NRA construed as a threat to the Second Amendment and civilian gun ownership that galvanised the organization internationally. With the Republican George W. Bush in the White House and the American UN negotiating delegation headed by John Bolton and senior members of the NRA, it appeared highly unlikely that the United States would sign up to the small arms programme of action. However, there were to be presidential elections in 2004, and a Democrat president might be more inclined to support the UN initiative, accordingly, while using the threat of the UN gun ban in its core fundraising and recruiting appeals, LaPierre took the NRA case 'on the road' in a series of filmed 'global gun debates'[59] to expose the claimed UN threat to US values, guns, and the Bill of Rights.

In his public debates and in a book written subsequently, *The Global War on your Guns: Inside the UN plan to destroy the Bill of Rights*, LaPierre outlined his assessment of the issues. From the outset, it is clear that LaPierre viewed the UN Programme of Action through an exclusively American lens. For, having failed to win the gun control debate in the United States, he argued, the 'global gun grabbers' were trying it again via the back door, through the UN. In his speeches and writings LaPierre invariably referred to the UN and the global gun control movement as 'socialists . . . and elitists', and people who 'think they know better than us how to live our lives, spend our money, educate our children and protect our homes'.[60] He insisted that 'Americans simply won't fall for it . . . we are the freest nation in the world' and that the right to bear arms was an inseparable part of that freedom, its fundamental guarantee.

A large part of LaPierre's account comprises a particularly one-sided reporting of the UN disarmament deliberations. Uppermost in the NRA-led US delegation's concerns were any limitations upon civilian ownership of firearms, any restrictions on firearm manufacture, any prohibition of sales to 'non-state actors' and any attempt to commit the United States to a regime of firearms registration to enable tracing and tracking of firearms sales. Transparency in firearm sales was presented as a prelude to wholesale registration, and registration part of a slippery slope to confiscation by a governing class that did not trust the people. LaPierre fulminated at length against the so-called demonization of legitimate gun owners. It all pointed to a global conspiracy to undermine the US Bill

59 The debates were filmed in front of invited audiences and distributed as DVDs or on subscription TV channels or NRA podcasts. I attended a debate between LaPierre and Rebecca Peters (of the International Action Network against Small Arms – IANSA) in London, in 2004. LaPierre's report of the event in his book (2006) bears little relation to the event as it happened. Eight years later, I took part in just such a debate myself: http://about.brighton.ac.uk/staff/profiles/pas1-wayne.pdf.

60 Wayne LaPierre, *The Global War on Your Guns: Inside the UN Plan to Destroy the Bill of Rights* (Nashville: Nelson Current, 2006), xxii. Elsewhere, 223, he describes the United Nations as a 'global thugocracy'.

of Rights and Constitution (an argument frequently levelled at gun control initiatives). However, what was lacking in LaPierre's account, despite the rhetorical flourishes and his persistent denouncing of the 'alien and elitist' UN, was any real understanding of UN governance. With G. W. Bush still in office, LaPierre could be confident there would be little support for the UN programme in the White House, but following the election of Barack Obama in 2008, the NRA leadership were less convinced their hard line would be supported. Despite the fact that a *Congressional Research Service Report* for the Library of Congress had been prepared as early as April 2005, stating clearly that UN arms control mandates would not be binding upon a country's domestic laws unless that country were to pass its own legislation to that effect, NRA lobbyists remained unconvinced. However, this has remained the position of the US State Department, and when Secretary of State, John Kerry, signed the Arms Trade Treaty on behalf of the United States on 25th September 2013, that position was reiterated:

> There will be no restrictions on civilian possession or trade of firearms otherwise permitted by law or protected by the U.S. Constitution. There will be no dilution or diminishing of sovereign control over issues involving the private acquisition, ownership, or possession of firearms, which must remain matters of domestic law.[61]

Despite such repeated assurances that national governments would continue to decide domestic legislation regarding the firearm rights of citizens, LaPierre and fellow NRA advocates were unconvinced. LaPierre dedicated substantial sections of his book to a tale of alleged UN corruption and policy failures, gun confiscations followed by genocide and, incorporating a strong version of republican individualism – sovereignty residing in the people, not the state – suggests that self-defence as self-determination is the only thing standing in the way of global barbarism. And it is at this point that a steadfast advocacy of the US Second Amendment slips neatly into step with Gingrich's global right to bear arms and Stell's specific assertion of handgun ownership rights. For, according to LaPierre, the right to self-defence (and implicitly the right to arms to assert it) 'is as old as civilisation itself and even a gift from God: part of the natural law that God inscribes on every human heart', for firearms 'are the birthright of all humankind' (226). Such a spiritual and essentialist reading of the Second Amendment perhaps helps explain much of LaPierre's fundamentalism. Any breach of these sacred principles leaves innocent people 'helpless against criminals' terrorists and tyrannical states (59); in turn, the gun becomes a global 'equalizer'.[62]

We have come full circle to Newt Gingrich's opening claim, for however resolutely US firearm advocates assert the foundations of their defence of the Second Amendment, in an equivalent sense they insist upon a similar global entitlement which they regard the United Nations as endangering. Unfortunately, unlike the UN, the abstract and anachronistic logic of the NRA's chief theorists invariably fails to take on board the well evidenced consequences of firearm proliferation. Greene and Marsh have done much to show how the proliferation of SALW has become a 'significant independent variable in processes of armed

61 Congressional Record, September 25 2013, 113th Congress, 1st Session Issue: Vol. 159, No. 128 at www.congress.gov/congressional-record/2013/9/25/house-section/article/h5827-5?r=37 (accessed March 16, 2017).

62 LaPierre, *The Global War on Your Guns*, 185, 226, 59.

violence, conflict, security or development'.[63] And, while guns may not directly *cause* violence, 'they do tend make it more likely, more lethal, more widespread, more harmful, more protracted, more entrenched, and more likely to recur.'[64] As US criminologist Elliot Currie likewise notes, it is 'hard to avoid the conclusion that, in conditions that are otherwise conducive to breeding violent crime, the wide prevalence of guns compounds and "lethalizes" those problems'.[65] A world awash with firearms is a potentially dangerous place; the proliferation of weapons in the world's poorest and most conflicted regions rather reiterates the point. Despite claiming to want to offer protection, Gingrich and his colleagues have only two things to bequeath to us – more guns and the right to shoot them.

63 Greene and Marsh, *Small Arms, Crime, and Conflict*, 250.
64 Squires, *Gun Crim in Global Contexts*, 4.
65 Elliot Currie, *The Roots of Danger: Violent Crime in Global Perspective* (Columbus, OH: Prentice-Hall, 2005), 108.

10 The universal right of self-defense and the auxiliary right to defensive arms

David B. Kopel

Do people have a right of self-defense? The answer does not depend on the American Second Amendment.

If there is a right of self-defense, there is necessarily an auxiliary right to the tools necessary for self-defense. William Blackstone, the most influential legal commentator in the English-speaking world, explained the concept for auxiliary rights. Some rights – such the right to own property or to enter into contracts – exist for their own intrinsic value. Other "auxiliary" rights, such as the right to petition government, exist in order the protect the primary rights. The right to defensive arms, which is enumerated in the English Bill of Rights, is another auxiliary right, according to Blackstone. As Blackstone acknowledged, there may be reasonable regulations on rights. For example, the right to arms for self-defense does not include every possible weapon.

This chapter will survey the universal human right of self-defense, from ancient China to the present. The chapter will not cite any American political philosophy. Professor Squires writes as if self-defense rights were invented in America, but his view is too narrow.

Part I of this chapter will present the UN's position: that self-defense is not a right, and the government must prohibit people from owning defensive arms. Parts II and III will present the alternative view, starting with Confucians and the Taoists.

Part IV will address the problem of genocide.

Part V will suggest some parameters of the auxiliary right to effective defensive arms. Societies have always varied in their defensive tools, such as clubs, swords, knives, bows, batons, firearms, chemical sprays, and electric stun guns. The minimum standard would be that *some* form of reasonably effective defensive arms must be lawful.

I. The United Nations

The preamble of the Arms Trade Treaty (ATT) declares itself "mindful of" the legitimate use of firearms for "recreational, cultural, historical, and sporting activities, where . . . permitted or protected by law." This is the only sentence in the thirteen-page treaty which recognizes any legitimacy for guns in non-government hands. Notably absent from the list of legitimate uses is defense of self and others.

The ATT is far from the first United Nations effort on gun control. In 2005, Brazil scheduled a nationwide referendum on whether firearms should be prohibited and confiscated. The United Nations Educational, Scientific and Cultural Organization (UNESCO) funded a public relations program in support of prohibition.[1] In the election, 64 per cent of Brazilians rejected prohibition.[2]

According to the United Nations Human Rights Council (UNHRC, or HRC), severe gun control was mandated by international law even before the adoption of the Arms Trade Treaty.[3] Namely, it is a violation of international law for a government to allow police or citizens to use guns against non-lethal attackers.[4] In other words, shooting a rapist is a violation of his human rights.

The HRC position applies equally to police and citizen use of force.[5] To prevent any crime that does not endanger the life of a victim, a law enforcement officer may never use deadly force, even when no lesser force would suffice to protect the victim.

The UN Department of Disarmament Affairs (DDA) has "officially designated" an organization to "coordinate civil society involvement to the UN small arms process."[6] That organization is the International Action Network Against Small Arms (IANSA), an umbrella network to which almost all national and regional gun prohibition groups belong. IANSA favors the confiscation of all handguns, and a ban on almost all rifles.[7] IANSA's director explained that when a man is trying to rape a woman, the woman "having a gun in that situation escalates the problem."[8]

The UN's 2015 implementation conference on the Arms Trade Treaty included a side event, sponsored by the governments of Mexico, Belgium, Germany, and the United Kingdom, celebrating the release of a new book, *Weapons and International Law: The Arms Trade Treaty*. The book takes the position that self-defense is not "an individual human right that can be commonly exercised." That is the central issue in the debate about UN gun control: Do people have the human right to defend themselves against ordinary criminals, and against criminal governments, such as perpetrators of genocide?

The UN's current view is not novel. In 1576, the French absolutist Jean Bodin, in *Six Livres de la République*, argued for arms prohibition to prevent "the immoderate liberty of speech given orators," and to prevent the people exercising sovereignty.[9] Early in the twentieth

1 Viva Rio, the Brazilian gun prohibition lobby, receives funding from UNESCO and UNICEF. Viva Rio, "Fight for Peace Sports Centre" (Rio de Janeiro, Brazil, 2004), 5 at www.globalgiving.com/pfil/807/projdoc.doc (accessed February 28, 2017).

2 "Brazilians Reject Gun Sales Ban", *BBC News*, October 24, 2005. http://news.bbc.co.uk/1/hi/world/americas/4368598.stm (accessed February 28, 2017).

3 See UN Human Rights Council, Sub-Commission on the Promotion and Prot. of Human Rights, 58th Sess., Adoption of the Report of the Fifty-Eighth Session of the Human Rights Council, U.C. Doc. A/HRC/Sub.1/58/L.11/Add.1 (August 24, 2006, report) at www.ohchr.org/_layouts/15/WopiFrame.aspx?sourcedoc=/Documents/HRBodies/CCPR/Discussion/2015/HRCConcluingObservations_UniversityMinnesota.docx&action=default&DefaultItemOpen=1.

4 UN Human Rights Council, Sub-Commission on the Promotion and Prot. of Human Rights, Prevention of Human Rights Violations Committed with Small Arms and Light Weapons, U.N. Doc. A/HRC/Sub.1/58/27 (July 27, 2006), 26 (prepared by Barbara Frey) at http://web.archive.org/web/20070724062031/www.geneva-forum.org/Reports/20060823.pdf (no defensive firearms use "unless the action was necessary to save a life or lives"; using a firearm against a non lethal threat is "violating another's right to life.") (accessed February 28, 2017).

5 Ibid., ¶¶ 28–29.

6 IANSA's 2004 Review – "The Year in Small Arms", at www.un-ngls.org/orf/cso/cso6/iansa_2004_wrap_up_revised.doc (accessed February 28, 2017).

7 *The Great U.N. Gun Debate*, King's College, London, DVD (Starcast Productions, Ltd., 2004); transcript at http://web.archive.org/web/20060821053654/www.iansa.org/action/nra_debate.htm (accessed February 28, 2017).

8 Ibid.

9 Jean Bodin, *The Six Books of Commonweale*, trans. Richard Knolles (London, 1606), 542–544 at https://archive.org/details/sixbookesofcommo00bodi.

century, Max Weber said that "the state is the form of human community that (successfully) lays claim to the monopoly of legitimate physical violence within a particular territory."[10]

By Weber's definition, a gang of robbers that believes it is entitled to other people's money and that rules the back streets of a city is a "state." A contrary view is that the only legitimate "states" are those which have the consent of the people.

Although the UN is presently Weberian, this has not always been so. The 1948 Universal Declaration of Human Rights recognizes the right of forcible resistance to criminal governments: "[I]t is essential, if man is not to be compelled to have recourse, as a last resort, to rebellion against tyranny and oppression, that human rights should be protected by the rule of law."[11]

II. The global tradition

A. *Confucianism*

Some undemocratic East Asian regimes – such as those in China and Singapore – have portrayed Confucianism as a philosophy of unlimited submission. Actually, Confucius (Master K'ung) sanctioned popular revolution: "The Head of the Ji Family was richer than a king, and yet Ran Qiu kept pressuring the peasants to make him richer still. The Master said: 'He is my disciple no more. Beat the drum, my little ones, and attack him: you have my permission.'"[12]

Mencius (371–289 B.C.) was the most influential developer of Master K'ung's thought. Mencius viewed rapacious governors as equivalent to ordinary robbers: "Now the way feudal lords take from the people is no different from robbery."[13] When Mencius was asked, "Is regicide permissible?" he replied,

> A man who mutilates benevolence is a mutilator, while one who cripples rightness is a crippler. He who is both a mutilator and a crippler is an 'outcast.' I have heard of the punishment of the 'outcast Tchou' [an overthrown emperor], but I have not heard of any regicide.[14]

In other words, killing a wicked king was not "regicide," but merely punishing a criminal.

In a story illustrating that one should only accept gifts when there is justification, Mencius recounted how someone had given him a justified gift: "a contribution towards the expense of acquiring arms" for self-defense.[15]

B. *Taoism*

Around 140 B.C., the *Huainanzi* ("The Masters of Huainan") was composed. The collection of sayings elaborated themes expressed by earlier Taoist authors. The *Huainanzi*

10 Max Weber, "Politics as a Vocation (January 28, 1919)", in David Owen and Tracy B. Strong (eds.), *The Vocation Lectures*, trans. Rodney Livingstone (Indianapolis, IN: Hackett, 2004), 33.
11 Universal Declaration of Human Rights, G.A. Res. 217A, at pmbl., U.N. GAOR, 3d Sess., 1st plen. mtg., U.N. Doc A/810 (December 12, 1948).
12 Confucius, *The Analects of Confucius*, trans. Simon Leys (New York: W. W. Norton, 1997), 11–17.
13 *Mencius*, trans. D. C. Lau (New York: Penguin, 1970) (book 5, part B), 154.
14 Ibid. at 68 (book 1, part B, item 8).
15 Ibid. at 88 (book 2, part B, item 3).

argued that governments are instituted for the security of the people, and when a government itself destroys security, the people have a right to overthrow the government:

> The reason why leaders are set up is to eliminate violence and quell disorder. Now they take advantage of the power of the people to become plunderers themselves. They're like winged tigers – why shouldn't they be eliminated? If you want to raise fish in the pond, you have to get rid of otters; if you want to raise domestic animals, you have to get rid of wolves – how much the more so when governing people![16]

Similarly, "When water is polluted, fish choke; when government is harsh, people rebel."[17]

C. *Greece*

According to Aristotle's *Politics*, each citizen should work to earn his own living, should participate in political or legislative affairs, and should bear arms. Aristotle criticized the theory of the philosopher Hippodamus, who wanted a strict division of roles between skilled labor, agriculture and defense. Aristotle found Hippodamus' division defective, because it would lead to the unarmed being ruled by the armed, "in effect, the slaves of the class in possession of arms."[18]

Of the essential elements of the existence of a state, "[t]he third is arms: the members of a state must bear arms in person, partly in order to maintain authority and repress disobedience, and partly in order to meet any threat of external aggression."[19] Dictators always disarmed their subjects: "It is from oligarchy that tyranny derives its habits of distrusting the masses, and policy, consequent upon it, of depriving them of arms."[20] In a good government, the king would have enough armed men so that he could defend the laws, but his collection of armed men should not be stronger than the people.[21]

The ancient Athenian law on self-defense was explained in a speech by Demosthenes.[22] The statute said: "If any man while violently and illegally seizing another shall be slain straightway in self-defence, there shall be no penalty for his death."[23] Demosthenes explained that "straightway" meant that the victim was had acted in immediate self-defense.[24] Demosthenes explained, "there is such a thing as justifiable homicide," for some kinds of homicide can "be accounted righteous."[25]

D. *Roman law*

Even after the Western Roman Empire fell in the fifth century A.D., Roman law remained a foundation of European law. As European law, Roman law later became part of the laws

16 Thomas Cleary, *The Taoist Classics: The Collected Translations of Thomas Cleary*, Vol. 1 (Shambhala Publications, 1999), 316.
17 Ibid. at 317.
18 *The Politics of Aristotle*, trans. Ernest Barker (Oxford: Clarendon Press, 1946) (book 2, ch. 8, § 8), 69–70.
19 Ibid. (book 7, ch. 8, § 7), 299.
20 Ibid. (book 5, ch. 10, § 11), 237.
21 Ibid. (book 3, chs. 11 and 15).
22 J.H. Vince, "*Introduction* to 'Against Aristocrates'", in Demosthenes, *Orations*, Vol. 3 (Cambridge, MA: Harvard University Press, 1935) (originally delivered in 352 B.C.), 212–213.
23 Ibid. (§ 69), 253.
24 Ibid. (§ 60), 253.
25 Ibid. (§ 74), 265.

of much of Latin America, Africa, and Asia. Roman law comes closer than any other legal system to being the common heritage of all mankind. Even in 1900, an international law treatise stated that deductions from Roman law provided "by far the greater part of the system of international law as it exists to-day."[26]

The foundation of Roman law was the Twelve Tables: twelve bronze tablets containing some of the basic legal rules, produced in final form in 449 B.C. They were placed in the Forum, so that every citizen could easily read them.[27] The self-defense rules are in Table VIII: "If a theft be committed at night, and the thief be killed, let his death be deemed lawful." In the daytime, killing a thief was lawful only if the thief defended himself with weapons.[28]

Cicero, the great Roman lawyer and orator of the first century B.C., wrote a speech that was studied for many centuries afterwards by almost everyone who learned Latin – almost every well-educated person. The law of self-defense is "imbibed from nature herself; a law which we were not taught, but to which we were made – which we were not trained in, but which is ingrained in us – namely, that if our life be in danger from plots, or from open violence, or from the weapons of robbers or enemies, every means of securing our safety is honorable. For laws are silent when arms are raised, and do not expect themselves to be waited for."[29]

The principle of self-defense led directly to Cicero's commendation of tyrannicide.[30] Self-defense against lone criminals and against tyrants were both applications of the natural "instinct of self-preservation."[31]

Around 534 A.D., the Byzantine Emperor Justinian ordered a compilation of all Roman law, which became known as the *Corpus Juris*. The *Corpus Juris* became the foundation of the legal systems not only in the Byzantine world, but also in most of continental Western Europe.

As the *Corpus Juris* explained, some laws were man-made for local circumstances, whereas the *jus gentium* was the natural law "which all human peoples observe." According to the *Corpus Juris*, the universal *jus gentium* includes "the right to repel violent injuries. You see, it emerges from this law that whatever a person does for his bodily security he can be held to have done rightfully."[32] "[N]atural reason permits a person to defend himself against danger."[33] Likewise, "Someone who kills a robber is not liable, at least if he could not otherwise escape danger."[34]

The most famous formulation was "it is permissible to repel force by force (*vim vi repellere licit*), and this right is conferred by nature." Thus, "arms may be repelled by arms."[35]

26 George B. Davis, *The Elements of International Law* (Harper & Brothers, 2005 ©1900), 19.
27 Titus Livius, *The Early History of Rome*, trans. Aubrey de Sélincourt (New York: Penguin Books, 1971), 192–248 (book 3, *8 – *59).
28 T. Lambert Mears, "Introduction", *The Institutes of Gaius and Justinian: The Twelve Tables and the CXVIIth and CXXVIIth Novels* Table 8, items 12–13 (The Lawbook Exchange, 2004, ©1882).
29 Marcus Tullius Cicero, *Speech in Defence of Titus Annius Milo, in Orations of Marcus Tullius Cicero*, Vol. 3, trans. Charles Duke Yonger (Colonial Press, 1899) (originally published 52 BC), 134, 158–159.
30 Cicero *De Officiis* [*On Duties*], trans. Walter Miller (Cambridge, MA: Harvard University Press 1975) (originally published 44 B.C.) (book 3, ch. 4, ¶ 19), 287; *see also* Ibid., 298 (book 3, ch. 6, ¶ 32).
31 ibid. (book. 1, ch. 4, ¶ 11), 13.
32 *The Digest of Justinian*, Vol. 1, transl. and ed., Alan Watson (Philadelphia, PA: University of Pennsylvania Press, 1985) (book 1, ch. 1, § 1, item 3).
33 Ibid., book 9, ch. 2, § 4.
34 *Justinian's Institutes*, trans. Peter Birks and Grand McLeod (Ithaca, New York: Cornell University Press, 1987), book 4, ch. 3.
35 *The Digest of Justinian*, Vol. 2, book 43, ch. 16, § 1, item 27.

The formulation is embodied in the modern Italian criminal code (*è lecito respingere la violenza con la violenza*), which recognizes self-defense as a justification, not a mere excuse.[36]

Under the *Corpus Juris*, carrying arms was also legitimate: "Persons who bear weapons for the purpose of protecting their own safety are not regarded as carrying them for the purpose of homicide."[37]

E. *Islamic law*

Shari'a is the main law in several countries, and broadly influential in many more. While there are several distinct schools of Islamic law, all agree that self-defense, including defense of property, is lawful. According to a modern scholar's summary of Islamic criminal law:

> There is a natural right to self-defense. One may defend oneself from a criminal act that poses an imminent threat to person or property, but only necessary force may be used. An intruder who might be repelled with a stick may not be shot and killed; neither may one pursue an intruder who has retreated and is no longer a threat. Violation of the limits of self-defense is aggression and renders one criminally liable.[38]

The right of resistance "by all available means" against the suppression of the "inalienable right to freedom" is affirmed in Universal Islamic Declaration on Human Rights.[39]

F. *Jewish law*

The book of Exodus absolved a homeowner who killed a burglar: "When a burglar is caught breaking in, and is fatally beaten, there shall be no charge of manslaughter."[40] Killing was not allowed if the homeowner were certain that the burglar was nonviolent. The *Talmud* explains the principle behind the law: "If someone comes to kill you, rise up and kill him first."[41]

Self-defense is not optional; it is a positive command. A Jew has a duty to use deadly force to defend herself against murderous attack. The *Talmud* also imposed an affirmative duty for bystanders to kill if necessary to prevent a murder, the rape of a betrothed woman, or pederasty.[42] Likewise, "if one sees a wild beast ravaging [a fellow] or bandits coming to attack him . . . he is obligated to save [the fellow]."[43] The duty to use force to defend an innocent is based in part on *Leviticus* 19:16: "nor shall you stand idly by when your neighbor's life is at stake."[44]

36 Coside Penale art. 52 (It.); *see also* art. 53 (legitimate use of arms as a justification).
37 *The Digest of Justinian*, Vol. 2, book 48, ch. 6, § 11; see also *Justinian's Institutes*, book 4, ch. 18.
38 Matthew Lippman, Sean McConville and Mordechai Yerushalmi, *Islamic Criminal Law and Procedure: An Introduction* (New York: Praeger, 1988), 56.
39 Universal Islamic Declaration on Human Rights, 21 Dhul Qaidah 1401, art. 2 (Sept. 19, 1981) at www.alhewar.com/ISLAMDECL.html (accessed March 1, 2017).
40 Exodus 22:2 *Modern Language Bible* (Peabody, MA: Hendrickson Publishers, 2005).
41 Babylonian Talmud, *Tractate Sanhedrin*, folio 72a. HEBREW-ENGLISH EDITION OF THE BABYLONIAN TALMUD: SANHEDRIN, 72a (London: I. Epstein ed. Soncino Press 1994).
42 Vilna Talmud, *Tractate Sanhedrin*, folio 73a. *Talmud Bavli: The Gemara: The Classic Vilna Edition With an Annotated, Interpretive Elucidation, as an Aid to Talmud Study. Tractate Sanhedrin*, 2nd ed., Vol. 2, elucidated by Michoel Wiener and Asher Dicker (Brooklyn, NY: Mesorah Publications, 2002).
43 Ibid., folio 73a[1]. Brackets in original.
44 New American Bible at www.vatican.va/archive/ENG0839/_INDEX.HTM (accessed March 1, 2017).

One of the greatest Jewish legal scholars of antiquity was Philo of Alexandria (ca. 20 B.C.–50 A.D.). Like the Romans, Philo viewed all forms of theft as mere variations on a single type of attack on society: an assault on the right of ownership of private property. Thus, a petty thief was no different in principle from a tyrant who stole the resources of his nation, or nation which plundered another nation.[45] Later, the Christian theologian Augustine of Hippo made a similar point, asking: "Justice removed, then, what are kingdoms but great bands of robbers?"[46]

The stories of the ancient Jews are full of stories of justified revolt against evil governments. The First and Second books of Maccabees describe a Jewish revolt against Syrian tyranny in the second century B.C. The books of Judges, Samuel, and Kings describe numerous justified revolutions, led by Jewish heroes such as Deborah the prophet.

In the First Book of Samuel, the Philistines captured extensive territories from the Israelite tribes. The Philistines imposed one of the first weapons-control laws in recorded history: "Not a blacksmith could be found in the whole land of Israel, because the Philistines had said: 'Otherwise the Hebrews will make swords or spears!'" To sharpen agricultural tools, such as plows, the Israelites had to pay for services from a Philistine ironsmith.[47] Disarmament was necessary to control a conquered people.

G. *Christian law*

1. *Canon law*

The Little Renaissance of the twelfth century saw much of the Western world begin to lift itself from the ignorance of the preceding seven. Universities were established in Oxford and Paris. The administration of law and of law-making was regularized by the creation of written laws and the diffusion of literacy.

Around 1140, Gratian of Bologna brought together numerous scattered sources to compile what became the unified text of canon law (church law): the *Decretum*. Heavily influenced by Justinian's *Corpus Juris*, canon law became a foundation of the Western legal system.

According to the *Decretum*, "Natural law is common to all nations because it exists everywhere through natural instinct, not because of any enactment."[48] Examples of natural law include

> the union of men and women, the succession and rearing of children, . . . the identical liberty of all, . . . the return of a thing deposited or of money entrusted, and the repelling of violence by force. This, and anything similar, is never regarded as unjust but is held to be natural and equitable.[49]

45 Edwin R. Goodenough, *The Jurisprudence of the Jewish Courts of Egypt: Legal Administration by the Jews Under the Early Roman Empire as Described by Philo Juedeaus* (Clark, NJ: Lawbook Exchange, 2002, ©1929), 230–231.

46 Augustine, *The City of God Against the Pagans*, trans. R.W. Dyson (Cambridge: Cambridge University Press, 1998) (book 4, ch. 4), 145.

47 1 Samuel 13:19–21 (New International Bible) at http://biblehub.com/niv/1_samuel/13.htm (accessed March 2, 2017).

48 Gratian, *The Treatise on Laws (Decretum DD. 1–20) With the Ordinary Gloss*, trans. Augustine Thompson and James Gordley (Washington, DC: Catholic University of America Press, 1993) (Distinction One, case 7, § 2), 6.

49 Ibid. (Distinction One, case 7, § 3), 6–7.

Self-defense is not a privilege granted by governments; the right is inherent in the natural order of the world.

An important feature of any civilized legal tradition is placing the government under the law. Canon law is a source of this idea. "It is just that the prince be restrained by his own ordinances," Gratian wrote.[50]

The principle of the rule of law underlies the right of revolution. It shows when their rulers are no longer a legitimate government: when they no longer obey the law. Thus, removing a tyrant is restoring the law.

2. Policraticus, *by John of Salisbury*

Published in 1159, *Policraticus* was perhaps the most influential political book written since the *Corpus Juris* six centuries before. The book "created an immediate sensation throughout Europe."[51] "For over a century *Policraticus* was considered throughout the West to be the most authoritative work on the nature of government." Thomas Aquinas, whose work later displaced Salisbury, consciously built on Salisbury's foundation.[52] The author of *Policraticus* was an English bishop, John of Salisbury. Throughout the Middle Ages, his "writings were extensively studied and repeatedly pillaged by jurists, preachers, reforming barons and humanists."[53]

Popes and kings had been vehemently arguing with each other about who had superior power. However, *Policraticus* focused on government's duties. In particular, what were the people's remedies when the government exceeded its rightful powers or failed to perform its duties? John argued that intermediate magistrates, such as local governors, had a duty to lead forcible resistance, if necessary, against serious abuses by the highest magistrate, such as the king.[54]

He explained that tyrants "disarm the law." They are guilty the serious form of "high treason" – destroying "the body of justice itself." So it is "equitable and just to slay tyrants" and "justice is deservedly armed against" them.[55] "As the image of the deity, the prince is to be loved, venerated, and respected; the tyrant, as the image of depravity, is for the most part even to be killed."[56] Therefore, tyrannicide was "honourable" when tyrants "could not be otherwise restrained."[57]

3. *Aquinas*

The *Summa Theologica* by Thomas Aquinas was the culmination of an intellectual movement known as Scholasticism. The Scholastics believed faith and reason, while separate, are complementary gifts from God. Viewing God is the "most perfect of intellectual

50 Ibid. (Distinction Nine, case 2), 29.
51 Harold J. Berman, *Law and Revolution: The Formation of the Western Legal Tradition* (Cambridge, MA: Harvard University Press, 1983), 276.
52 Ibid., 278–279.
53 D. E. Luscombe and G. R. Evans, "The Twelfth-century Renaissance", in J. H. Burns (ed.), *The Cambridge History of Medieval Political Thought* (Cambridge: Cambridge University Press, 1988), 325–326.
54 John of Salisbury, *Policraticus*, trans. Cary J. Nederman (Cambridge: Cambridge University Press, 1990); Douglas F. Kelly, *The Emergence of Liberty in the Modern World: The Influence of Calvin on Five Governments From the 16th Through 18th Centuries* (Philipsburg, NJ: P&R Publishing, 1992), 30.
55 John of Salisbury, *Policraticus*, (book 3, ch. 15), 25.
56 Ibid. (book 8, ch. 17), 191.
57 Ibid. (book 8, ch. 18), 205.

beings," the Scholastic movement helped foster the belief that government too should be rational.[58]

As to "Whether it is lawful to kill a man in self-defense?" Aquinas answered: Killing a person in self-defense is not murder, because the defender has no intention to kill. His intention is just to protect himself, which is proper and reasonable. The defender intends the legitimate effect of preserving his own life. The second effect, the death of the attacker, is not culpable, because the defender was not intending that result.[59]

"Whether sedition is always a mortal sin?" Aquinas said it was, because it destroyed social unity. When a tyrant misruled a city, and the people overthrew him, the people were innocent of sedition. "Indeed it is the tyrant rather that is guilty of sedition."[60]

THE GOLDEN BULL, MAGNA CARTA, AND STRUCTURED RESISTANCE TO TYRANNY

In light of the widespread recognition of the right of the people to remove a tyrannical "government," laws which attempted to set up good government began to provide structured mechanisms for doing so.

In England in 1215, the barons forced King John to sign the Magna Carta. Section 61 authorized a limited right of revolution. If the king disobeyed Magna Carta, and refused a request from a committee of barons to redress their grievances, then all barons had the right to summon forth the entire armed nation. Led by the barons, all free persons, bearing their personal weapons, would seize and hold the king's castles, without harming the king or his family.[61]

Similarly, in Hungary in 1222, the nobles forced King Andrew II to promulgate a "Golden Bull," in which legal process was regularized and the government made subject to law. Like the Magna Carta, the Golden Bull recognized the right of enforcement. If a king violated the Golden Bull, "the bishops and the higher and lower nobles" would have "the uncontrolled right in perpetuity of resistance."[62]

The principle of authorized resistance (*jus resistendi*) was also recognized in Spain. Castile's Pact of 1282 agreed that towns had a right of revolution if the king violated the Pact.[63] Aragon, Spain's other major kingdom, acknowledged the right of nobles to depose a king who violated judicial procedures or other legal rights.[64]

In short, the natural right of self-defense was universally recognized. As international law began to be developed, the personal and collective right of self-defense was elaborated and fortified. Persons who today deny the existence of the right are turning their back on the human rights heritage of humanity.

58 Friedrich Heer, *The Medieval World*, trans. Janet Sondheime (Dublin: Mentor Books, 1963), 268–269. (New York: Mentor Books, 1963; first published as *Mittelalter* in Germany, 1961).

59 Thomas Aquinas, *Summa Theologica*, trans. Fathers of the English Dominican Province (Cincinnati, OH: Benzinger Bros., 1947), Second Part of the Second Part, Question 64 at www.ccel.org/a/aquinas/summa (accessed March 1, 2017).

60 Ibid., Question 42.

61 David I. Caplan and Sue Wimmershoff-Caplan, "Magna Charta", in Gregg Lee Carter (ed.), *Guns In American Society: An Encyclopedia of Politics, Culture, and the Law*, Vol. 2 (Santa Barbara, CA: ABC-Clio, 2002), 371–372. Article 61 was omitted in reissuances of the Magna Charta from 1216 onwards. Faith Thompson, "The First Century of Magna Charta" (1925), excerpted in James C. Holt (ed.), *Magna Carta and the Idea of Liberty* (New York: Wiley, 1972), 64 n. 4.

62 Berman, *Law and Revolution*, 294.

63 R. Altamira, "Magna Carta and Spanish Medieval Jurisprudence", in E.H. Malden (ed.), *Magna Carta Commemoration Essays* (London: The University Press, 1917), 227–243.

64 Ibid., 237; Geronimo Zurita, "Anales de la Corona de Aragón 323", 1610 at http://ifc.dpz.es/publicaciones/ebooks/id/2448 (accessed March 1, 2017).

III. The classical founders of international law

The above global legal, political, and philosophical traditions were integrated into the creation of international law during its classical period, through the eighteenth century.

A. Francisco de Victoria

Francisco de Vitoria was the greatest professor at what was then the greatest university in the world, the University of Salamanca. His classroom became "the cradle of international law."[65] "Victoria proclaimed the existence of an international law no longer limited to Christendom but applying to all States, without reference to geography, creed, or race."[66]

For example, in 1532 he argued that the Spanish had no right to enslave or take the property of Indians in the New World. That the Indians were pagans did not deprive them of their natural rights, including their right to defend themselves against Spanish depredations.[67] The pillage of the Indians had been "despicable," and the Indians had the right to use defensive violence against the Spaniards who were robbing them.[68]

Self-defense included the right of a child to defend himself against a homicidal father, the right of a subject to defend himself against a homicidal king (as long as the defense would not produce chaos in the kingdom), and even the right of self-defense against an evil pope.[69] Deadly force was permissible when necessary to prevent a major robbery, but not a trivial one.[70]

Victoria's *On the Law of War* closely analyzed what should be the laws of war, based on the laws of personal self-defense. As recognized in the *Corpus Juris*, because force may be repelled by force, self-defense of persons and property is lawful.[71] By extrapolation, defensive war is lawful, because it is a form of collective self-defense.[72]

The law of personal self-defense shows that it was wrong to kill innocent non-combatants in war. Such killings could not be just, "because it is certain that innocent folk may defend themselves against any who try to kill them."[73] Because self-defense by innocents is just, the killing of innocents is unjust. Thus, "even in war with Turks it is not allowable to kill children" and women.[74]

B. Francisco Suárez

Francisco Suárez (1548–1617) taught in Salamanca, Rome, and Coimbra.[75] Author of fourteen books on theological, metaphysical, and political subjects, he was widely

65 James Brown Scott, *The Spanish Origin of International Law: Francisco De Vitoria and His Law of Nations* (Oxford: Clarendon Press, 1934), 75.
66 Ibid. at 10*a*–11*a*. (His name is spelled "Vitoria" or "Victoria.").
67 Francisci de Victoria, *De Indis et de Iure Belli Relectiones*, ed. Ernest Nys and trans. John Pawley Bates (Washington, D.C.: Carnegie Institution of Washington, 1917), 115–149.
68 Scott, *The Spanish Origin of International Law*, 79–81.
69 Francisco de Victoria, *On Homicide & Commentary on Summa Theologiae*, trans. John P. Doyle (Marquette University Press, 1997), 195–197 (article 7, item 3); Brian Tierney, *The Idea of Natural Rights* (Grand Rapids, MI: Eerdmans, 1997), 296.
70 Victoria, *On Homicide & Commentary on Summa Theologiae* (article 7, item 6).
71 Victoria, *De Indis et de Iure Belli Relectiones*, 167.
72 Ibid., 168.
73 Ibid., 178–179.
74 Ibid.
75 James Scott Brown, "Introduction", in Francisco Suárez, *Selections From Three Works of Francisco Suárez*, Vol. 2, ed. Gladys L. Williams (Getzville, New York: William S. Hein, 1995), S.J. 5a – 8a.

recognized as one of the preeminent scholars of his age, and one of the founders of international law.[76]

Self-defense is "the greatest of rights," wrote Suárez.[77] It was a right which no government could abolish, because self-defense is part of natural law.[78] The irrevocable right of self-defense has many important implications for civil liberty: A subject's right to resist a manifestly unjust law, such as a bill of attainder (a legislative act imposing criminal punishment on an individual), is based on the right of self-defense.[79]

Unlike some modern scholars, Suárez did assume that "the state" was identical to "the government." Rather, the state itself could exercise its right of "self-defense" to depose violently a tyrannical king, because of "natural law, which renders it licit to repel force with force."[80]

Like individual self-defense, collective self-defense in warfare must "waged with a moderation of defence which is blameless" – that is, not grossly disproportionate to the attack.[81] For the individual and for the state, defense against an aggressor was right *and* a duty – such as for a parent, who is obliged to defend her child.[82]

British historian Lord Acton wrote that "the greater part of the political ideas" of John Milton and John Locke "may be found in the ponderous Latin of Jesuits who were subjects of the Spanish Crown," such as Suárez.[83] Suárez was also a major influence on Grotius.[84]

C. *Hugo Grotius*

The Dutch scholar Hugo Grotius (1583–1645) was a child prodigy who enrolled at the University of Leiden when he was eleven years old. Hailed as "the miracle of Holland," he wrote over fifty books, and "may well have been the best-read man of his generation in Europe."[85] *The Rights of War and Peace* has "commonly been seen as the classic work in modern public international law, laying the foundation for a universal code of law."[86] It was "the first authoritative treatise upon the law of nations, as that term is now understood."[87] "It was at once perceived to be a work of standard and permanent value, of the first authority upon the subject of which it treats."[88] Thus, "in about sixty years from the time of

76 Tierney, *The Idea of Natural Rights*, 301.
77 Ibid., 314.
78 Francisco Suárez, "A Treatise on Laws and Gods the Lawgiver", in *Selections From Three Works*, Vol. 2, 273 (quoting the *Constitutions* of Pope Clement, book 2, title 11, ch. 2.).
79 Ibid., 101.
80 Francisco Suárez, "Defensio Fidei Catholicae Adversus Anglicana Sectae Errores" [Defence of the Catholic Faith Against the Errors of the Anglican Sect], 718 (1613) at www.aristotelophile.com/Books/Translations/Suarez%20Defense%20Whole.pdf. See also Francisco Suárez, "A Work on the Three Theological Virtues of Faith, Hope, and Charity", in Suárez, *Selections From Three Works*, Vol. 2, 854–855 (the state is superior to the ruler, and has a natural right of self-defense against a tyrant; the state also has the right to enforce the implicit term of its contract with a ruler – namely that the ruler act for the good of the public) at www.aristotelophile.com/Books/Translations/Suarez%20Defense%20Whole.pdf. p718.
81 Suárez, "A Work on the Three Theological Virtues", 804.
82 Ibid., 802–803 (citing Pope Gregory IX, *Decretals*, book 5, title 39, ch. 3).
83 John Dalberg Acton, *The History of Freedom and Other Essays* (Brooklyn, New York: Gryphon, 1993), 82.
84 Brown, "Introduction", Suárez, *Selections From Three Works*, 18a–19a.
85 David B. Bederman, "Reception of the Classical Tradition in International Law: Grotius' De Jure Belli Ac Pacis", 10(1) *Emory International Law Review* 4–6 (1996).
86 Hugo Grotius, *The Rights of War and Peace*, Vol. 2 (Carmel, IN: Liberty Fund, 2005), inside jacket.
87 George B. Davis, *The Elements of International Law* (London: Forgotten Books, 2016, ©1900), 15.
88 Ibid.

publication, it was universally established in Christendom as the true fountain-head of the European Law of Nations."[89] In short, "it would be hard to imagine any work more central to the intellectual world of the Enlightenment."[90]

The purpose of *The Rights of War and Peace* was to civilize warfare, especially to protect non-combatants. Grotius started with the right of personal defense: "Grotius grounded his theory of laws, or rights, in 'the design [*intentio*] of the Creator' as manifested in the constitution of the natural world. Two principles were uppermost: self-defense and self-preservation."[91]

As Grotius observed, even human babies, as well as animals, have an instinct to defend themselves.[92] Self-defense was essential to social harmony, for if people were prevented from using force against others who were attempting to take property by force, then "human Society and Commerce would necessarily be dissolved."[93]

Self-defense is appropriate to preserve life; to prevent the loss of a limb or member (mayhem); against rape,[94] and against robbery: "I may shoot that Man who is making off with my Effects, if there's no other Method of my recovering them."[95]

"What we have hitherto said, concerning the Right of defending our *Persons* and *Estates*, principally regards private Wars; but we may likewise apply it to publick Wars, with some Difference," Grotius explicated.[96] For example, pre-emptive war is usually forbidden, because national war contains the personal self-defense requirements of "immediacy" and "certainty."[97]

In *The Free Sea* (*Mare Librum*), a foundational book of maritime law,[98] Grotius explained that natural law is immutable, and cannot be overturned by governments.[99] Suárez had made the same point explicitly, and the point is implicit in the other writers discussed previously. Accordingly, if a government purported to enact a law abolishing the right of self-defense – or to constrict the right into a practical nullity – that law is void *ab initio*.

D. Samuel Pufendorf

Swedish scholar Samuel Pufendorf was the first person ever appointed as a Professor of the Law of Nations – a position created at the University of Heidelberg for Pufendorf to teach Grotius's text.[100] Pufendorf also served as a counselor to the King of Sweden and the King of Prussia. In 1674, his eight-volume magnum opus was published: *Of the Law of Nature*

89 Robert Ward, *An Enquiry into the Foundation of the Law of Nations in Europe From the Time of the Greeks and Romans to the Age of Grotius*, Vol. 2 (London: Forgotten Books, 2016) (1795), 374–375.
90 Richard Tuck, "Introduction" to Grotius, *The Rights of War and Peace* 1, xi.
91 Grotius, *The Rights of War and Peace* 1, inside jacket.
92 Ibid., 183–184 (book 1, ch. 2, § 1.3).
93 Ibid., 184–185 (book 1, ch. 2, § 1.3) (quoting Cicero, *On Duties*, book 3, ch. 5).
94 Ibid., 401–402.
95 Ibid., 408.
96 Ibid., 2, 416.
97 Ibid., 25–26.
98 David Armitage (ed.), "Introduction" to Hugo Grotius, *The Free Sea*, trans. Richard Hakluyt (Carmel, IN: Liberty Fund, 2004) (originally published 1609), xii.
99 Ibid., 6, 38, 43.
100 Jean-Jacques Barbeyrac, "The Life of Hugo Grotius", in Grotius, *The Rights of War and Peace*, Vol. 1, 69.

and Nations.[101] Grotius and Pufendorf "together quickly became the equivalent of an encyclopedia of moral and political thought for Enlightenment Europe."[102]

If people could not defend themselves, then it would be impossible for them to live together in a society. No forcible defense would make "honest Men" into "a ready Prey to Villains."[103] "So that, upon the whole to banish *Self-defence* though pursued by *Force*, would be so far from promoting the Peace, that it would rather contribute to the Ruin and Destruction of Mankind."[104] The "the *Law of Nature*, which was instituted for a Man's Security in the World," certainly did not favor "so absurd a Peace as must necessarily cause his present Destruction, and would in fine produce any Thing sooner than *Sociable* life."[105]

There was no requirement that a defender use arms no more powerful than the arms of the aggressor.[106] "For Example, if a Man is making towards me with a naked Sword and with full Signification of his intentions toward me, and I at the same time have a Gun in my Hand, I may fairly discharge it at him whilst he is at a distance."[107] Similarly, a man armed with a long gun may shoot an attacker who was carrying a pistol, even though the attacker is not yet within range to use his pistol.[108]

Lethal self-defense is permissible against a non-deadly aggressor who would maim the victim, or who would inflict other less-than-lethal injuries.[109] Lethal force is also permissible to prevent rape, assault, or robbery.[110]

Some people claim that because the prerogative of punishment belongs exclusively to the state, self-defense must be forbidden. Pufendorf disagreed. Retribution after the crime had been completed is exclusively a state function. "But Defence is a thing of more ancient date than any Civil Command," and accordingly, no state can legitimately forbid self-defense.[111]

Following the methodology of other classical international law scholars, Pufendorf extrapolated from personal self-defense the broader rules of national warfare, including: Just Cause, no attacks on non-combatants, no execution of prisoners, no wanton destruction of property, and limits on what spoils might be taken.[112]

Self-defense was a right against all violent criminals. So if a ruler makes himself a manifest danger to the people, then "a People may defend themselves against the unjust Violence of the Prince."[113]

Pufendorf approvingly repeated Grotius's point that a people would never enter into a social compact that forced surrender of right to resist unjust and violent government. It would be better to suffer the "Fighting and Contention" of a state of nature than to face "certain Death" because they had given up the right to "oppose by Arms the unjust Violence of their Superiors."[114] The genocides of the twentieth century would provide deadly confirmation of this point.

101 Samuel Pufendorf, *Of the Law of Nature and Nations* (Clark, NJ: Lawbook Exchange, 2005) (1672).
102 Tuck, "Introduction", xi.
103 Pufendorf, *Of the Law of Nature and Nations*, 184 (book 2, ch. 5, § 1).
104 Ibid.
105 Ibid.
106 Ibid., 191 (book 2, ch. 5, § 9).
107 Ibid., 191 (book 2, ch. 5, § 8).
108 Ibid.
109 Ibid., 186 (book 2, ch. 5, §11), 192 (book 2, ch. 5, § 10).
110 Ibid., 186, 192–194, 198 (book 2, ch. 5, §§ 3, 11, 13, 16).
111 Ibid., 190, 198 (book 2, ch. 5, §§ 7, 16).
112 Ibid., 833–848 (book 8, ch. 6).
113 Ibid., 721–723 (book 7, ch. 8, §§ 6–7).
114 Ibid., 723 (book 7, ch. 8, § 7).

IV. Genocide

How much harm is done by arms, and how much is done by arms prohibition? University of Hawaii Professor R. J. Rummel compiled the demographic data regarding genocide. He estimated the total number of victims of mass murders by governments from 1901 to 1990 at 169,198,000.[115] The figure does *not* include deaths of soldiers or civilians from war. With 169 million deaths due to mass murder by government, the risk to life from criminal governments is overwhelmingly larger than the risk to life from lone criminals.

In 1967, the International Society for the Prevention of Crime held a Congress in Paris on the prevention of genocide. The Congress concluded that

> defensive measures are the most effective means for the prevention of genocide. Not all aggression is criminal. A defense reaction is for the human race what the wind is for navigation – the result depends on the direction. The most moral violence is that used in legitimate self-defense, the most sacred judicial institution.[116]

Genocide is almost always preceded by a careful government program to disarm the future victims. Genocide is almost never attempted against a well-armed population. Bosnia, Cambodia, China, Guatemala, Rwanda, the Soviet Union, Sudan, Uganda, and Nazi Germany are among the places where genocidal tyrants made very sure that the victim populations were first disarmed. Only after disarmament did genocide begin.[117] When genocide is initiated against populations which have been incompletely disarmed, as by the Ottoman Empire against the Armenians during World War I, many more people survive.

A. *Mass shootings in gun-free zones*

Everyone is familiar with the problem of mass shootings by extremists and by persons who are dangerously mentally ill. (The two groups significantly overlap.) The vast majority of these crimes are perpetrated in so-called gun-free zones. This continues a historical pattern. Initially, Nazi genocide was carried out by mass shootings. As soon as the Nazi invasion of the Soviet Union began on June 22, 1941, special SS units called *Einsatzgruppen* were deployed for mass killings. All the Jews or Gypsies (Roma) in a town would be assembled and marched out of town. Then they would all be shot at once.[118]

115 Rudolph J. Rummel, *Death by Government*, 2d ed. (New Brunswick, NJ: Transaction Publishers, 2000), 15.

116 V. V. Stanciu, "Reflections on the Congress for the Prevention of Genocide", in Livia Rothkirchen (ed.), *Yad Vashem Studies on the European Jewish Catastrophe and Resistance*, Vol. 7 (Jerusalem: Yad Vashem, 1968), 187.

117 See for example, Stephen P. Halbrook, *Gun Control in the Third Reich: Disarming the Jews and "Enemies of the State"* (Oakland, CA: Independent Institute, 2014); Aaron Zelman and Richard W. Stevens, *Death by "Gun Control": The Human Cost of Victim Disarmament* (Hartford, WI: Mazel Freedom Press, 2001); David B. Kopel, "Book review of Aaron Zelman et al., Lethal Laws", 15 *New York Law School Journal of International and Comparative Law* 355–398 (1995); David B. Kopel, Paul Gallant and Joanne D. Eisen, "Firearms Possession by 'Non-State Actors': The Question of Sovereignty", 8 *Texas Review of Law and Politics* 426–435 (2004) (Bosnia); David B. Kopel, Paul Gallant and Joanne D. Eisen, "Is Resisting Genocide a Human Right?", 81 *Notre Dame Law Review* 1275–1346 (2006) (Sudan); Nicholas J. Johnson, David B. Kopel, George A. Mocsary and Michael P. O'Shea, *Firearms Law & the Second Amendment; Regulation, Rights, and Policy*, 1st ed. (New York: Aspen Publishers, 2012), online chapter 13, 255–258 (Bosnia) at http://firearmsregulation.org/FRRP_2012_Ch13.pdf.

118 Yehuda Bauer, "Jewish Resistance in the Ukraine and Belarus during the Holocaust", in Patrick Henry (ed.), *Jewish Resistance Against the Nazis* (Hartford, WI: Mazel Freedom Press, 2014), 485–493.

Within a year, the 3,000 *Einsatzgruppen* (aided by several thousand helpers from the German police and military) had murdered about a million people, concentrating on small towns in formerly Soviet territory (including recent Soviet conquests of the Baltic states and eastern Poland).[119] Such a feat which would have been impossible if the intended victims had not been long-disarmed by Communist and Tsarist arms control decrees. In pre-war Poland and in the Soviet Union, "no firearm, not even a shotgun," could legally obtained without a government permit. For the most people, "such permits were impossible to obtain."[120] "Not to allow the peasants to have arms" had been the policy "from time immemorial."[121] In this regard, Lenin and Stalin carried on the Russian Tsarist traditions.

Because of the psychological damage to the *Einsatzgruppen*, the Nazis invented extermination camps with huge gas chambers, which were more efficient at mass killing, and which created a larger physical (and, consequently, psychological) distance between the murderers and their victims.

Many genocidal regimes have lacked the infrastructure capabilities of the Nazis. For them, mass murder was mainly by bullet, or by machete (as in Rwanda). Always, the victims were first disarmed.

To the extent that the European Jews in the Holocaust were able to obtain arms, they fought. They participated in partisan resistance at a far higher rate than any other group in Europe. Armed Jews shut down the extermination camps at Sobibor and Auschwitz. The Jews who did fight, usually by escaping into the woods, had a much higher survival rate than did those who stayed behind in the ghettos.[122]

B. Non-state actors

At the United Nations, many Americans have resisted proposals for a ban on arms transfers to "non-state actors." Such a ban would make it illegal to transfer arms to non-government persons who were not approved by the existing regime. According to Professor Squires, the opposition means that Americans favor providing arms to "insurrectionists" and "terrorists."

Historically, the "non-state actor" ban would have outlawed aid to anti-Nazi guerillas during World War II, anti-communist rebels during the Cold War, and the American rebels during the War for Independence.[123] It could even prohibit arms sales to the army and navy of Taiwan – which the UN officially considers to be a province of China.[124]

119 Hillary Earl, *The Nuremberg SS-Einsatzgruppen Trial, 1945–1958: Atrocity, Law, and History* (Cambridge: Cambridge University Press, 2009), 4–8; Reuben Ainsztein, *Jewish Resistance in Nazi-Occupied Eastern Europe* (London: Paul Elek, 1974), 222–225.

120 Ibid., 304; see also Chaika Grossman, *The Underground Army: Fighters of Bialystok Ghetto*, trans., Schmuel Beeri (New York: Holocaust Library, 1987), 3.

121 Ainsztein, *Jewish Resistance in Nazi-Occupied Eastern Europe*, 304.

122 David B. Kopel, *The Morality of Self-Defense and Military Action: The Judeo-Christian Tradition* (Santa Barbara, CA: ABC-Clio, 2017).

123 See, for example, David B. Kopel, Paul Gallant and Joanne D. Eisen, "Firearms Possession by 'Non-State Actors': The Question of Sovereignty", 8(2) *Texas Review of Law & Politics* 373–436 (2004); David B. Kopel, "The UN Small Arms Conference", 23(1) *SAIS Review* 319 (2003).

124 Ted Bromund and Dean Cheng, "Arms Trade Treaty Could Jeopardize U.S. Ability to Provide for Taiwan's Defense", Heritage Foundation issue brief no. 3634 (2012) at www.heritage.org/research/reports/2012/06/arms-trade-treaty-and-the-us-ability-to-provide-for-taiwans-defense (accessed March 1, 2017).

V. The auxiliary right to arms

Common sense is embodied in the legal maxim, "When the law gives a man anything, it gives him that also without which the thing itself cannot exist." If people have a right to the free exercise of religion, then they necessarily have the right to possess, buy, and sell the scriptures of their religion, and related religious writings. If people have a right to freedom of the press, then the people must have a right to possess, buy, and sell newspapers and magazines.

If there is a right of self-defense, there must necessarily be a right to possess some defensive arms. Otherwise the right would be a practical nullity. How can a small woman defend herself against a pair of large rapists if she cannot use arms? How can a frail eighty-five-year-old man protect himself against three young men who are intent on robbing and killing him? Not everyone has the capability of learning an empty-handed martial art so well that defensive tools are unnecessary.

Firearms are ideal defensive arms. As the International Committee of the Red Cross observes, firearms are among the types of weapons that "are easy to handle effectively with a minimum of training."[125]

The most thorough study of defensive arms use against violent criminal attack found that "[a] variety of mostly forceful tactics, including resistance with a gun, appeared to have the strongest effects in reducing the risk of injury."[126] Thus, "the best available evidence indicates that victim resistance to crimes is generally wise."[127] Further, "armed and other forceful resistance does not appear to increase the victim's risk of injury."[128] While social scientists have many disagreements about firearms issues, the above results have not been challenged.

This is not to suggest that there is necessarily a universal right to firearms under all circumstances. One circumstance in which there certainly is a right to firearms is resistance to genocide. The Genocide Convention is *jus cogens* – which means that it trumps any contrary law. Accordingly, providing firearms or other defensive arms to people who are actively resisting genocide is lawful, even if lesser international laws, such as the Arms Trade Treaty, forbid it.[129] The utility and necessity of defensive arms against genocide is well established – including by the assiduous efforts of *genocidaires* to disarm their intended victims.

In other contexts, the particular arms which are covered by the auxiliary right to arms may vary. In some contexts, defensive sprays or stun guns might be sufficient. What kind of firearms might or might not be included would depend on the availability of equally effective substitutes.

The sanctity of the home against violent and unexpected invasion is a widely expressed fundamental human right all over the world.[130] Accordingly, the self-defense right and its auxiliary are at their apex in the home. Laws which impede home defense are especially egregious violations of human rights. National and international arms control laws should respect all human rights, including the right of self-defense.

125 International Committee of the Red Cross, "Arms Availability and the Situation of Civilians in Armed Conflict", ICRC, 1999, 21 at www.icrc.org/eng/resources/documents/publication/p0734.htm (accessed March 2, 2017).

126 Jongyeon Tark and Gary Kleck, "Resisting Crime: The Effects of Victim Action on the Outcomes of Crimes", 42 *Criminology* 861 (2004).

127 Ibid., 904.

128 Ibid., 902.

129 David B. Kopel, Paul Gallant and Joanne D. Eisen, "Is Resisting Genocide a Human Right?" 81(4) *Notre Dame Law Review* 1275 (2006).

130 David B. Kopel, Paul Gallant and Joanne D. Eisen, "The Human Right of Self-Defense" 22 *BYU Journal of Public Law* 43, 143–147 (2008).

Index

For Product Safety Concerns and Information please contact our
EU representative GPSR@taylorandfrancis.com Taylor & Francis
Verlag GmbH, Kaufingerstraße 24, 80331 München, Germany